A WILDER LIFE

A WILDER LIFE

Journey of an adventuring doctor

JOAN LOUWRENS

Jonathan Ball Publishers
Johannesburg · Cape Town · London

© Text 2020 Joan Louwrens
© Published edition 2020 Jonathan Ball Publishers

Originally published in South Africa in 2020 by
JONATHAN BALL PUBLISHERS
PO Box 33977, Jeppestown, 2043

This edition published in 2021 by Jonathan Ball Publishers
An imprint of Icon Books Ltd, Omnibus Business Centre,
39-41 North Road, London N7 9DP
Email: info@iconbooks.com
For details of all international distributors, visit iconbooks.com/trade

ISBN 978-1-77619-112-3
eBook 978-1-77619-061-4

Author photograph by Jeff Topham, www.jefftopham.com
Front and back cover photos by Joan Louwrens.
    Front, top: Svalbard archipelago, Arctic.
    Front, bottom: Tswalu Kalahari Reserve, Northern Cape, South Africa.
    Back: *SA Agulhas II* lying off Gough Island, South Atlantic Ocean.

Every effort has been made to trace the copyright holders and to obtain their permission for the use of copyright material. The publishers apologise for any errors or omissions and would be grateful to be notified of any corrections that should be incorporated in future editions of this book.

Printed and bound in Great Britain
by Clays Ltd, Elcograf S.p.A.

For my far-flung patients — always my best teachers.

Contents

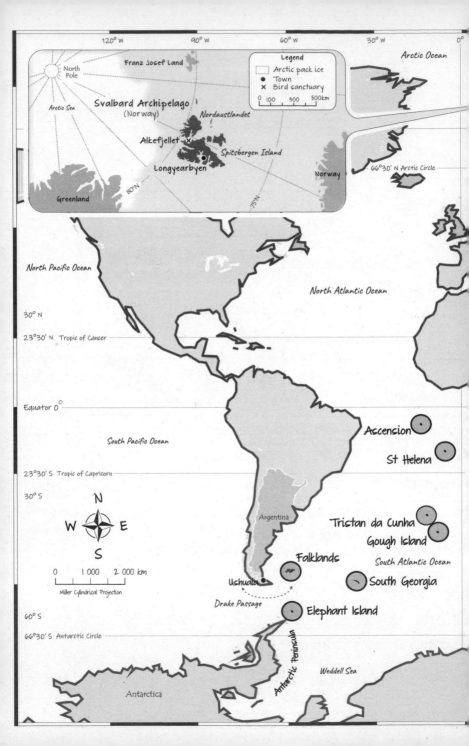

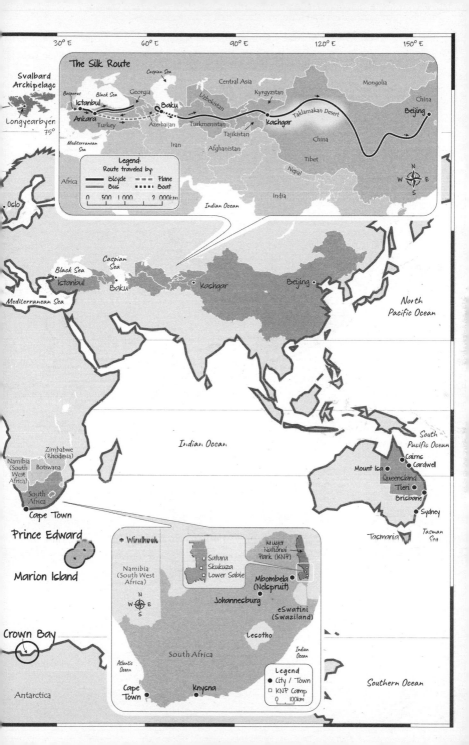

Prologue

'Do what you can, with what you've got, where you are.'

– Squire Bill Widener of Widener's Valley, Virginia, USA, quoted in
  Theodore Roosevelt's autobiography, 1913.

The Lowveld, Swaziland, March 1980

I'm crouched over a dangerously pale, groaning patient. The
stagnant air trapped in the back of the ambulance reeks of past
calamities. The siren, obviously defective, wails in outbursts in time
with the bouncing of the wheels over the potholed dirt road.

I'm having trouble keeping the first three fingers of my left hand
where they should be, which is securing a fluid line into the rectal
passage of the patient. His buttocks are raised on pillows in an
effort to keep the fluid running downhill to his head. Much of it is
seeping out in a brown watery mess.

Gingerly, I press the fingers of my right hand against his wrist.
Can I feel a thready pulse beat? Yes! His life may yet be saved – if
we both survive the trip to the Good Shepherd Hospital in Siteki,
Swaziland.

I ease myself into a position more compatible with a prolonged, uncomfortable ambulance ride, left hand still firmly at the patient's anus, clutching the plastic line administering the lifesaving fluid. Swallowing a rising feeling of nausea, I reflect on my present unenviable position.

I'm a 27-year-old recently qualified medical doctor. I completed a harrowing internship in an unpredictable and wildly busy hospital in Windhoek, South West Africa, and then 'recuperated' doing a year of well-ordered pathology in Denver, Colorado, USA, while my husband, Peter, completed a Master's degree in the relatively new field of agricultural and environmental engineering.

A blissful six months of adventurous and somewhat dangerous travel through Central America followed, during which Pete and I cemented our passion for each other and wild, rough outdoor living.

Our next choice seemed entirely appropriate: we returned to our beloved Africa, to Swaziland, where we were both employed at a new sugar estate, Simunye, in the early days of its construction. Despite my youth and inexperience, I was the acting senior medical officer – the truth was that no one else wanted the job – and Pete was the agricultural engineer. Our first daughter, Mary, was born here, but I soon returned to work, along with Mary, who had many willing carers in the form of the wonderful nurses at the clinic.

I was just becoming a little more confident in my bush-medicine role when I was called, this morning, to a tractor accident in the sugarcane fields. My heart was pounding and my palms sweaty as I scrambled over the red clods of earth and stubbled stalks of cane towards the oddly silent crowd of bedraggled cane cutters standing in a circle, craning their heads forward.

There lay my patient, dead still. He'd been run over by the tractor and no doubt had serious internal haemorrhaging ... but the minutest movement of his chest showed that there was hope.

'Let's get an IV line up!' I shouted with authority – to nobody in particular, as I had no helpers. His life was ebbing away. I needed to replace blood-volume-boosting electrolytc-containing fluid to give him a fighting chance of survival.

I scrabbled around in the emergency box, placed and replaced tourniquets, and pulled them tighter. Then I slapped, pummelled and thumped the arms of my patient, trying to get a vein to stand out. I stuck him mercilessly with an intravenous needle, many times without success. I was failing in the most basic and simplest of medical procedures, the securing of an intravenous access for life-saving fluid.

I sank back on my heels. I wiped the sweat (or was it tears?) from my eyes with the back of a grubby hand. I'd never felt so helpless, so totally incompetent.

Then a voice, very quiet and respectful, came from behind me. 'Ma'am? Why don't you stick it up his arse?'

I turned to see a short, pale, scruffy young man – I later learned he was the manager of this section of the estate – dressed in a khaki shirt and shorts, wearing sandals made of old tyres. 'I was a medic in the Bush War in Rhodesia,' he continued. 'We only had a two-week training course but we did learn a few tricks. We saved lives by rehydrating per rectum.'

'Come and show me how, please!'

With steady hands and slow movements, he removed the needle from the intravenous-administration set. He carefully rolled the patient onto his side, pushed a few bundles of sugarcane under his hip to keep him steady, and inserted the line into his anus. He opened the tap of the fluid bag and a steady stream of drops ran down the line and into the patient.

I watched, spellbound. The fluid seemed to be staying inside the patient's rectum, hopefully to be rapidly absorbed into his bloodstream.

'Thank you. Thank you so much,' I murmured.

My saviour stood up, brushing his hands off on his shorts. 'Only a pleasure. Glad to be of service. We need to help each other in this Africa.'

He had no idea just how much he had helped me, how his act of kindness based on so little theoretical knowledge would influence my medical career – my life – from that point on. With his compassionate willingness to help in this scenario of unpredictable medical demand, he opened my path to adventure medicine.

The ambulance slows as we head through the gates of the Good Shepherd Hospital. The back doors swing open and amid a chorus of chatter many hands reach for the stretcher. Finally, I can remove my left hand, and my patient is whisked into the casualty ward.

I stumble out into the unruly garden and take refuge from the oppressive heat under the shade of a spreading acacia. My area of responsibility is over. I rate myself on my performance: ten out of ten for panic; nine out of ten for care, concern, compassion and being there; two out of ten for skill and expertise. Still, despite the stressful and unpredictable nature of the episode I've just lived through, I feel intensely alive. Teamwork and 'making a plan' won through.

My vague thoughts of specialisation in a clean, un-emergency-based speciality like ophthalmology or dermatology now seem strangely inappropriate. Maybe, just maybe, I'm better suited to this, I ponder. Apparently, I thrive on problem-solving with minimal assets at my disposal.

The roar of a diesel Land Rover engine shakes me from my reverie. It's Pete and Mary coming to take me home. He declines to hear the sordid details — he has a squeamish disposition despite the fact that his wife, sister and mother are all medical doctors.

But for me it's been an epiphany. I can handle the unexpected. I'm always willing to take help when my own ability is lacking. I'm dogged: I don't give up. Despite high levels of anxiety, I revel in the adventure of this kind of medicine.

I sit back, shut my eyes and chuckle. Medicine should never be an adventure; medical practitioners are trained to always know what to do, or to work out a good solution. But it's an imperfect world and just today I've been shown the inadequacy of my training in circumstances nobody could have predicted.

※

The Lowveld, South Africa, October 2015

I feel an overwhelming sense of wellbeing. It's a returning, after about thirty-five years, of the soul and the spirit to a niche where life felt complete, where all my senses were in overdrive, where I was a wife, a mother and a doctor, and I felt fairly bulletproof.

We all dance to the beat of nostalgia. I was then in my 20s, when life had not yet had a chance to get too heavy and unpredictable; or I was just too naïve to know any better. Now in my 60s, a private vulnerability lurks.

I'm driving slowly towards Skukuza, the largest rest camp in the

Kruger National Park and also the site of the village that houses the administration, veterinary, service and research personnel, and therefore all the ancillary services like schools, shops, clubs, clinics, churches, recreational facilities and the obligatory golf course. I'm about to start a two-month general medical practice as 'locum tenens' – a temporary fill-in doctor – for the clinic in the park, relieving my beautiful young doctor friend Nicki, who has just had her first baby, a gorgeous girl child named Isabella.

Unknown to me, Nicki is embroiled in her own medical crisis: her father, Mark, who was visiting his first granddaughter, has fallen hard off his mountain bike and is now lying with multiple serious traumatic injuries in the intensive-care unit (ICU) of a hospital in Nelspruit, the closest large town. Nicki and her mother are at his bedside. My expectations of having my friend to ease me into the hurly-burly bush medicine of the Kruger Park are an illusion soon to be shattered.

In blissful ignorance of what lies ahead, I pull over to the side of the road. I'm watching a choreographed display of a family of warthogs as they forage and frolic, throwing up puffs of red dust in their wake. Some have their pencil tails erect, suspended as if by a magical force. How perfect and often ignored are the small and familiar creatures in our world.

I'm resolving to practise a heightened sense of mindfulness in my privileged stay in this wilderness when the shrill tone of my cellphone shatters my musings.

'This is Anna-Marie from the clinic. Welcome ... but where are you?'

'Hello, Anna-Marie. I'm doing well and will be with you, as promised, in two hours' time.'

A tense silence. Then: 'Can you get here sooner? It is an emergency and our doctor has had to leave. A young girl is injured and bleeding ... and there are other problems.'

'I'll do my best but there's a speed limit—'

'Yes, yes,' Anna-Marie breaks in. 'I will explain if the park cops catch you.'

'And the elephants?' I try – and fail – at some humour. The phonecall is over.

I take a deep breath. Despite the fact that I've thrown myself repeatedly into the medically unknown, I'm filled with deep apprehension, and I wonder fleetingly what it is that drives me, a 60-something doctor, to continually place myself in the line of fire.

I start my car and roll off into the dust.

I have trouble locating the clinic in Skukuza but finally spot the low thatched-roof building outside of which, in a random, haphazard fashion, is a variety of vehicles; an ambulance is drawn up to the door. Groups of subdued people are milling around, some checking their watches, others muttering into cellphones.

I park on the opposite side of the dirt road and walk briskly across. Elbowing my way through the crowds at the door, I walk into a somewhat dark and airless waiting room where a ceiling fan is performing very slow revolutions.

A young girl is sprawled across the lap of an older woman, clutching her bandaged and bloodied forearm. She's whimpering.

'Doctor Joan! Please come through. I am Anna-Marie.'

Anna-Marie is the practice manager, a neat, businesslike, 40-something woman who carries an air of authority despite her evident relief at seeing me. She gives me a two-minute tour of the clinic layout, asks that I write up my notes using a computer program I've never seen or used before, and points to the dispensary down a distant corridor. The stitching trolley and patient are then wheeled into a consulting room and, simultaneously, Anna-Marie turns on her heel and departs, shutting the door firmly behind her.

All I can do is smile calmly, introduce myself, swallow my rising sense of panic, and squelch the mental image from another life, of that patient in the sugarcane fields. Here, at least, I have the privilege of being able to wash my hands, and this I do, methodically and slowly, as I consciously keep my voice low, using the time to reassure mom and daughter and lower the emotional temperature in the room.

I hear how Magda, my 13-year-old patient, while playing rough and tumble with her brother, had fallen onto the fence of a barbed wire enclosure. I peel the blood-soaked bandage off her right forearm to expose a long, jagged, gaping laceration which immediately begins oozing as the pressure of the dressing is released. My patient begins to whimper again, between staccato intakes of breath. Mother looks green and averts her eyes.

'We can fix this easily,' I lie.

I marvel inwardly at how over the years of unpredictable medical practice I've learned to play-act as the need demands. Here I need to be confident, engage my patient to take an interest in the repair ('So how many stitches do you think we'll need here?'), be honest about the procedure being a little uncomfortable ('Just a few pinpricks') and marvel at how well she's coping. Forty-five minutes and twenty-one stiches later, the drama is over.

Mother and daughter beam at me and gush thanks, astounding me, as always.

I sink into a chair as the door closes and wish a cup of coffee and a cheese sandwich would materialise. Instead, a young female park ranger, eyes wide with fright, scurries in, holding high a bandaged right hand: she's smashed a finger in the door of her Land Rover.

My examination reveals a nail in fragments, some finger pulp missing and an edge of bone exposed. Now I feel like whimpering.

'We can fix this easily,' I lie, again, and add, more honestly, 'but it will take quite a long time and you'll have to come back often to the clinic for dressings.'

I rely on the magic of local anaesthetic as I perform a ring block to totally deaden all sensation in her finger and, while salvaging what I can of her finger, I keep the park ranger chatting about her very special job. The diversion tactic works and she departs, arm in a sling, with packets of pills, pain free and with a note booking her off work for ten days. (Her youth and my good luck result in near-perfect healing, with function fully restored within a month.)

The remainder of the day passes in a blur as I endeavour to empty the waiting room. From tuberculosis to thorns in fingers, panic attacks to depression, piles to constipation, I need to draw on all my inner resources to administer care and compassion. In each case, I hope that the patient leaves the clinic with the problem on the road to being resolved.

As the sun is setting I stagger across to my new home, almost tripping over a geriatric warthog who's snuffling, nose in a hole, bum in the air.

That night I lie in the flimsiest of underwear, spreadeagled across my bed, watching the ceiling fan stir the oven-warm air. I think back over my hectic day of medical practice. Although totally spent,

I feel a sense of rejuvenation, a return to youthful energy and thought. Could it be that in our chosen professions, as in life, we go through a given set of stages and then return to the beginning again?

My choice of medicine as a career has coloured my life in unimaginable ways and rendered huge rewards. Perhaps I no longer need my profession to define who I am – but I have to acknowledge that my unconventional path of what I now term 'adventure medicine' needs some scrutiny.

How, when my desire was to contribute to the greater body of medicine, specialise, and become really good at a well-defined field, did I end up as a jack of all trades and master of none?

CHAPTER 1

Kruger National Park: 2015

'Youth is not a time of life; it is a state of mind; it is not a matter of rosy cheeks, red lips and supple knees; it is a matter of the will, a quality of the imagination, a vigor of the emotions; it is the freshness of the deep springs of life.'

– from the poem 'Youth' by Samuel Ullman, 1918

THERE'S ACCESSIBLE MAGIC ON OUR PLANET. It took me, wrapped me in a glass cocoon, and allowed me, 'high in the sunlit silence, hovering there' (in the words of Second World War fighter pilot and poet John Gillespie Magee Jr), to view land and water with the eye of a dancing winged creature.

This magic is helicopter flight.

I was always, from childhood, fascinated with small planes, and embarked on obtaining my private pilot's licence, starting flight training at the tender age of 17 in Rhodesia, where I lived then. My parents had little to say about this except that the funding was my responsibility. They knew that I had small means, and still being at school didn't allow too much in the way of employment.

Perhaps they knew me better than I knew myself: I found the small cockpit of the Piper Cherokee to be intensely claustrophobic, and the dreaded airsickness intervened. I flew solo once — and never again.

But now, to hover, twirl and swoop, with only glass between me and the ether, and to be almost unlimited as to where gentle landings could occur, was sheer magic.

I'd been summoned, as usual at short notice and before sunrise, in that time when the sky seemed an impossible blue and in the east there was the hint of gold and pink. The reason for a doctor being called to board the helicopter in the Kruger National Park was never a joyful one: it usually meant that there'd been contact between park rangers or the rhino anti-poaching-unit personnel, and poachers. Shots had been exchanged, and someone lay injured, dead or dying.

Much money and effort went into slowing the killing rates of these defenceless animals, whose misfortune is having a horn made of inert keratin rising like a noble beacon from their skulls.

The barbaric slaughter of rhinos contaminated the lives of all who worked in the Kruger Park. Rangers who were trained to cope with dangerous animals now had to face dangerous armed criminals. The risk factor of their jobs had risen exponentially. They could also be drawn into the dark underworld of bribery and corruption when massive money became too hard to resist.

Helicopter pilots were asked to fly in suboptimal conditions because a colleague lay dying. Doctors had to deal with gunshot wounds in the veld and, if the wounded person was a poacher, work under the scornful, disapproving glares of the rangers whose lives had almost been ended by that very patient. There was no fairness.

I knew all this, but for a few minutes I suspended knowledge, for the thrill of watching a herd of wildebeest kicking up clouds of red dust as they stampeded to cover. Vultures, alarmed by the noise of the strange flying machine, spiralled upwards off the bones of a kill. Two hyenas skulked into the shadows.

We followed a small watercourse. It disappeared into a wooded grove from which granite koppies arose. In an open sandy clearing lay a dead rhino, a gaping bloody hole where her horn had been.

I felt a physical pain in my chest. There was a baby rhino trotting aimlessly around, towards its inert mother and then away again, spinning in a circle, then standing, head drooping to the ground.

The pilot radioed these findings to the veterinary team. They would follow in another helicopter. For this small creature, there was some hope.

I saw a ranger near a khaki-coloured bakkie below us. He pointed to a suitable landing spot, and the pilot settled the chopper with barely a jolt. I offloaded my well-equipped emergency bags and a portable stretcher, while a member of the anti-poaching unit, who'd flown in with us, conversed in isiZulu with the chief ranger. I gathered that we needed to climb to the top of the koppie, where there were two casualties.

The ranger indicated to his subordinates to carry my gear. We walked in silence, negotiating boulders and flesh-tearing thorn trees. I was led to a body wedged between two boulders. The person was unconscious and breathing irregularly. There was a mound of bleeding ragged tissue over his left thorax — the entry site of a bullet. A torn T-shirt covered his torso and around his waist I noticed colourful plaited woollen cords — his lucky amulets. His blue jeans were filthy.

Travelling to work by helicopter.

I dropped to my knees and felt for a pulse in his neck. I imagined I detected a slight pulsation. I called for my bag and unzipped it in haste. I checked his eyelids to assess colour and make some estimate as to blood loss.

There was a sudden heave of his chest – and then nothing. He died as I sat with my fingers on his pulse.

Behind me there was agitated conversation. I saw the rangers moving farther up the hill. I followed.

The second poacher was propped up against a rock. His wrists were bound together in front of him with thick black cable ties. He was ordered to stand up, which he did with difficulty. His right arm showed an entry-and-exit bullet wound. The bone may have been fractured and he was bleeding actively. I needed to get an intravenous line up and replace fluids.

The chief ranger said they would assist him down to the bakkie and then I could work with greater ease down there. The atmosphere was angry and hostile. My only relief was that no ranger had been shot – and then I reprimanded myself for not staying impartial.

The poacher was lifted and carried, none too gently, down the hill. I sat him in the back of the bakkie with his back against the cab. He showed intense gratitude when I let him drink from my water bottle; the rangers showed their open disapproval.

I got a drip up and gave him a morphine injection. He kept his gaze low.

The body of the other poacher was carried down on a stretcher and dropped in sight of my patient. Nothing covered him. His eyelids weren't fully closed.

The chief ranger addressed my patient in isiZulu but I didn't need to understand the language to understand the message. He leant over and took the chin of my patient in his hand. He twisted his head and forced his gaze to fall on his dead friend. An animated monologue followed, during which the chief ranger edged his boot under the dead body to give it a small lifting movement. He pointed at my patient, then jabbed his finger at the body while his tirade continued at great speed and volume. Once finished, he kicked at the earth in anger, turned his back and strode off.

I was informed that the wounded poacher would be taken to the closest hospital, so I scribbled my findings and medications given on Skukuza notepaper and sealed it in an envelope. The corpse was placed in a khaki body bag and hoisted onto the bakkie, and my stretcher was folded and returned to its case. Two rangers climbed into the cab, revved the engine into life and headed south across the veld. There was no road.

The helicopter already had its rotor spinning and we did the leopard crawl back into the cockpit. In moments we were airborne.

We flew in silence. Then the pilot, as if talking to himself, muttered, 'What a shit job it is now, being a ranger. Always in the firing line. Dead people, dead animals. No justice. Do you know what the chief ranger told me?'

I shook my head.

'That dead poacher – he knew him. He comes from Mozambique but lives somewhere locally. The ranger has personally caught him poaching before. He was arrested and taken to prison. Then he was released on bail, awaiting trial. Well, it's too late for that now.'

⁂

I was phoned late one afternoon by the head of the anti-poaching unit, who had a reputation for being direct and efficient. It was his responsibility to despatch the chopper for any valid reason, not only those linked to poaching.

'Doctor Joan. This is Bernard. You know who I am?'

'Indeed. You're well known around here.'

'I'll get straight to it, then. I've been phoned by the resident manager of Satara Rest Camp. There's a party of schoolkids at their camp swimming pool and they've just hauled one out – suspected drowning. He wants you to fly up ASAP.'

'Can I speak to the manager, please?'

'I'll get him to phone you immediately.'

I stood in the evening light, sweating, and answered my cell at first ring. 'Doctor Joan here.'

'Yes, Doc. Charles Dlamini here.' He spoke softly and hesitantly. 'We need you and your medicine to save a child, right now.'

'Charles, I need some information. Is the child breathing? Does he have a heart beat? Was he pulled out from the bottom of the pool? Has anyone tried mouth-to-mouth?'

'Ah, Doctor, I am not sure. Yes, he was lying at the bottom. Nobody noticed him sink. Too many children. I was called there. He is very still. They have tried to help him. Please come.'

'Charles, listen carefully,' I said. 'You've had first-aid training. Go and use it. Bernard and I will try to get some medical help there but ...' I hesitate in stating the painful truth '... the child may not be alive. It will take me about forty minutes, even in the helicopter, to get to you. That is too long. Keep your cell with you. I will phone back very soon.'

A frenzy of phonecalls resulted in Bernard locating a psychiatrist who was a guest at Satara. He consented to examine the child – while it was way out of his comfort zone, he had the training to be able to pronounce on life or death.

I phoned Charles. 'A doctor in your camp is coming to help now. He'll check the child and decide if I should come to fetch him and take him to hospital.'

'The child ... he does not breathe,' Charles admitted. 'But, Doctor, come with the helicopter and save him.' There was real agony in his voice.

Minutes later the psychiatrist phoned. On examination he'd

found that the child's pupils were already widely dilated – he'd been dead for some time.

I spoke to Charles again. 'I'm so sorry, Charles. You did your best.'

There was a long pause, then Charles said, 'Doctor, you should have come with the helicopter.'

Charles was crediting me and the helicopter with magic we sadly did not possess.

The tragic drowning of that young schoolboy was the first death during my time in Kruger Park. I had dealings with four more. I had to confirm death by gunshot wounds of two poachers. The other two deaths, to this day, leave me with lingering questions.

Emergencies seldom happen at convenient times. An elderly Indian man came into my surgery late one afternoon. He was accompanied by his obviously wealthy and authoritative son, who did all the talking. He told me that his father had a long history of hypertension and angina but that this had worsened to the point that he had become nauseous and had pain radiating down his left arm.

I wasted no time in doing an ECG – an electrocardiogram, which is a recording of the electrical pulses of the heart. It confirmed that the old man had suffered a myocardial infarct – a heart attack. Blood flow through his narrowed coronary arteries had been severely restricted and the heart muscle, without a supply of oxygen, was dying.

I explained that he needed immediate admission to an ICU and to be under the care of a physician. This I could arrange for them in Nelspruit, and I could organise for an ambulance to take them there.

'Oh, that won't be necessary, Doctor,' the son told me. 'I can drive him there myself.' Then he added, 'But we live in Johannesburg and my dad is under the care of a cardiologist there. I'll phone him and get his opinion.'

I stressed that time was of the essence and offered to phone the cardiologist myself. The son declined but I phoned Dr Shepton, the physician, in Nelspruit immediately and arranged for admission of the father and further assessment.

As I was busy writing a letter of referral for Dr Shepton, the son left the room. His dad lay quietly on the examining couch. I gave him an aspirin, which, as simple as it sounds, is the immediate treatment for a heart attack, as it may prevent more blood clot from depositing in the coronary arteries. Reassurance I poured out in copious amounts.

His son returned. I handed him the referral letter, complete with directions to the hospital in bold print on the envelope.

'Thank you, Doctor. We came from Lower Sabie Camp. I'll go back there and pick up some things first—'

'No!' I interrupted. Although it was only a 45-kilometre trip, it would take him about an hour and a half to get back to Lower Sabie, sticking to the park's speed limits; then it would be a further two-and-a-half-hour trip on to Nelspruit. 'Get out of the park as fast as you can. I can get you an escort if you want one. Head to Nelspruit without delay.'

'Okay, Doctor,' the son said. 'An escort is not necessary. We will go now.'

They departed, the elderly patient not without first taking my hand in both of his and giving it a tiny squeeze.

That night I lay thinking of my patient. There was something about the attitude of the son that made me feel uneasy. Perhaps he was just a chauvinist and not used to taking instruction from a woman.

Early the next morning I phoned Dr Shepton. 'How's my patient that I sent in last night?' I asked.

I heard a slow sigh and feared the worst. 'Same old story,' the physician said: 'Everyone knows better. They arrived quite late, and before I could do a full examination, the son became edgy and said he would prefer to go to their cardiologist in Johannesburg. I warned him of the dire consequences of this action. He didn't hear me.'

'And?' I prompted but I already knew the answer.

'Dad apparently had another episode of massive chest pain and died in the back of the car somewhere near Pretoria.'

Dr Shepton and I shared another patient who posed uncomfortable, unanswered questions that I wrestle with to this day.

This painful tragedy began with a phonecall late on a Friday afternoon from a visitor to the park. 'Good evening, Doctor. I need some advice. My name is Hans but I am phoning about my wife, Greta,' he said in a heavy German accent. 'She is a healthy, fit lady of 56, but yesterday she told me that her left lower leg was painful, and we saw that it was swollen. It is not red. She still walks easily. Maybe she just pulled a muscle ...?'

I wanted to talk to Greta personally, but Hans said that her English wasn't good enough. He was phoning from the office of the camp manager, from whom he'd sought assistance. They were staying at Lower Sabie Camp. I, the only doctor on call, was at the Skukuza surgery, an hour and a half away by car.

I went straight into interrogative mode. Had they recently flown out from Germany? What medication was she on? What previous medical problems had she had? I felt myself stiffen as I got the answers. They'd had a long-haul flight three days ago; no, she hadn't taken any aspirin as a precaution; yes, she was on hormone-replacement therapy. This last response made me even more uncomfortable – oestrogen hormones used in menopause increase the incidence of blood clotting.

My brain went into overdrive to deal with the unique set of problems I was facing. 'Hans, there's a chance that your wife has developed a thrombus, a blood clot in her leg. It would be best if I was able to examine her but to drive up here is wasting valuable time, and anyway I don't have the equipment to make a conclusive diagnosis. It would be better if you took her to the Nelspruit hospital where they can do the necessary investigations.'

There was a long pause. Sensing his discomfort at the idea of driving in the fading light through Big Five territory to a large, bustling hospital in a foreign land, I added, 'Let me phone the physician there and get his opinion.' I already knew what that would be but I was buying time and regimenting my thoughts. 'I'll get back to you.'

I called Hans back a few moments later to confirm what I already knew: Dr Shepton had said he must bring her through, and that he'd arrange for her admission. 'I'll arrange for you to get an escort through the park,' I added.

'But Doctor, can't we go through first thing tomorrow morning?' Hans said. 'Greta is not really sick. We will leave at first light. Surely that will be okay? What is the worst thing that can happen if we just wait a few hours? Can't I just give her some aspirin in the meantime?'

I took a deep breath. I was treading a narrow line between doling out complacency and causing wild anxiety. I needed to be gentle and understanding but blatantly honest. I believe now that my choice of words and tone fell short of the need.

'Hans, I do understand how you feel,' I said. 'I may not be correct in my proposed diagnosis, but if your wife does have a deep-vein thrombosis, there can be serious consequences. A deep-vein thrombosis occurs when a blood clot forms, usually in the lower leg, as in your wife. This alone is not dangerous. However, the clot can become dislodged and travel up the vein to the large veins in the lungs, where it can cause a blockage, so preventing blood from entering the lungs and getting re-oxygenated. It's a risk to wait.'

'How big a risk?'

'The worst scenario is that if the clot moves up to her lungs she will experience excruciating chest pain and have difficulty breathing. It is called a pulmonary embolus.' I paused then added, 'She can die from it.'

Silence, then, 'Thank you, Doctor. We will discuss this.'

Hans handed the phone to the camp manager, who gave me all Greta's details for the letter for Dr Shepton, which I faxed to the camp office. I also got permission for an escort.

The night passed quietly but my phone rang early the next morning, a Saturday. 'Joan, Shepton here. This morning I was doing my rounds and noticed the curtains drawn around a trolley in the emergency resuscitation room. It was your patient.'

Dr Shepton went on to tell me that Greta and Hans had arrived at the hospital in Nelspruit in the early hours of the morning after an episode at the camp of acute chest pain and shortness of breath

— the classic symptoms of a pulmonary embolus. 'The camp manager sent her in with the portable oxygen. She made it here still breathing but not for long,' the physician said.

'But ... they left before sunset.' My brain was beyond grasping all this.

'No, Joan,' the doctor said. 'It was their decision to wait until the morning. Bad decision. Sorry.'

❋

'Okay, so you have a patient who's had a spitting cobra blast into his eyes.'

The patient, the head chef of a nearby exclusive private game camp, was howling in agony as he was helped onto the couch by two chattering, terrified assistants. His eyes were squeezed tightly shut.

The phone clamped to my year, I could barely hear the voice of Neil, the ophthalmologist in Nelspruit, above the noise in my consulting room at Skukuza.

I tossed the bottle of anaesthetic eye drops to the nursing assistant, who rapidly instilled copious drops into both eyes of the patient. Within minutes the cacophony had ceased and relative calm descended.

'Hang his head over the edge of the couch,' Neil instructed when I could hear him more clearly. 'Put a basin underneath it on the floor. Set up a bag of saline with an administration set. Open the tap fully and irrigate his eyes continuously. Repeat with a second bag. Then put some antibiotic ointment in and pad up both eyes. See him tomorrow. He'll be fine.'

It sounded almost too easy but I followed Neil's instructions to

Skukuza surgery, Kruger National Park.

the letter, and the next morning I was amazed to find the patient with the pads off his eyes and a huge grin on his face.

'Yo, Docta! I thought I was blind! But everything now, I can see it!'

He still had slight swelling of his eyelids, and his conjunctivas were inflamed, but his vision was perfect.

'Here, I bake bread for you. You are a good sangoma,' he said and thrust a still-warm loaf of delicious-smelling bread wrapped in a dish-cloth into my hands. He danced out cheering, skipping and waving.

I gave thanks for the small joys of my profession.

It wasn't the first and it was most certainly not the last time I sought advice from Neil.

'Now for something completely different,' I said to him on the phone a few days later. 'I have a young Asian lad from Singapore. He was fixing his glasses with superglue, and somehow he got a fair bit in his one eye. His lids are stuck together.'

'Wow, that's a first,' Neil said. 'Okay, no panic. Try irrigation again but warm up the saline a bit. Use some careful massage of the lid and see if you can loosen an edge. Try peeling it off. No worries if he loses a few lashes. Don't worry, the glue wouldn't have stuck to his conjunctiva – it's wet. And you won't damage his cornea.'

While I arranged the equipment for the irrigation, Neil caught me up on a couple of the patients I'd sent him recently. 'The one who got the kebab stick in his eye – lucky for him there was no penetrating wound, just a small area of ulceration, which I'm treating. And you did a good job with the patient who had a foreign body stuck under his contact lens. It must have been there for days; he has a corneal ulcer at the site of the bit you removed but it'll heal totally with treatment.'

He took a deep breath. 'Where do you find all these customers?'

'Thanks, Neil.' I laughed out loud. 'I'll keep sending them.'

I didn't tell him about an elderly American patient I'd seen recently whose story was bizarre and disturbing; her problems needed more than an ophthalmologist. She'd come into my consulting room, requesting that I remove her contact lenses and replace them with a new set. My knowledge and experience with contact lenses were close to zero but I did know that patients usually learned to cope well with the removal and insertion themselves.

The woman seemed healthy and calm, and her vision was good.

She could see that I was puzzled. 'My optician back in the States usually does it for me. I was worried that I wouldn't be able to come on this trip but he assured me that any doctor would do it for me.'

I lay her down, scrubbed my hands, fitted my head torch and performed the very simple procedure.

'I can teach you how to do this yourself,' I said. I'd have liked to save her the monthly visit to a doctor.

'I can't do it, Doctor,' she said in a quiet voice. Then, as if reciting a script she'd learned by heart, she continued, 'I'm horribly claustrophobic. I can't bear to touch my eyes or even have anything close to them. I get fearful. I panic.'

I waited for her to continue. Her story was suddenly very important to hear.

'When I was a small child I was in the bath and my mother pushed my head down into the water. She wasn't okay. I was always scared of her and her shouting. She yelled and yelled and tried to drown me. I struggled and slipped out of her grasp. My nanny saved me. After that I never saw my mother again and my father never spoke of her.'

She gave me a sad smile. 'I've never learned to swim properly. I can't get my face into the water. I was 60 years old before I could even splash water on my face to wash it. I really am much better now.'

When I could trust my voice, I thanked her for sharing this with me.

I sat for a few moments after she left and reflected on something she probably would never know. She had altered my behaviour forever. I would be more tolerant and understanding of the irrational, strange phobias and fears I encountered in my work. I would respect the dignity of even those I failed to comprehend. I would encourage the telling of more stories.

❊

When I arrived to do my three-month locum in the Kruger National Park, I'd recently been awarded my diploma in tropical medicine and hygiene. I'd loved working for it and gaining vast quantities of new knowledge concerning infectious diseases, malaria, tickbite fever and bites from all sorts of other creatures. I was keen to put it all into practice.

I wasn't disappointed. But what made the job uniquely unusual for me was the vast cross-section of humanity with whom I worked. There were the employees of South African National Parks, who ranged from the top administrative leaders and research scientists to the lowly cleaners and manual labourers. I took care of all their families, so newborns, toddlers, teenagers and geriatrics all lined up for appointments.

Guests in the park came from throughout South Africa and all over the world. Language posed its own barriers. It was impossible to locate translators for languages I'd sometimes not even heard of. Sign language and the internet helped.

These people didn't choose me as a doctor: their needs forced them into my consulting room, often reluctantly or in a fraught emergency situation. The range of their socioeconomic standings went from top multimillionaire CEOs of global companies like Microsoft, and famous actors and authors, to the old retired couple who scraped together enough for an annual camping holiday in the bush.

Day visitors posed their own challenges, some of them eating and drinking to excess in the well-appointed restaurants, then exceeding the speed limit racing to make gate-closure time, and crashing recklessly en route, writing off cars and maiming themselves.

So my consulting room, adorned with photographs of lions, elephants, rhinos, warthogs, green mambas, scorpions and birds, and a massive close-up of the malaria-bearing mosquito sucking blood, became my centre of adventure medicine. Hardly a day passed when I wasn't confronted with an entirely new scenario or some totally unlikely event, like having to race out one morning to the Kruger Gate, where a cash-in-transit heist had occurred, leaving a driver with a minor gunshot wound, but with a big satisfied grin on his face because he'd outwitted and out-aced the robbers.

Even familiar injuries had unusual causes. A ranger hobbled in one day with a badly sprained ankle. His attention had wandered from the rhino that had just been darted and the animal had toppled over onto his leg. He was lucky to escape with such a minor injury.

Not so another ranger, who was closing the tailgate of a rhino truck when the rhino inside barged against it. He didn't get his fingers out in time and two were sliced off at the end joints.

I didn't relish dealing with traumatic injuries but one unique form I got proficient at was monkey bites. Monkeys in the Kruger Park have become a persisting menace, and while I was there, an attempt was being made to gain knowledge as to the incidence, severity and provoking factors involved in these bites. What was common to all was the presence of food, but the guests were usually not to blame. Often they were just carrying plates of food out to picnic tables, when the monkeys would descend and grab the food, and bite if any attempts were made to prevent this.

A monkey's teeth are sharp but small, and its jaws are also small, so the wounds inflicted were relatively superficial. The mental trauma was worse and tested my diplomatic skills. The visitors' pleasant game-viewing day and picnic had been ruined; they'd had to drive to see the doctor, a consultation for which they were obliged to pay; they were concerned about tetanus, for which I gave them an injection, and then rabies always loomed.

When it came to rabies, I had expert input. Dr Lucille Blumberg, the rabies specialist at Wits University and our lecturer in the subject for the diploma, assured me that monkeys had never been responsible for the transmission of rabies to humans in South Africa. I did my utmost to pass on this piece of information in the most convincing way.

My first brush with rabies had been during my housemanship at Katatura State Hospital in Windhoek in 1976. I was on an intensive-care rotation with one other intern. Traditionally, the ICU rotation was seen as a bit of a time out – the hopelessly inexperienced interns were regarded as pretty useless among all the high-tech instrumentation and super-well-trained staff, and we took turns to cover the duties and so get some extra desperately needed sleep.

But on this morning we stumbled in, having changed into our green surgical scrub uniforms, and were instantly aware of a hushed, sombre mood in the ward.

The head sister tiptoed towards us and addressed us in a low, sad voice. 'Doctors, we have a patient here, and I hope that in the long medical career that lies ahead of you, you never see another one with this diagnosis. Our patient has rabies.'

Rabies! We knew enough to know that it carried a 100% mortality rate if diagnosed only when symptoms appeared. It's one of the oldest and most terrifying of the world's infectious diseases: it's been present for 4 000 years on all continents except Antarctica. With appropriate intervention it can (especially nowadays) be totally preventable, but this was 1976, when the disease, the very name of which means 'madness' in Latin, was claiming more than 50 000 lives annually, the bulk in Africa and Asia.

'Our patient is an 8-year-old boy who was brought in from a remote rural area. His father says that he was bitten by a stray dog that rushed into their village and attacked without warning. The bite was not too bad so the parents did their own first aid. They took him to the nearest clinic only when he started to get agitated and show abnormal movements some ten days later.'

She pushed open the door of the private ward. 'Follow me quietly,' she said.

We could hear the erratic breathing of the young boy in the dimly lit ward. He lay curled up against the protective railings of the bed. He was naked except for underpants. He seemed to be asleep.

Resting her hand on the bedrail, the sister looked down at him. 'He is sedated now. He was hallucinating and having violent spasms.'

Then, suddenly, a leg shot out. He grimaced. Saliva dribbled from his mouth. And in a single movement, he lurched forward and sank his teeth into the hand of the sister. Blood immediately oozed from the broken skin. She gasped in pain and terror but then, in a display of unbelievable calm, she backed away from the bed, asked us to leave, and pushed the alarm button.

For days afterwards the hospital was abuzz with the news of the horrific incident we'd witnessed. The sister's life was now at risk and we heard the possible interventions that were to be attempted. The rabies vaccine was still in its infancy and claimed not to be 100% safe: it had an outside chance of actually giving the disease to the patient to whom it was administered as a lifesaving attempt. She could die with or without the vaccine.

She opted to receive the vaccine, a series of painful injections into the muscle of her abdominal wall. Her wait must have been interminable, and more so when she was informed that the young boy had died, but she continued her role as wife and mother, maintaining a semblance of normality.

The sister survived – miraculously, many thought.

There had been no gross negligence. The situation was tightly controlled, the players experienced, and yet in a split second a demon had been released. And that demon, which feasts on ignorance, poverty and fear, roams still.

Rabies still claims at least 30 000 lives annually, and this is probably an under-reported figure, as most deaths occur in vulnerable remote rural areas in Africa and Asia. About 40% of victims are children younger than 15 years.

There is cause for optimism, though. The vaccine is now highly effective, and if correct protocol is followed, survival is 100%. So I was only minimally fazed when a thin, middle-aged, slightly bewildered patient who'd sustained a dog bite was escorted into my consulting rooms in Skukuza in the middle of the Monday-morning chaos.

The translator had already obtained the patient's story. 'This man, who is employed as a cleaner for the park, went home over the weekend to his distant village. His neighbour's dog bit him on the thigh,' he told me.

I questioned patient and translator alike as to whether this was a family pet, whether the attack was provoked, whether the dog appeared ill, and other details. The only piece of information I really required, however, was whether or not the dog had been immunised against rabies in the current year.

I was somewhat surprised when it transpired that the patient had, in fact, asked his neighbour as to the immunisation status of the dog, and that his neighbour had reassured him that the dog's vaccinations were up to date. The rabies education and awareness programme is showing results, I thought, and relaxed a little.

I wanted proof of this vaccination status, however, and I managed to arrange for the patient to be transported to his home, where he would visit his neighbour and return with a copy of the vaccination certificate. I then inspected the dried, bruised but rather unimpressive bite site, and applied a suitable dressing.

According to my training, I administered a tetanus booster vaccine, and enquired as to the availability of the rabies immuno-globulin and vaccine. The immunoglobulin would be injected at the site of the bite to mop up any accessible virus, while the multidose vaccine served to prime the patient's immune system into further protection against the potentially invading virus.

'Oh no, Doctor Joan, we don't keep it in stock. Too expensive. We can order it and it will be here in a day or so ...'

So much for the urgency of rapid action post suspected rabid-dog bite. Were we here in South Africa ever going to achieve a rabies-free country? Japan had achieved this in 1957, despite having had a vast portion of its health infrastructure destroyed during the horrific bombings and nuclear attacks of the Second World War.

My patient returned, not the next day, as requested, but a few days later. He produced a grubby and crumpled piece of paper bearing the letterhead of a local veterinary clinic. The neighbour's name and the dog's name appeared in block capitals. It was an invoice for deworming and a distemper vaccination.

A wave of nausea passed over me. I had to sit down. The patient before me, despite all my learning and good intentions, may be carrying the lethal rabies virus, and now it was too late to do anything about it.

I asked him to return to the clinic in three days but, again, he showed up much later – ten days later. Although by that time he might have started to show signs of rabies if he was infected, his symptoms were vague: he had a temperature, but then so did almost every patient I saw that day, as we were in the midst of a very virulent flu outbreak. Trying to hide my anxiety, I administered appropriate treatment, gave him sick leave and asked him to return the next day.

I slept little that night, and the next morning in my consulting room I sat in a state of fear awaiting his visit.

He never appeared, then or ever. I sent a driver to his home. He reported that the family had left suddenly. The neighbour knew no more. Nobody seemed to know what had happened or where he'd gone. All leads went dead.

The thought that he was also dead would forever haunt me.

※

For the average urban dweller, a visit to the wilds of the Kruger National Park was a step out of their comfort zone, although if basic rules were adhered to, their safety wouldn't be compromised. The rewards were the magic of the bush, the extravagant splendour of birds and towering ancient trees, and allowing a little wild spice to season the thoughts. If sightings of the Big Five – lion, leopard, rhinoceros, elephant and Cape buffalo – could be ticked off, it was a bonus.

There was a small armoured creature, seldom seen, that scurried around, particularly at night, in murky recesses under firewood and in other dark, dank places such as roof crevices and inside shoes. It wasn't sought after. It wasn't a new tick for a sighting, but it could become the dinnertime talking point for some visitors – perhaps the highlight (or painful lowlight) of the entire experience.

I talk of the scorpion, that prehistoric-looking bearer of claws and a tail that can inflict a sting, the pain of which can be no worse than that of a thorn piercing the skin or can spoil an entire week. When encountered, the scorpion assumes an aggressive stance, raising its claws, arching its tail and exuding a sense of danger way out of proportion to its size. Death from a scorpion bite is exceedingly rare and only tiny babies are truly at risk. But it was the fear factor that often complicated my task.

The phone shouted me awake at 2am. I was instantly alert and scared. These calls were never good news.

'Doctora! Doctora! Come quick! I am going to die! I have been bitten! Dolor! Dolor!

My mind jumped instantly to venomous snakes: adders, mambas, cobras.

'Did you see the snake?' I asked calmly, despite my wild tachycardia.

'No! No! No! Not snake! The tail that bites! El escorpión! Dolor! Dolor!'

I was hugely relieved, even if the patient wasn't. Amid the

deluge of Spanish-accented words I gathered that the young patient and his partner were Chilean and lived in downtown Santiago, but were at the moment temporary residents of a rondavel in Skukuza.

'I'll meet you at the clinic now,' I said.

I strode across, taking a second to send gratitude up to the ethereal glow of the full moon. The elegant couple were already seated on the outside bench, the patient burying his tear-streaked face in the hairy chest of his shirtless partner, who was clutching a plastic bag and whimpering.

'Gracias, gracias,' they both stammered as they entered my consulting room, and with a flourish the partner emptied the bag onto my desk. It yielded a very dead and badly mutilated black scorpion.

'Well done for catching the culprit,' I said with a smile.

I was then entertained by a very graphic description of events. The couple had been in the throes of passion when something had dropped out of the thatch above them, onto the naked buttocks of Pedro. The scorpion took aim and plunged his tail spike into the soft flesh. The excruciating pain catapulted Pedro in a wide arc onto the cement floor. The scorpion hit the adjacent wall and slid earthwards. The unaffected partner leapt up, and pounded all life out of the tiny black creature, before attempting to console his wailing partner.

I examined the site of the sting, then the remains of the scorpion. I was happy to reassure them that the scorpion had huge pincers and a small tail: it therefore had very low venom, both in potency and amount. If the tail had been broad and fat, and the pincers puny, its sting would have been infinitely more toxic and viciously painful.

'So no injection? Nothing against the poison?' my patient asked.

'The pain will soon ease off,' I said, and slid a packet of painkillers across the desk. These and the scorpion carcass were stowed in the plastic packet, which Pedro tied closed and held aloft in victory.

Even the trees and plants in Kruger could inflict trauma. The tamboti tree, which is common in the park, is well known for its milky latex which is poisonous to humans but not to animals. I had to use Neil's eye-irrigation technique a few times when firewood gatherers had been careless in protecting their eyes from the latex and sawdust while chopping.

Less well appreciated is that even the smoke of these trees is toxic. I had to minister to a rural wedding-party group who had chosen to make their braai with this wood. All suffered from severe vomiting and diarrhoea.

The viciously thorny acacias, truly iconic African trees, got the better of my doctoring skills on a few occasions. A young, tough Austrian endurance athlete entered my consulting room and pointed to a massive thorn embedded in her wrist. It had broken off and its point was barely visible. I administered local anaesthetic and began to try to cut some tissue away to get better exposure. The more I dug, the more it bled, obscuring the thorn end. Each time I grasped a tiny piece of it, it broke off.

I put on my magnifying glasses. I began to sweat. Clear focus became impossible.

I called in the young nursing assistant to assist in swabbing. He did this carefully and meticulously.

Finally, I handed him the forceps. Without a word, he bent close, poised the forceps for a second above the wound, and, like a bird going for a worm, gripped the thorn firmly and eased it out gently.

I was grateful, both to my able nursing assistant for his young eyes and calm expertise, but also to the patient, who'd remained stoic and silent throughout the procedure.

✳

My younger daughter Anna is a wildlife veterinarian. While I was doctoring in Kruger, she came to gather data for her PhD, which involved developing a new, safer anaesthetic cocktail with which to

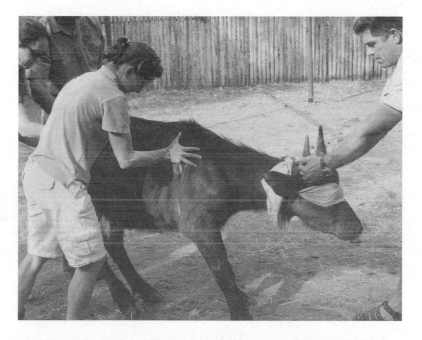

Wildlife veterinarians, my daughter Anna (pictured here) included, were among my trauma patients.

knock out rhinos and other large herbivores for the purpose of translocation or veterinary intervention.

I was occasionally permitted to lurk on the periphery of a game capture and observe diminutive Anna, darting rhinos from a hovering helicopter, and then leaping out as the chopper approached ground level, to orchestrate the required interventions on the now swaying rhino. I was massively impressed at the confidence she showed, and her ability to get the many assistants operating like a fine-tuned machine. The unconscious rhino would be measured, collared, tagged and injected, its skin biopsied, its blood sampled, ticks removed, then photographed, before being given an antidote to enable it to awaken, stagger to its feet and trot off.

Our different professions had so many parallels, and yet here lay the great divide, and one against which I often struggled. Humans have a mind, healthy or not, and can exert free will. Animals have a mind, the workings of which we can only guess at and which we often choose to override, and their free will is often dependent on our needs. In my medical life there have been many maladies of the human body which I've grown confident to treat with good results; the maladies of the mind can still leave me floundering.

Veterinarians need to know much more about drugs and their effects than us doctors of humans. We deal with a single species; vets have to be acutely aware of differences in drug action across a spectrum of species.

In the course of my medical career in under-resourced places, I have on occasion been called on to assist with the medical needs of animals. My interventions haven't always been a success.

I recall an episode in Swaziland when I was a young and inexperienced but confident doctor. A dear, ancient lady hobbled into my makeshift clinic, cradling an equally ancient, bedraggled tabby cat.

'It is his time,' the old lady whispered through her tears. 'He is 19 years old and sick and won't eat, won't drink. He has been my best friend. He must go to heaven. There is no vet near. You must give him the injection.'

I gently took the cat and tiptoed through to my consulting room, indicating that it would be best if she waited outside. The chief reason for this was that while I really wanted to help this old woman who had made such a painful decision, I had no idea how to perform the euthanasia. I reasoned that if a vial of morphine could sedate a human and suppress respiration, then three vials would kill a scrawny cat.

I carefully shaved fur away from a vein in the leg of the inert cat, filled a huge syringe with morphine and pushed it in fast. Saying a little prayer, I laid my hand on the chest of the cat and waited. To my horror, the cat took a flying leap and embedded its claws into the nearby curtain. He scurried up onto the pelmet and raced across it and down the other curtain.

I dove for him and missed. He shot under my desk, growling and hissing. Clearly, I needed help.

I stepped into the waiting room, closing the door firmly behind myself, and told the old dear that she should go home and I would visit when it was all over.

'Bring him with you, please,' she said.

I nodded.

I nipped back into the room to find the cat scattering the vials of medication off the trolley. It had a hounded look in its eyes, and was panting and lashing its tail.

I phoned the only veterinarian I could find in the phone book.

'Oh no! What a mess up!' he laughed. 'Cats are exquisitely sensitive to morphine. It hypes them up big time.' And he kindly advised me what drugs I should have used.

Much later, with assistance, I caught the cat and followed the vet's highly effective instructions.

It was lunchtime in the surgery and the fans were sluggishly stirring the tepid air. A dust-covered young ranger sprawled softly snoring on a plastic chair. The duty receptionist jerked her head towards my consulting room. 'Doctor Joan. You have a problem.' Then she shouted in isiZulu at the sleeping ranger to pull himself together and follow me.

All was calm and quiet in my consulting room – so quiet that I almost missed the still mound on the examining couch. A young black woman in a bright pink T-shirt and a torn yellow skirt was lying on her back, arms rigidly at her sides, her gaze directed up to the ceiling. Her calloused feet were bare. She was breathing.

I greeted her in my halting isiZulu. There was no response. She remained immobile.

The ranger, whom I presumed to be her husband, came to stand beside her and, with his face about five centimetres from hers, shouted her name. No response.

I took her arm gently and elevated it above the bed, then released it – and it stayed in the position at which I had let it go. I moved her arm across her body into an impossibly uncomfortable posture and released it. It stayed.

I was witnessing the first patient I'd ever seen with stuporous catatonia, a neuropsychiatric syndrome that manifests in aberrations of movement and behaviour including immobility, staring, mutism, rigidity, withdrawal and refusal to eat, along with more bizarre features such as posturing, grimacing and automatic obedience.

I gently eased the woman's arm back down to the couch. During all this time the patient had not once acknowledged my presence.

I called the receptionist to act as a translator. The first few questions I asked the terrified-looking husband were met with garbled responses. He was in shock.

Eventually I gathered that the patient was his second wife and that she had for a few weeks been spending a lot of the day sleeping and had been acting increasingly strangely. She had a young baby, who was now in the care of her mother – she had become incapable of caring for the little girl. She wasn't on any medication he was aware of. He presumed she was possessed by evil spirits.

I vaguely recalled from my psychiatric-student days that cata- tonia could be linked to schizophrenia or severe depression – possibly post-natal depression in this patient? I sat at my desk and opened my computer, and scanned all the latest information on stuporous catatonia. I realised I was way out of my depth. This woman needed to be admitted to a psychiatric unit. This would require a lot of phonecalls and pleading with specialists in the local government hospital in Nelspruit.

I read up on treatment. The recommendation was benzo- diazepines – the anxiolytic group of drugs into which Valium falls. I gave her a dose, then ordered an ambulance, made some phonecalls and began writing a referral letter.

Within half an hour she'd sat up and begun conversing normally. If I hadn't known better, I would've sided with the husband in pronouncing that the evil spirits had been chased out. But I knew it would be a short-term gain, and that she needed admission, psychiatric evaluation and long-term medication.

When I ushered her out of my room and into the ambulance, I wondered at the letter I'd written. None of what I'd described in that referral was now present in the patient in front of me. What incalculable mysteries the human mind presents!

And the day was not yet done with mental mysteries.

I answered the phone with my mouth full of a delicious hamburger I was enjoying at the golf club. 'Hang on,' I said, then chewed vigorously and swallowed. 'Okay, how can I help you?'

I recognised the voice of one of the senior administrative clerks, Veronica, a woman I'd seen fairly often as a patient, and someone I liked and respected. She asked after my health and commented on the weather while I surreptitiously continued to eat my dinner, then said, almost casually, 'It's my husband, Joshua. Please can you see him, Doctor? He's tried to commit suicide.'

I nearly choked on my mouthful but managed to get out, 'I'll meet you at the clinic in fifteen minutes.'

They were there together when I arrived, sitting quietly on the bench outside, dappled evening light slanting through the trees and falling in patterns on their heads. I greeted them, then continued to the side door and fumbled with my many keys to gain access. 'Please follow me,' I said, leading the way to my consulting room, switching on lights as I went.

Veronica came in and sat down. Joshua lingered at the door.

'Please,' I said to him and pointed. 'Take a seat.'

As he moved into the room and sat down, his head bowed, I

became aware of a strange smell. It wasn't subtle but it wasn't entirely unpleasant.

Veronica told me that Joshua had been depressed. 'I understand him but he sometimes doesn't understand things himself,' she said. He was ...' I could see she was struggling with the words '... abused by his father as a child. He sees it as his fault.'

Joshua raised his head and looked at me with an expression of such vulnerability I had to look away. To my surprise, he spoke. 'I think it may be better if I am not here,' he said. 'Veronica is so good to me, but I am a burden.'

Veronica clucked in the background. She had heard this many times before.

'I drank the methylated spirits in the kitchen,' Joshua continued. 'There was only half a bottle, so then I drank three bottles of Veronica's perfume.'

I was catapulted to high alert on hearing the words 'methylated spirits'. As a student I'd had to do a case report on a patient who was a derelict alcoholic and had consumed a bottle of meths as it was the cheapest manner in which to feed his addiction. The methanol content had destroyed his sight and resulted in kidney failure, which later killed him. I learned later that immediate treatment may have saved him but I couldn't recall in detail what that treatment was.

'Excuse me for a moment please,' I said, and hurried to the reception phone clutching my little black book of all crucial medical information and relevant contacts. I phoned the poison centre at Tygerberg Hospital. I was breathless with anxiety as I related the details of my patient.

'Is that it?' the young-sounding doctor on call asked as I paused

33

to take a breath. Without waiting for a response, she cleared her throat and added, 'Can I ask you a personal question? When did you graduate?'

'In 1975,' I said. I was irritated – what did this have to do with anything?

'Okay, that explains it. You grew up when meths was mainly ethyl alcohol, with ten per cent methanol added as a poisonous component to discourage consumption. They also added that wonderful colour. Emergency departments started to see more and more poisonings in addicts who soaked it in bread to remove the colour, because of course the methanol remained and caused all the damage. About fifteen years ago there was a Health Department directive to prohibit the addition of methanol in meths. They now add some other ghastly-tasting chemical, but it has no serious toxicity. Your patient may be a bit hungover but he'll be fine,' she concluded.

'So it's still called meths but it contains no methanol?' I could hardly believe what I was hearing.

She chuckled, but kindly. 'Yes. Is there anything else I can help you with?'

'No, thank you, I said. 'Your help has been way better than all my years of experience.'

I returned to Veronica and Joshua. Although there was a long journey ahead for him, there was no immediate danger. How wonderful it was to share news like that.

I made an appointment for the following day for them both to see me. I suggested that I'd like to refer them to a psychologist for counselling, but that I'd still remain in close contact with them and always be available to talk. Of course, I wouldn't be: I'd be leaving in a few weeks but I trusted that someone would step into my shoes.

They left, hand in hand, heads close, and I hoped one step nearer to a peace.

＊

My phone was ringing. In the confusion of waking I knocked it flying off my bedside table. The sun had yet to rise. I checked my watch: 5am.

'Joan. This is Jackie. I met you briefly at the school concert a few nights ago.'

I was racking my brain to put a face to the voice when she continued, 'My son is dying.'

Instantly, I was sitting upright.

'I have identical twin boys of 19. They both suffer from insulin-dependent diabetes. They've just arrived from KwaZulu-Natal, where they work. Jason brought Kyle because he was sick and getting sicker. He looks bad, really bad, and I've been through this many times. They're headed for the clinic now.'

The phone went dead.

I threw on clothes and ran across the road to the clinic. As I was unlocking the front door, a bakkie raced towards me, throwing up loose gravel as it screeched to a halt. A tall, dark-haired figure climbed out on either side. I felt relief wash over me.

The patient was conscious, although leaning on his brother as they came into the consulting room. Kyle went directly to the examining couch and lay down.

'Hello, Doc,' his brother said. 'I'm Jason and that's Kyle.' He pointed to the couch and Kyle lifted one hand at the wrist. 'We're both type-one diabetics.' This kind of diabetes is genetic; it isn't caused by eating the wrong food or too much sugar, or being overweight.

'This is our usual regime of medication,' Jason continued, thrusting a card with close-set typed words into my hand. 'Kyle got really bad gut rot and hasn't been so good with eating and drinking. And we've been partying big time. Not sure if he's been checking his sugar levels regularly.'

'Sort of,' muttered the body on the bed, then he shouted, 'Bring a dish!' and just in time I got a kidney dish under his chin. He gasped and retched. Slimy green gastric contents filled the container. He leaned back and closed his eyes.

I checked his pulse, his temperature, his rate of respiration, his hydration status, his blood-sugar level. I detected the sweet telltale smell of ketoacidosis, a serious complication of diabetes caused by insufficient insulin in which the body produces excess blood acids, called ketones. Kyle needed intravenous fluids and insulin – fast.

The cannula slid easily into his vein. I strapped it down securely and sent up quiet thanks.

Their mother entered the room. Despite much background chatter, I tried to stay focused on Kyle. The emergency treatment was the easy part here. Once he was rehydrated and his blood sugar had returned to normal, his electrolytes and kidney function needed regular monitoring. He needed to be admitted, for a day at least, into a high-care situation in a hospital in Nelspruit.

I detected immediately that this wasn't a popular suggestion. The pair, with the bulletproof confidence of youth and their mom as backup, were used to handling their illness. They were confident that they could take care of themselves in this new emergency, as they had done before.

Using all the diplomacy I could muster, I praised their self-reliance and their optimism but, uncharacteristically for myself, I painted a series of possible disastrous complications. I just didn't want any more surprises.

I was grateful that Kyle still felt wretchedly nauseous and consented to go to the hospital. I gave him an injection to still his nausea for the trip.

By this time the clinic staff had started to arrive for work. My colleague, Rob, stuck his head into my consulting room and was greeted warmly by the brothers and their mother. They looked to him to possibly reverse my decision but he supported me.

As they exited, with the intravenous line dangling from Kyle's arm, Rob placed a supportive hand on my shoulder. 'Well done,' he said. 'Lovely folk, but not easy to deal with. Kyle has been on the point of death a few times.' He smiled. 'We've always saved him.'

For the rest of the day I pondered over the seesaw dilemma of self-sufficiency and interdependence. The ideal was cultivating both. The intricacies and dark recesses of the human mind often messed up the balance.

My last patient of the day was a tough middle-aged khaki-clad game tracker sporting a big, genuine, toothy grin. I understood that he lived and worked in the bush, far from Skukuza. He explained that a few days before, he'd sliced into his left index finger with his skinning knife.

I was puzzled. I saw no sign of a bandage on his finger.

He raised his hand and extended his fingers. I noticed a seven-centimetre laceration along the length of his finger, but the edges of the skin lay cleanly and firmly next to each other, held together by what looked like stitches of fishing line. The wound wasn't bleeding or septic.

'Who did this?' I asked.

He looked sheepish. 'I was tracking in the bush, Doc. It was bleeding a lot. I cleaned it and sewed it up.'

'Wasn't it very painful to put all those stitches in?' I couldn't get over that he'd done it himself and how he'd achieved such a perfect result.

'Ah, a bit,' he admitted, and chuckled.

I examined his finger and established that, within the limitations of pain and a bit of swelling, all movements were intact, indicating no tendon damage. 'Well, I can't do any better. You've fixed it,' I told him. 'Leave the stitches in for about ten days. You can go to your closest clinic to get them taken out.'

He looked down, shifted in his seat, and stated the obvious: 'But, Doctor, I can take them out.'

Of course he could.

CHAPTER 2

Tristan da Cunha: 1991–1992

'I am fundamentally an optimist. Whether that comes from nature or nurture, I cannot say. Part of being optimistic is keeping one's head pointed towards the sun, one's feet moving forward.'

— Nelson Mandela in his autobiography, *Long Walk to Freedom*, 1994

MY MEDICAL RESPONSIBILITIES ON THE SMALL Danish cargo vessel *Arktis Carrier* started almost immediately after we left Cape Town, setting out on the 2 800-kilometre sea voyage to Tristan da Cunha, an archipelago of volcanic islands in the Atlantic Ocean, midway between the southern tip of Africa and South America.

The little vessel was yawing and heaving over the notorious Cape rollers and my sea legs were buckling. Nausea was mounting when the captain called me up to the bridge, the highest deck of the ship with the greatest motion. There, on the captain's chair, sat a burly seaman with an impressive paunch and a short neck encased in adipose rolls. His head was tilted at an unnatural angle.

'He has this sore lump,' the captain said, indicating a malevolent red protuberance on the seaman's hairy neck. Even from a distance, the diagnosis was simple: it was an abscess on the point of rupture.

On stable dry land, in a clean and well-lit environment, with a nurse at my side and lots of swabs and cotton wool available, lancing an abscess is my most intensely disliked procedure. Apart from the sight of the glutinous greenish-yellow bloody pus that exudes, the stench defies description. My seasickness was already almost at a point of no return; how was I going to complete the task at hand without emptying my stomach contents all over the navigation instruments?

I had to just vasbyt, as they say in Afrikaans, and then, as soon as the deed was done, beat a hasty retreat to the closest toilet, ignoring the captain calling me back to share a cup of tea.

The events that brought me to this place had begun unfolding seven years before, in December 1984, when my husband and best friend died of brain metastases from a melanoma. Pete was 32; our elder daughter Mary was 4½ years old; our baby Anna was just five months.

Pete, ever the realist, had called me to sit with him a few days before his death. His vision from his deep, sunken, stricken eyes was already blurred. I held his gaze through curtains of wobbling wateriness.

'Joan, I would never have married you if I thought you couldn't cope,' he said. 'I'm leaving you our girls in the full confidence that you'll nurture them into great women. You just show them how it's done, even if the path you lead them on is wild.' Pete saw me as the extremist of the partnership, the risk taker, doing it differently while his was always the voice of reason. But he always trusted me.

After Pete died, I pulled in all my horizons, my plans and dreams, and looked only to getting to the end of each day. I had a job to do – I had children to raise. I fooled those around me into thinking I was making progress out of the clogging treacle of loss and paralysing grief. In private I cried daily for a year. I hung on to the forward motion of others, of my girls, and hoped that some balance would evolve.

I was grateful for my medical qualification: thoughts of a career were far too lofty, but I was confident that I'd always find employment to fit in with my more important occupation of child rearing. And it would put bread on the table.

I worked part-time as a medical officer in the outpatients and casualty departments of the Knysna Provincial Hospital in the Southern Cape. The job was hectically busy, unpredictable and demanding, but a great training ground for rapid and accurate decision-making and self-reliance. I became a better, more efficient, more experienced doctor.

The Knysna years were punctuated with some travel, even over the seas, with Mary and Anna, and frequent weekend exploring excursions into the Garden Route and farther into the wide expanses of the Karoo.

But a journey of a different kind also had its origins in Knysna. It was a medical adventure into the shadowy and frightening world of death and dying. No-one ever escapes a brush with this world, and yet we're reluctant to talk about it, to delve into painful, dark areas when we don't have the means or words to offer solace.

I'd just emerged from walking with my Pete along the path of his terminal illness, and his death had altered me. At first I felt as though a limb had been amputated, that I would never walk again, but slowly I came to know that I would walk again, even run, but with a different gait.

Sue Waller, an elegant, vivacious, beautiful mother of small daughters, approached me one day in the car park where we were both collecting our kids from nursery school. She was in a crisp white uniform held at her slim waist by a maroon belt. I knew that she was a nursing sister running a home-care service in nearby Sedgefield.

'Joan, I need your help,' she said. She avoided my gaze. Doctors come to recognise this giveaway body language: the request would be a medical one.

I smiled as graciously as I could. 'Go for it, Sue!'

'Joan, I have many old and doddery patients. Those are easy for me. It's the ones who're suffering from cancer where I feel helpless. And their GPs seem just as inadequate. They have so many symptoms beyond control. They know they're going to die; they just can't stand the thought of the suffering involved in getting to that release. They often withdraw and then their loved ones suffer hugely. Communication breaks down just at the time when so much may need to be said.'

I dreaded what I was pretty sure she was going to ask, and quickly rallied my thoughts and donned my armour.

'Frank has a cancer of his throat,' Sue continued. 'Pain cripples him. He needs some potent analgesia. His doctor is hesitant to prescribe morphine.'

And here she struck a chord in me that resonated. During Pete's illness I'd made contact with the fledgling St Luke's Hospice in Cape Town, and learned techniques of giving opioid analgesia and tricks to deal with the side effects. It had enabled Pete to regain dignity and peace. He was able to talk of his death, even acknowledge that it was a rare privilege to know just when he would be dying, and so close the circles.

Sue drew a deep breath, smiled, inclined her head and said, 'Please would you visit Frank and help him?'

I had never achieved Pete's level of peace and acceptance. His shadowy world scared me. It seemed a miracle to me that he could reassure me as to my future on earth while he was departing it.

'Sue, it's too soon,' I said. 'It's still too raw. I can't do it yet.'

'Please, Joan. You have the expertise – and the personal experience. Just one visit to help him?'

Visiting Frank showed me that I had the medical knowledge to relieve his pain. Of greater value was that Pete had left me with an ability to face pain, mental and physical, in others, acknowledge it, and invite the patient to open his heart and mind, and talk. I realised that I could make a difference.

Out of that single visit arose the Knysna Sedgefield Hospice. Today it's a noble institution, well loved, respected and generously supported by the community. It was, and remains in my life, a medical adventure of huge significance.

Seven years after Pete died, I made the mistake of remarrying.

I was back in Cape Town by then, and life was proceeding well enough, but I was lonely, lacking intimacy, adult male company and maybe just plain sex. It was painful always being the social misfit, the threatening unattached female, the extra wheel at a time when other families were sending down deep roots for the future.

The girls were hostile towards Jeff from the outset. I convinced myself that part of Anna's problem was that she'd never had a father with whom to interact, and this inclusion of male influence in our little trio was desirable.

On the day we married, I went out for a morning run. I wasn't excited. I was uneasy and frightened. Some thought, some voice, some surge within stopped me in my tracks. It took my breath away. I had to sit down. Nausea came in waves as I faced the mistake I was making.

'Don't be ridiculous, Joan!' taunted my bullying voice. 'This is all pre-wedding nerves. How feeble are you? So maybe you don't love him as much as you loved Pete, and the sex isn't so good. So? You've made your promise. Just get on with it and make it work.' And then, more kindly, 'You've faced more difficult challenges and won.'

I was too much of a coward to call the whole thing off, and I decided I would enter this new phase of life with optimism and hope. Our beloved country was also entering a time of great change: President FW de Klerk, in dramatic fashion, had announced the unbanning of the African National Congress, the Pan Africanist Congress, the South African Communist Party and 33 other 'illegal' organisations. Nelson Mandela had been released from the Victor Verster Prison in Cape Town on 11 February 1990 amid huge celebrations and joy.

My personal new venture was far less successful. The marriage lasted a year and a half. We were divorced on 13 December 1991. In that short time we did harm, to ourselves, each other and my children. I emerged with no self-esteem, massive guilt at my failure and broken promises, and the disappointment of many.

It was during this ragged time that a colleague mentioned to me that the remote island of Tristan da Cunha required a doctor for six months. For me, this was potentially a dream come true: in October 1961, as a 10-year-old schoolgirl, at home in what was then Rhodesia, I'd sat glued to a small black-and-white TV set watching the volcano on that island erupting. The film footage had been taken by a Dutch passenger on the Royal Interocean liner MV *Tjisadane*, which had been diverted to assist in the mercy mission of the evacuation of all 264 inhabitants. The drama had been palpable: men, women and children, with dogs and sheep in tow and as much as they could carry on their backs, stumbled through billowing smoke and ash to board their small fishing craft and head out to nearby Nightingale Island, where they intended to find safe refuge until the ship could take them on board. No lives were lost and they were transported to Cape Town, and then eventually to their unhappy urban home in Calshot near Southampton.

To the surprise of the British government, they elected to return to their beloved island in late 1963. Tristan remained a dependency of St Helena and therefore part of a British Overseas Territory, so a British Administrator was installed and Britain took on the task of rehabilitation and the improvement of the island's infrastructure. This included the upgrading of the local hospital and the ongoing employment of imported doctors.

I was to take the place of the Englishman earmarked for the post, who had reneged at the eleventh hour. South Africans were still considered politically undesirable, but great need always overrides politics, and I was granted the job after a hasty, three-minute, almost inaudible telephone interview with a faceless bureaucrat in London.

The girls – 12-year-old Mary and 7-year-old Anna – and I boarded the *Arktis Carrier* along with schoolbooks, medical tomes and what was later to prove a frivolous choice, bicycles. Family and friends gathered to cheer us on and wave us off. I did notice a few surreptitious glances and private mutterings between some; I knew that it seemed a crazy, impetuous and maybe even dangerous decision. But for me, I was in motion again, an adventure of unknown proportions lay ahead, and the medicine I needed to practise would alter my view on my medical work forever.

We were given the captain's study as our cabin. It had only two bunks to be shared between the three of us but this inconvenience was far outweighed by having an en-suite toilet. How had I been so naïve as to disregard seasickness when I knew I was embarking on an eight-day sea voyage? Especially me, who as a child had always volunteered to look after the dog when all the other kids were whooping it up on various nausea-inducing funfair rides that dived and swooped and went in circles?

Anna related that down in the dining mess it was a challenge to keep food and crockery on the table. Chairs were chained to the floor. The safety barriers around the table edges were raised and bolted into position. I discovered that my best chance for survival was lying horizontal and immobile, ignoring the cupboard doors slamming and the drawers rolling in and out as the ship lurched and heaved in sea conditions threatening our forward progress. The crew, tucking into vast plates of food, just tut-tutted on hearing of the doctor's imminent demise.

Three days later, the seas still enormous, I awoke with an overwhelming hunger. I was cured, and remained so for the rest of the voyage. Who knows how the body adapts? Do those semi-circular canals in the middle ear just get tired of reacting to the motion stimulus?

Back on my feet, I learned a great deal on that voyage to Tristan. Although I hadn't set eyes on any ocean until I was 12 years old, I felt a strong connection with it now. It was its wilderness quality that captivated me. Wild places pull my soul and there, to the far horizon, on all sides, extended a wild place. We didn't set eyes on any other form of civilisation during the entire voyage. The world belonged to the creatures of the sea and the sky.

I saw my first giant of the skies, a soaring wandering albatross that didn't flap its wings for the entire fifteen minutes of my spellbound observation. Humpbacked whales appeared from the depths like magical genies and cavorted and blew alongside us in what seemed like an attempt to connect.

The shimmering light of sunrise over the water, and the sea shot through with reds and golds at sunset, gave me an extravagant pleasure in being alive. I would creep up on deck at night just to observe the impossibly bright stars and revel in the exhilaration of the moment.

My susceptibility to the wonder of the ocean was replaced by fear and foreboding as we approached Tristan, however. The weather was still abysmal, with howling wind, horizontal rain and an angry sea. Our arrival would be delayed, I was informed. The *Arktis Carrier* was to seek a safe anchorage in the lee of a small rocky outcrop with the discouraging name of Inaccessible Island. No landing at Tristan was possible, as there was no more than a small-boat harbour and the transfer from our ship to a launch would be too dangerous.

This all seemed routine to the crew, who were happy for the extra fishing time, and my children watched countless videos, an activity denied to them back home.

Three days later, we finally stepped onto Tristan da Cunha, the most remote inhabited archipelago in the world.

Approaching Tristan da Cunha.

The transfer to the launch had been hair-raising and dangerous. That we arrived unscathed seemed nothing short of a miracle. The evil voice in my head had snarled repeatedly, 'Yes, Joan, this time you've gone too far. It's your choice to endanger your own life but the lives of your children?'

Those children, however, were bursting with curiosity to see their new home and I held my head high as I marched them up from the harbour towards the small hospital nestled against the dark cliffs of the base of the central volcanic cone, Queen Mary's Peak.

'Welcome, Doctor Joan!' A middle-aged woman in jeans and gumboots, greying blonde hair streaming out behind her, was hurrying down the concrete road towards us. Smiling, she grabbed both my hands. She seemed very pleased to see me. 'I'm Doctor

Rosemary. You'll be taking over from me.' I detected the pleasant lilt of an Irish accent.

She looked down and greeted each child just as effusively, then said, 'I have three days to show you the ropes, and then I'm going home.' And with a sigh she added, 'Thankfully.'

Seeing my face freeze, she quickly said, 'No, don't get me wrong. You'll have a marvellous, exciting time. And what happens, happens.' She gazed east to the distant horizon. 'It's just so far from the rest of the world.' Then she gave us another of her beaming smiles. 'Come, let me show you where you'll be living.'

I couldn't complain about my proximity to work: our bungalow was within shouting distance of the hospital, and I could hear squeals of delight as Mary and Anna cavorted with the neighbour's sheepdog.

Doctor Rosemary was a gynaecologist and obstetrician, and was way out of her comfort zone with the humdrum problems of general medical practice. 'It'll be so much easier for you,' she remarked while giving me a tour of the hospital, named Camogli after the village in Italy that was the birthplace of Andrea Repetto and Gaetano Lavarello, two sailors who were shipwrecked on the island in 1892 and decided to remain.

She waved dismissively at the two wards. 'We seldom use these,' she said, 'but here's the dental room, often in use.'

I'd been informed that my responsibility covered dentistry, and before we left Cape Town I'd spent a day at the elbow of a local dentist. I started sweating.

'And here's the theatre, and here's the maternity ward.' These looked clean and bright and well ordered.

'Did you have any deliveries?' I asked her.

'Unfortunately not but I'll introduce you to Joanne Green who'll be delivering soon. She's a primip.'

She used the medical term for a first pregnancy. Now I was really sweating. I'd done no post-graduate training in obstetrics, and a day before departure I'd had a day's tuition and hands-on practice doing a Caesarean section.

'But I was told there's a midwife on the island?' My voice sounded like a whine.

Rosemary laughed. 'Yes, there is, but you need to hope any deliveries are early in the day, before she's settled down with her favourite tipple. There are also two untrained nurse aids but effectively you're on your own.'

This job was going to be a unique adventure, and probably well above my capabilities. Survival mode was required. I'd stay on good terms with everyone, I decided. I'd get to know every inhabitant personally – there were only 297 folk and a mere seven surnames to remember. Those housebound would get a home visit.

Also, as Mary and Anna would be attending school, I'd aim to be the perfect helpful parent. I'd offer to run an after-school sporting activity.

I needed to be accepted on all fronts because when things went wrong – as I anticipated they would – I'd need the support and friendship of the island's inhabitants, not their anger.

❋

I was gazing through my consulting-room window at a ship slipping slowly over the horizon. It was taking Doctor Rosemary home. I had a hollow feeling in my belly.

A knock on the door interrupted my reverie. I smiled, as I always try to do at my patients.

A girl, clearly in her teens and obviously pregnant, waddled in. My smile froze. This wasn't Joanne Green, the pregnant patient I'd already met. This was an unknown.

Involuntarily I glanced out the window again, my eyes searching for the ship carrying the obstetrician into the blue. It wasn't miraculously going to reappear.

'Please sit down,' I said to my new patient. Maybe she was just fat ...

In the quaint old-fashioned accent of a local she got straight to the point. 'I have not seen my period for eight months or so,' she said, stating the obvious.

Our house on Tristan da Cunha, with Anna and dog, and the hospital behind it.

'When was your last menstruation?'

'Don't know.'

'Have you been pregnant before?'

'No,' she said, looking shocked. 'But I can't be pregnant.'

I ignored this. 'Let me examine you, please.'

With some difficulty she climbed onto my examining couch. It took only a few seconds to confirm my presumed diagnosis. I even felt foetal movement. There was no need for a pregnancy test. 'Yes, you're pregnant,' I told the girl.

She avoided my eyes and just nodded.

'It's difficult for me to assess when this baby will be born,' I continued. 'We have no dates to go on and feeling the size is only a rough measure. I guess you're about eight months pregnant.'

That gave me about a month to follow her closely, do all the usual checks, give her an antenatal crash course, prepare her for a potentially difficult delivery, and scrutinise the obstetric textbooks.

I asked her about any other medical problems.

'None,' she said, and she certainly did look a healthy 18-year-old, of average height and with a wide hip girdle – all positive factors for baby delivery.

I handed her a packet of antenatal vitamins. 'Let me see you in a week, please.'

She looked tearful. Her world had also been shaken.

I didn't get to see my patient again for an antenatal check. A few days later, in the midst of a traditional Tristan birthday party to which almost the entire population had been invited and where alcohol was flowing abundantly, she sidled up to me and whispered, 'My pee burns.'

That sounded manageable: a urinary-tract infection, a common complication of pregnancy.

'Collect a sample of urine and meet me later in the clinic,' I told her.

Wine glass drained and thanks given, I stepped out into the night, revelling as always in the exuberance of the heavens. As I neared the hospital an eerie wailing accosted me. I broke into a run and arrived breathless and panting – but not nearly as breathless and panting as my patient, who lay sprawled across a couch in the waiting room, in fully established labour. Delivery was imminent.

'Help me get her onto the bed,' I barked at her startled boyfriend, the soon-to-be-father. I added, hopefully, 'Fetch the midwife!'

But the infant whose existence had only been discovered five days previously now wanted to make her entry into the world, and she did so in dramatic fashion. Her head popped out, tearing her mother's perineum. Then the worst complication imaginable happened: medically known as 'delayed second stage', it's when the baby's shoulders become wedged in the birth canal. This can kill the infant by asphyxiation, and the mother can suffer severe soft-tissue damage or worse.

Fighting back the nausea of terror, I reached for a large pair of scissors and cut a massive episiotomy – a surgical cut at the opening of the vagina – to enlarge the birth canal. There was nothing elegant or wondrous in my actions of heaving the baby, my knee against the mattress and yelling at the mother, between her screams of agony, to 'Push! Push harder!!'

I pulled using a force I'd never used in any previous deliveries. A snapped collarbone in the baby would be the least of my problems. This tug-of-war seemed interminable. I inched her forward, the incremental movements taking seconds but feeling like hours, and finally, suddenly, the infant emerged, followed by a gush of blood and amniotic fluid.

Silence.

And then that repeated miracle: the baby cried lustily. As did we all.

My second delivery, I handled like a professional. Or rather, the mother did. Joanne Green, also with no previous experience of childbirth, intuitively knew what to do. It helped that she'd been closely monitored and coached by Doctor Rosemary.

She was a tall, muscular woman, and proceeded through labour pacing slowly around the ward. This felt comfortable to her and, being a doctor who believes the patient is always right, I encouraged it. It would bring the baby's head well down and hasten labour.

About fifteen minutes prior to delivery, Joanne announced, 'My baby is coming,' and lay down.

With Joanne breathing deeply and pushing by turns, I controlled the crowning of the head of the baby, just as the textbook instructed. With a fair bit of panting, coaxing and reassuring, Joanne was delivered of her first son, Jason. There was no cutting or tearing or excessive bleeding.

Joanne, washed with a satisfied dreaminess, took Jason in her arms and looked into my moist eyes. 'Thank you, Doctor Joan,' she said. 'Please will you be his godmother?'

I nodded vigorously, not trusting my voice. It was I who needed to thank Joanne. She and Jason had restored my confidence in my ability to be a doctor – a priceless gift.

Dentists, universally it seems, strike fear in the hearts of their patients. Perhaps this is born of an intense feeling of vulnerability: the patient lies, exposing a rather private part of their anatomy to the masked and goggled medical practitioner while he/she inflicts pain. There's no chance to voice any objection, and any grimacing, groaning, twitching or fist-clenching goes apparently unnoticed.

Nonetheless, on Tristan, I loathed and feared being a dentist. I'd much rather have been a patient.

Within a few days of my arrival, a lanky shepherd, Sogneus, came in and pointed to one of his front premolars. It had a grey hue. 'This tooth,' he said, tapping it: 'pull, please.'

I tried to convince him that he'd already lived with it for ages, and that the nerve was probably dead, and that as it was no real bother, he should ignore it.

'No, Doc,' he insisted. 'Pull.'

I came clean. I admitted that my experience was limited and that I'd take a long time to complete the task. He was unfazed: smiling patiently and shaking his head, he tapped the tooth again. There was no escape.

While my patient got comfortable in the dentist's chair, I hauled out the very comprehensive dental textbook and balanced it on the dental light table. I was relieved to note it had superb diagrams and step-by-step instructions as to how to proceed with an extraction. And I was deeply grateful that the dentist who paid an annual visit to Tristan was a conscientious fellow who had numbered all the extraction forceps to correspond with the illustrations and instructions in the textbook.

Injecting the local anaesthetic in strict accordance with the instructions went relatively smoothly. I picked up the number 11 forceps, a beautiful tool. I positioned it, clamped it shut and pulled. Nothing budged. I heaved again, bumping the light table and sending the textbook flying. But there had been some movement.

I re-read the technique for applying the force for extraction, and added a few modifications like placing my foot against the dental chair. Finally, the tooth reluctantly parted company from its gum.

By now I was dripping with perspiration, but my extraordinarily diplomatic patient ignored this, shook my gloved and bloodied hand, and thanked me. He departed with the offending tooth encased in bloody tissue in his fist.

Sandra, a 20-something woman, was my next memorable dental patient. By now I'd gained some expertise and confidence, and wasn't totally thrown when she stated that her wisdom teeth had been causing her discomfort and that she wished to have them removed.

After a careful examination and consultation with the textbook, I agreed to do the extraction of all four, but in two sessions. I was still in possession of my wisdom teeth, and my children were too young to have any, so I had zero experience of the pitfalls that so many folk relate when having wisdom teeth removed.

Wisdom teeth are in a very hard-to-reach part of the mouth – right at the back. Instilling the local anaesthesia was a challenge. My hands seemed too big and clumsy to reach where the forceps needed to grasp. I carefully sliced away some of the gum covering the biting surface of the tooth to get better purchase, and with grim determination I pulled. The crown came away, leaving the remainder of the tooth and the root firmly embedded. This was the worst outcome imaginable.

'What's happened, Doctor Joan?' enquired Sandra.

'There's a problem, Sandra. Give me a moment, please.'

I took my trusty textbook into my consulting room. Searching under 'Complications of wisdom tooth removal' I read, with dread, the paragraph relating to a broken tooth: 'A patient who suffers this complication will require immediate referral to a dental surgeon with experience in surgical extractions.'

How simple that would be if I were sitting in a suburb of Cape Town. And how impossible it was now, sitting on a volcanic outcrop eight days from Cape Town by ship, if one was even available.

I had the sense to know my limitations and desist from any further attempts on that tooth, or any of the remaining three.

I returned to face Sandra. 'I'm so sorry, I've failed to extract your tooth, and I've broken it,' I told her. 'It will need to be extracted by an oral surgeon in Cape Town. As you well know, there could be some delay in getting you on a ship. I'm confident that I can put you on antibiotics and some painkillers and there should be no further problems.'

I'm a perennial optimist and I was in luck. So was Sandra. She gave me an anaesthetised, lopsided grin, and said cheerfully, 'That's okay, Doctor Joan. I've wanted to go to Cape Town for a very long time.'

Many weeks later, after her successful return to Tristan, with a complete new set of trendy outfits and a broad, beautiful smile, she skipped into my consulting room bearing a gift of six lobster tails and a carefully handwritten card of thanks. She opened her mouth wide and leaned in to show me that all four offending wisdom teeth were no more.

That night I reflected on this accepting attitude of the Tristanians. It has to be born from living where there's limited choice;

where so much is dependent on forces beyond the control of the inhabitants; where loss and hardship have to be faced and then used as stepping stones to move forward. The Serenity Prayer came to mind: 'God grant me the serenity to accept the things I cannot change, the courage to change the things I can, and the wisdom to know the difference.'

I tiptoed into the bedroom of my sleeping children. Our time on Tristan would be a positive experience, and one from which I hoped they would learn a few unique life lessons. I had to think in this vein to mask my guilty feelings: I'd wrenched them, without asking, out of a good suburban school where they were secure and happy, to accompany me and attend a school along with 37 kids of widely ranging ages. The teachers were kind and willing but lacked formal training.

Mary, who from a young age respected accuracy of knowledge, had got into a dispute with her teacher when learning about the ostrich. Naturally, Mary was familiar with these birds. Her teacher correctly taught that it was the largest living species of bird, and laid the largest eggs. Where she and Mary differed was that teacher said it could fly. Not shy to speak up, Mary questioned this until told to sit down and keep quiet.

Where Mary gained hugely in ornithological knowledge was from a project with which we assisted. Weekends saw us struggling up to The Base, the region between the sheer cliffs that encircle Tristan and the central peak cone. It's a steep, slippery 600-metre climb. Here, the Atlantic yellow-nosed albatross nests, and our job was to extricate the fluffy chicks without being lacerated by the sharp beak of the mother or covered in regurgitated fish as she showed her wrath. We then attached a leg ring and took countless measurements of the chick, valuable information for ornithologists back at the University of Cape Town (UCT).

Bird numbers on Tristan have been under close scrutiny since rats, arriving originally in 1882 off the wrecked American barquentine *Henry B Paul*, had feasted on eggs and chicks. Cats were then introduced. They were spoiled for choice – rats or birds. A concerted effort to rid the island of cats followed. Now there were no more cats, but the rats remained a menace.

One of the duties of the resident doctor was to be the adjudicator on Annual Ratting Day. This was a celebration that got the entire population moving. Teams were drawn up and set off at first light. Any method of rat-catching was permitted and competition was keen.

I was drawn aside by the Chief Islander, the elected head of the Island Council, just before I had to do the count of tails at the end of the day, and told to scrutinise each tail for freshness. There'd been cheating in the past, in which rat tails were frozen and served up the following year!

A doctor duty I relished was that I had to visit all incoming vessels, meet the captain and crew, and declare them free of any transmissible disease. I was painfully aware of the limitations of this exercise, given a virus's skill at concealment, but I never passed up an opportunity to head out over the waves and make the first contact with folk from the outside world.

Given how isolated we were, I was astounded by the number and variety of vessels that passed. There were tiny yachts on trans-ocean missions, fishing boats, the RMS *St Helena*, the *SA Agulhas*, two square-riggers called *Eye of the Wind* and *Søren Larsen*, a Royal

Navy vessel called the RFA *Gold Rover* and some battered cargo vessels that had never intended to visit but had been sent in search of shelter by foul weather. All had passengers keen to disembark but sometimes the weather prevented this, or they failed to get permission from the Administrator, the person appointed by the British Overseas Territories to oversee the business and politics of the island.

There was always a feeling of common purpose when we shared reasons for finding ourselves on this dot in the ocean. It defied description. The best I could come up with was a need to escape, to experience wild places, a testing of resilience, of bowing to the magnificence of nature. We all felt intensely privileged.

Although I loved the excitement of a visiting vessel, I was made acutely aware of its unwanted cargo when, after a visit from a couple on a yacht, almost the entire population came down with a virulent upper-respiratory-tract infection, the causative agent being an imported yacht virus. Tristanians have limited immunity to the world's plethora of viruses, and they also have a genetic trait of asthma. A common-cold virus can cause serious exacerbations of asthma that require intensive intervention.

I'm a chronic asthmatic, well controlled on daily medication, and I felt fairly confident in managing the outbreak. The sheer volume of patients soon overwhelmed me, however, and there simply wasn't enough medication available. I had to make difficult decisions and ration the meds, keeping a few vials of life-saving drugs for myself in case I went into an acute attack. A dead doctor was the worst scenario.

As it happened, my life was never threatened, but the life of Martha, the mother of the Chief Islander, was. She was carried in one evening, and from down the passage of the hospital I could hear her frantic wheezing efforts to get air in and out of her lungs. The small pipes leading to her air sacs, the bronchi and bronchioles, had gone into spasm and the virus infection had also caused the linings of those pipes to swell up. The net result was that the diameters of the airways were all greatly diminished and airflow had come to a virtual standstill. Martha couldn't get air into her lungs, the blood couldn't exchange carbon dioxide for oxygen, and she ran the risk of dying from insufficient oxygen.

Martha was blue around the mouth and terrified. Her level of consciousness was waning. Fortunately, I was prepared for such an emergency. I clamped an oxygen mask and nebuliser onto her nose and mouth, and inserted an intravenous line, and within seconds I'd administered injectable bronchodilators and the magic bullet, a massive dose of corticosteroids.

She responded, but too slowly for my liking, and later that evening I repeated the intravenous drugs, adding powerful anti-biotics in case a secondary infection resulted in her deterioration.

She became drowsy and incoherent. The ominous wheezing persisted but it was quieter: less air was moving through her lungs.

I asked to speak to the Chief Islander, her son, in the privacy of my consulting room. 'Martha is seriously ill,' I told him. 'I've done everything I possibly can do to save her life but her brain may have been starved of oxygen for a while. I'll contact a specialist in Cape Town for any further advice, but for now we need to have courage, and wait and hope.'

'And I'll pray,' her son added quietly.

Getting a second opinion from a consultant in Cape Town was a difficult undertaking. I had to head down to a small hut called the

Radio Shack, and book a scheduled time for a radio transmission with Cape Town Radio, the communication service used by all ships in the vicinity. Cape Town Radio would then redirect my call to the desired number.

How can something as finite as time expand and contract so? The wait to make the connection seemed interminable. But finally I made contact with consultant pulmonologist Dr Joe Grobbelaar, a friend and highly respected colleague. I'd seen him just prior to our departure and mentioned that I was off to Tristan. 'Watch out for all the asthma there,' he'd said glibly.

Now he sounded very serious as he wrestled with the radio etiquette. 'Joan? Is that you? Where are you? On Tristan? Over.'

'Yes, Joe,' I said as the static swelled to blot out all voices. 'I need help. I have an elderly woman who's responding poorly to all the usual treatment. She's had loads of steroids. She's almost in status asthmaticus. What more can I do?' Status asthmaticus is a severe condition in which asthma attacks follow one another without pause.

A long, crackly pause followed. Perhaps he was waiting for my 'over'.

'Joe? Are you still there?'

'Yes, Joan,' came the reply, then Joe ran through all the interventions I'd already tried. 'There's no magic,' he concluded. 'Ventilating her without ICU support would be tricky and still may not save her life. Over.'

I didn't mention that, even were that a possibility, neither I nor the equipment on hand was in any way up to it. I waited.

'Could you possibly transfer her to City Park Hospital here in Cape Town?' Joe asked.

'No,' I said, with regret. 'There's no plane link. The journey is eight days by ship, if there's one on hand, and the patient would have to travel without medical back up. I can't leave and there's no nursing care.' Then, in a strangely high voice, I heard myself say, 'Thank you. I can only keep trying.'

'Good luck, Joan,' came Joe's last words. 'Over and out.'

Feeling desperately alone, I thanked the radio operator. His eyes, round and dark, showed the fear I felt.

There was no getting around this. I'd said yes to the challenge of this adventure in medicine. I'd had no idea of how agonisingly lonely it would be at times, how my confidence in my medical ability could quickly be replaced by an overwhelming feeling of hopelessness and despair.

I walked back to the hospital. I paused once to gaze up at the stars and fill my lungs with the air Martha so badly needed. Giving up wasn't an option.

For three days and three nights, I sat beside Martha. Her aged, very deaf husband was my constant shadow-like companion. He sat in silence, almost motionless, at the head of the bed, clasping his wife's cold, pale hand. The minuscule nuances in her breathing sounds were my markers for further intervention. The background music was the hiss of the oxygen.

I thought that I was a reasonably experienced doctor in the treatment of asthma, and being a chronic asthmatic myself, I felt I had inside information. But this was dangerous, uncharted territory. I injected more potent bronchodilating drugs and steroids than was safe; then I had to counteract undesirable side effects, like a racing heartbeat, with more drugs. The nebuliser ran incessantly. Martha remained minimally responsive, but breath continued to pass, in tiny increments, in and out of her lungs, and her heart beat on.

On the third day, as I rested my head on the bed next to her, I felt a hand touch my hair. It was her husband, smiling, and holding her hand aloft as Martha stirred in the bed, rolled her head and gazed slowly around. She had stepped irrevocably back from death, and she recovered without alteration to her mental state.

For the next few days the ward was a centre of joyous celebrations.

※

Life on Tristan had a rhythm that captivated me. Although intermittently super-stressed in my medical life, I fell into the pace of the island with ease and relief. It made me joyful, restored my self-esteem following my disastrous marriage, and gave me time to revel in the magic of children.

And it reconnected me with nature. There was no TV, no telephones, no traffic. The island's rhythm was dictated by that of the natural world. Awakening at first light, I would lie in bed wondering if it was a day of sunshine or rain, listening for the women calling their cows for milking, checking for roof rattles that could mean a strong-enough wind to cancel school.

I had, a few weeks prior, caused great hilarity and some scorn among the islanders when, in true Calvinistic fashion, I'd sent my kids off in a howling gale – wind was never an excuse to miss a day's school. But when they returned an hour later, shivering, eyes large with fear, and with stories of hanging onto poles to stop being blown away, I knew I'd made a bad call.

Then there was the scuttling around at night to get all the chores done before the electricity ended. I liked the rhythm of having only sixteen hours of power, generated by the massive central diesel generator whose fuel consumption had to be carefully monitored, as a supply was brought in by ship only every four months. Late-night reading by the soft glow of candles held a romantic pleasure.

There were also those annual days of celebration of the harvests: taking the long boats around to Sandy Bay to pick apples, heading to Nightingale Island to harvest the chicks of the greater shear-water, whose young bodies would then provide enough cooking fat for the next year – a practice that might have been regarded as somewhat barbaric and inhumane but which brought into stark relief that we were on the world's most remote inhabited archi-pelago, and practices frowned on in less isolated parts of the world were, there, a necessity.

Another carnival day, and one that filled me with great anxiety, was the shooting of the heifers on a distant part of the island, to provide meat for the coming year. I was permitted to attend one of these shoots, to be on hand for any accidents. Despite what seemed, to my unpractised eye, frighteningly random shooting that left huge scope for gunshot injuries, the only casualties were the animals. The carcasses, with heads removed, were loaded into the dinghies, and the return of the flotilla to the harbour was festive.

Fishing, a less gruesome pursuit, was always there in the background. Everyone fished. The crystal-clear waters around the island were far from exploitation by unscrupulous trawlers, and the variety of fish seemed boundless. Lobster catching was also easy. These activities were both recreational and essential for keeping food on the table.

Then there was the industry around potatoes, the standard crop of Tristan. Everybody grew potatoes in an area called the Potato Patches about two kilometres from the main settlement, Edinburgh of the Seven Seas. Many folk also had a shack at the Potato Patches that was the equivalent of their holiday home. It was even closer to nature: no power, cooking over peat and dung, and water collected off the roof.

The doctor was well cared for, and the girls and I lived off the kindness of the islanders, with frequent gifts of fish, lobster and potatoes.

I also had time to develop new friendships, with both people and animals. We inherited a sheepdog, Susie, and a ram with a good pair of horns, whom Anna rescued from the pot. The ram became the keeper of the gate when patients came to seek my help, and was enough of a deterrent to keep the malingerers at bay.

Dougie Withers was an English professional diver involved in a pilot study to assess the feasibility of enlarging the harbour, and as we were the only two singles of a similar age on the island, we formed a lasting friendship. He showed me that I still had some hidden desirability, although he had to dig deep to haul it out! His magic was an amazing sense of humour and a joy in the absurd – a little reminiscent of Pete. Dougie was relaxed and kind to my girls, and the four of us embarked on memorable excursions on land and sea.

The simple pleasures of sex did lure us into bed, but not without a lot of fun and laughs. It wasn't a serious business. Despite, as usual, being blinded by my usual naivety and not having contemplated such a happening, the first time we found ourselves beyond the point of no return I was nonetheless savvy enough to know that we must use a condom. So proceedings were halted as I dashed off into the night, into the adjacent clinic, to rummage around in drawers by torchlight to find the essential foil-packaged object.

I became mildly obsessed with the history of Tristan and the South Atlantic Ocean in which we now lived. I learned that the island was part of the British Overseas Territory comprising St Helena, Ascension and Tristan da Cunha islands. It had been discovered by a Portuguese admiral, Tristão da Cunha, in 1506, while he was exploring a sailing passage around Africa.

Its first inhabitants, three obstreperous and mutinous sailors off a Yankee whaler, Jonathan Lambert, Thomas Currie and a man known only as Williams, only set foot on the island in 1810. Lambert was so delighted with his new home that he published a proclamation in the *Boston Gazette*, claiming the islands for himself and his heirs, naming them The Islands of Refreshment. His sovereignty was short-lived, however: he and Williams drowned in 1813.

The British, fearing that the French might occupy Tristan to organise the escape of Napoleon, who was imprisoned on St Helena (the island's nearest neighbour at 2 400 kilometres distant), annexed the islands in 1816, suddenly focusing the world's attention on this small dot in the South Atlantic. Lord Charles Somerset, Governor of the Cape of Good Hope, was instructed that the islands were to be taken over as a precautionary measure, and he organised a garrison to be stationed there. This was maintained until 1817, but on its withdrawal, William Glass, originally a Scot, requested to be left behind with his wife from the Cape, Maria Leenders, their two children and two other volunteers. So began the present settlement.

Mary and Anna getting close to nature.

Shipwrecked sailors, mutineers, disillusioned American whalers and freed female slaves from St Helena swelled the numbers to the 250 souls of today.

I was standing at a height of 2 060 metres above sea level, the summit of the central volcanic cone of Tristan, Queen Mary's Peak. I'd slogged my way up with Sogneus, he of tooth-removal fame, and also the husband of Margaret, my housekeeper and bread baker. I was greatly privileged: he'd never before escorted a woman to the summit.

My exhilaration spilled over as I twirled 360 degrees, stopping to imagine where St Helena lay, and Gough Island and Marion Island, and far down there to the south — terra incognita, the

Antarctic. I felt an overwhelming need to complete my South Atlantic island education – I wanted to visit and work on all of these islands. I now knew I had the ability and the confidence to undertake this.

I spotted an albatross gliding effortlessly over the dark waves that stretched on all sides to the horizon. How I wanted to be more in its world, to become familiar and knowledgeable about sea birds, marine mammals and fish. They felt like magical creatures from another planet. Could my profession, my very ordinary medical degree, in some way open doors for me?

I laughed out loud. Sogneus smiled at my obvious joy.

'That thar is pretty, and not too many folks has bin up here to look,' he said, pointing to the crater lake, shimmering blue on the edges, white with ice in the middle. I drank in this view.

My mind was made up. These far-flung places with their aura of mystery and unpredictability drew me in. I was going to seek out medical opportunities in remote locations and hope that either my credentials would suffice, or such positions held such small appeal that competition would be minimal.

Soon, however, there was an incident that should have dissuaded me from practising 'remote' adventure medicine ever again. It should have chased me into a clean, cool, white consulting room, protected by a bossy receptionist, practising a well-ordered speciality like dermatology. This event tested my medical skills, my negotiation skills, my patience, my bravery and my optimism. It was a combination of a serious medical condition and seriously bad weather, and it proved that the management of the practical issues around a medical problem could be the deciding factor in a patient's survival.

Basil Lavarello, a man in his early 60s and an islander of some influence, walked into my surgery one day. I looked up and gasped involuntarily. He was egg-yolk yellow. He stood in great discomfort, scratching – his arms, his legs, his face – and causing angry red excoriations to erupt.

'Doctor Joan, I'm going mad with them itches.' It was a vast understatement.

'And how long have you been yellow?' I asked. I thought it an obvious question, but he looked puzzled and I realised that he was unaware of his appearance. It was just the physical discomfort that was bothering him. But his yellow coloration, the jaundice, bothered me hugely. The cause was most likely a blockage of his biliary ducts. This obstructed the flow of bilirubin, a yellow fluid, from his gall bladder into his gut, and it was therefore being reabsorbed into his blood. Excess bilirubin in the blood results in its being deposited in the skin, causing intense itching.

None of the causes of obstruction of the biliary ducts, I knew, were easily remediable without surgery. Worse still, any number of serious complications could occur. We were in for a torrid time.

Days later, in the Radio Shack, I was once again struggling to enlist the help of a specialist thousands of kilometres away. 'Yes, Dr Jeffrey, he is on intravenous antibiotics, but he continues to spike a temperature and his jaundice is worsening. Over,' I shouted.

Silence.

'Are you still there? I'm having trouble hearing you.' The dreadful quality of the radio transmission was exacerbated by the wind outside, howling and whistling. I struggled to hear his next sentence, but I'd already anticipated it. 'Well, there's nothing else to do but get him to Cape Town. You'll lose him otherwise.'

'Yes, I do think he'll die if he stays here, but he may die getting to you – it's eight days by ship and he goes on his own, maybe with a relative, but not with a medically trained person. And I need to find a ship. Over.'

'Sounds like you have your hands full,' said Peter Jeffrey, my surgeon friend in Cape Town. 'Good luck. I'll expect him. Over and out.'

Dr Jeffrey, in his comfortable, warm, modern consulting room in a big city on the mainland, expressed a confidence in me that I certainly didn't feel. I had to rise to this occasion. I looked up. The radio operator had his head bowed and his eyes fixed on the dials. He was becoming accustomed to me and my pending disasters, although I did sense his extreme anxiety.

'Please send out a general SOS to all shipping channels,' I instructed him. 'Ask if any ship heading east is close enough to Tristan to divert to collect a patient for Cape Town. Tell them it's a matter of life or death. I'll be back this evening for news.'

Stepping out into buffeting wind and horizontal stinging rain, I felt isolated and vulnerable. For a moment, I was the soaring albatross observing this mere mortal, way below on a tiny speck of land, slap-bang in the middle of the heaving Atlantic Ocean. Nothing, no-one, could be more insignificant. But I was of no consequence right now. My task was to reassure Basil that all was in hand and that plans were afoot to get him safely to Cape Town.

Back at the Radio Shack in the evening, the news wasn't good. Although a ship had responded to our SOS and had altered course for Tristan, it had collided with another vessel in the terrible seas. In between the static, I listened with growing dread as the captain told me his ship had been badly damaged and that he was heading directly for Cape Town.

'Thank you, Captain, and good luck,' I said. Then I had a sudden thought. 'Wait — what's the name of the ship you hit?'

As I heard the reply, the pins and needles of an adrenaline surge coursed through my body. The other ship in the collision was the second of three vessels that had answered our call for help, and was also limping its way to Cape Town. We therefore still had one potential rescue ship.

To the radio operator I said, 'Get that ship on the air. Beg them. Tell them we'll expect them ASAP and I'll get Basil prepared.'

The following day, before the sun rose, I was out in front of the Radio Shack. The small harbour lay below me, the open fishing boats tugging at their moorings. The sea beyond the breakwater was vicious. Waves crashed and plumes of foam shot skywards. Gulls twisted and dived.

The skipper of the transfer launch was ready. Basil, a bent yellow reed, was gazing out from the cliff above the harbour, searching for his saviour.

And there she was — a small cargo vessel out in the open sea, disappearing behind huge swells, and then pulling her bow up out of the crashing waves. It was a terrifying sight. Transfer of a passenger would be hazardous, perhaps suicidal.

'Come now,' came the voice of the captain over the radio. 'We'll make a lee for your launch.'

The action went into fast-forward as the launch skipper and his team rushed up to talk to the captain. Basil elbowed his way in. Andy, the radio operator, was trying to maintain radio etiquette, and I stood rooted to the spot outside.

There were loud and frequent exchanges on the radio, and finally from the launch skipper: 'The launch will not go out. Too dangerous. Too many lives at risk. Thank you for trying. Over and out.'

I stood, a barely breathing statue. Basil edged in next to me. In silence we watched the small ship swing around and disappear into swirling, death-shroud mist.

'I knows it from the start. Tristan says I must die here.'

'No, Basil. I will get you off.' I said this with confidence and bravado, but then – as must be fairly obvious to the reader by now – doctors need to be fair actors. I strode off, head down, in the most abominable weather I'd ever experienced.

At the residence of the Administrator, hanging onto the door post, I beat the door with my fist in an attempt to be heard above the roar of the wind. 'Sir? I need to talk to you urgently,' I shouted.

The door opened a fraction. An arm shot out, grabbed mine and pulled me inside. 'Doctor Joan! What are you doing wandering around in this?'

'Sir, I desperately need your help. I mentioned to you a few days ago the serious illness of Basil Lavarello. You're aware that I was trying to get a ship to take him to Cape Town but there's no ship available – except maybe the one that cruises around the island catching lobster for the Tristan Investment Company.'

The Administrator, who had been avoiding my eyes, now gave me his full attention. 'But that one isn't due to return to Cape Town for a few months, and anyway it's required to return with a full load of lobster. It would be hugely costly to the company, and to Tristan, if it returned ahead of schedule.'

'Sir, this is a life-or-death emergency.' I paused, then caught and held his gaze, before continuing slowly and deliberately, keeping my voice low. 'There is so much I don't know. But I know, without any doubt, that without further treatment in a hospital setting, Basil will die a horrific and painful death.'

Having made my case, I refused to dwell on negative thoughts. I battled my way to the hospital, and wrote the best referral letter of my life, to my surgical colleague in Cape Town. I wanted him to know that I had tried hard but failed. This was a last gamble.

One hour later I got a call from the Administrator: 'Tell Basil to pack and be ready to leave at 10 tomorrow, weather permitting.'

As massive as this was, this was just the first step for Basil. He needed to survive eight days on the ship, without any trained medical input. I gave his wife, who would accompany him, a hurried teaching session on how to manage his pain and other symptoms on the journey, packed all the necessary drugs and other medical equipment, and compiled endless lists and easy-to-follow instructions.

Basil's departure day dawned grey but still, as was the entire population of Tristan, who had gathered to bid him farewell. I looked into his eyes, the sclera a deep egg-yolk yellow. 'Good luck, Basil. My thoughts are with you,' I said.

He frowned, shook my hand, and turned to step into the launch. Then he paused momentarily, looked up to the heavens, and raised his right arm in a sort of farewell salute.

My next eight nights were sleepless. My daily contact with the ship was always fraught but Basil remained alive. From Cape Town harbour he was whisked away by ambulance to the Kingsbury Hospital, where he underwent scans and biopsies that revealed a tumour blocking his bile duct. Surgery was scheduled, and the malignant biliary tract carcinoma was fully removed, with additional radiotherapy in an attempt to prevent a recurrence.

He made a fast, uneventful recovery, lost his yellow colour and ceased itching. In a few months, he was back on his beloved Tristan. I had departed by then, and I never saw him again.

❋

In May 1992 Mary and Anna and I departed tearfully from the volcanic cone protruding from the Atlantic Ocean, each nursing our private losses of parting, and placing them on the scales of experience gained. The return sea journey, on the same fishing vessel that had carried Basil to Cape Town, was uneventful.

For the first time in five months I was off duty. I meditated, I dreamed. I even had the courage to look cautiously into a future that previously had felt like a sporadically flickering candle at the end of a wind tunnel.

My experience on Tristan felt otherworldly. I'd been removed from the pain of mourning Pete, from the fractured self-esteem caused by my failed marriage to Jeff, and even from the uncomfortable solo-parent status in a world dominated by couples. The only expectation the kind folk of Tristan had of me was to be a caring and competent doctor, and despite my many glaring failures, I'd passed this test, usually under suboptimal conditions.

My world had been opened up to oceans and islands. I wanted to string them together with the trace of an albatross. Medical expertise could give me the wings to do this, if I had the courage.

I was free to make my own decisions, perhaps the only advantage of Pete's catastrophic death. I now wanted to gain more skills to equip me for this peculiar genre of medicine, one practised in remote locations with limited resources and assistance.

On Tristan, where I'd had the advantage of slower-moving, less demanding days, I'd watched my girls, played with them, baked with them, knitted with them, talked easily with them and really enjoyed their company. They had shown themselves to be strong, resolute and independent thinkers. They would be okay in spite of any unusual work choices I might make. And anyway the day would come when they would head off without me: I would always want them to feel I was sufficiently independent that they could forge ahead without too many concerns regarding the wellbeing of their aging, eccentric mother.

There could also be shared adventures. They now seemed so relaxed and attuned to shipboard travel … perhaps other ships could take us off to new destinations.

I didn't want to lose this feeling of optimism, confidence and curiosity. But I was prepared to lose sight of the shore.

That night I wrote in my journal:

Life is precarious and tricky, and has the potential to be achingly lonely. Strive to be happy, giving and healthy. Looming in a nebulous future, there are hooks you can hang on to:

1. Keep dreaming. Anything is possible.

2. Know that timing is never perfect. Accept this and work with it.

3. Saying 'yes' always reaps greater rewards than saying 'no' (well, nearly always).

4. Keep looking for the 'point of wonder'– that special moment that lifts a day, giving it a charge and enough momentum to look forward to the next day.

CHAPTER 3

St Helena: 1993 and 1995

'Life is either a daring adventure or nothing.'
– Helen Keller in *Let Us Have Faith*, 1940

I'D CLIMBED TO AN ARID, ROCKY high point above Jamestown, the capital and historic main settlement of St Helena island. The town lies on the northwestern coast of this volcanic outcrop, some 4 000 kilometres east of Rio de Janeiro, and nearly 2 000 kilometres west of the Angola/Namibia border.

I was scanning the horizon for a small mail ship, the RMS *St Helena*, which was bringing my daughters from Cape Town to spend three months with me. I had engineered another working island adventure, which included their attending school here for a while – 13-year-old Mary at the senior Prince Andrew School, and 9-year-old Anna at Pilling, the closest of the seven junior schools.

I had preceded my girls by four weeks, leaving in early November 1993; they'd needed to finish their school year and would then follow in December. I had an exciting but circuitous route – a flight to Brize Norton, the Royal Air Force (RAF) base near Oxford, then a flight across the Atlantic in a RAF TriStar to Recife in Brazil, from where I was shepherded onto a Hercules as the only female passenger and flown to a shortened runway under repair on Ascension Island.

Finally, I'd stepped aboard the RMS *St Helena* and we'd set a course for Jamestown, home to about 630 of the total population of St Helena of 4 534 souls. I was one of three resident doctors on the island – the generalist, the tasks of surgery and anaesthetics fortunately being the responsibility of my two colleagues.

St Helena lies within the tropics. The island is not, however, of the lush palm-fringed sparkling-seas white-beach variety. Its black-sand beaches reveal its violent volcanic origin, and the only tropical vegetation grows at mist-shrouded elevations that snag the trade winds, coaxing them to deposit their watery load. From these heights the land falls away to the ocean in deep-sided rocky valleys edged by hunchbacked hills interspersed with pockets of land suitable for grazing.

Environmental damage inflicted by goats, and man felling trees, and by clearing for the flax industry, had left only one third of the island under indigenous vegetation. The flax industry, encompassing the growing, harvesting and manufacture of rope and twine, was the engine of the island's economy from 1907 until 1966, when competition from synthetic fibres made it unprofitable. The legacy of acres of land supporting rampant flax plants was a painful reminder.

I saw the white dot of the RMS *St Helena* appear on the horizon, and I scampered down the hill, singing and whooping. I had missed my girls and filled the gap their absence had caused with uncharacteristic anxiety. How had they survived the five-day voyage from

Cape Town? Would they make friends on the island? Would they get lonely? Would their schooling here be adequate? Could I make up for all they would be missing?

Ships arriving at Jamestown anchored out in James Bay, and all passengers and cargo were transferred to smaller craft which then pulled alongside the harbour wall. Passengers had to pass through immigration and customs, a three-hour-long process that felt interminable to me, but finally Mary and Anna emerged, laughing and skipping, and it was as if our time apart hadn't happened at all.

All islands are swathed in unique mysteries, protected by a tacit agreement between the residents. This state of affairs may be born from centuries of isolation and self-sufficiency, and on St Helena I became aware of the defensive pride the locals had in their outcrop of volcanic rock in the Atlantic Ocean.

St Helena was discovered in 1502 by Portuguese navigator João da Nova, and named after Helena of Constantinople, the mother of Emperor Constantine the Great. She, appropriately, became the patron saint of new discoveries.

The island became a rendezvous point and source of food and water for ships travelling around the Cape of Good Hope from Asia to Europe. The Dutch claimed it in 1633 but didn't establish a settlement there. It was left to the English East India Company, in 1657, to settle a colony, after being given a charter to govern by Oliver Cromwell.

The Dutch took exception to this and took the island by force for a short period in 1673, but the English repossessed and held on to it. It became the second-oldest British Overseas Territory after Bermuda.

Mary and Anna perched on fortifications near Jamestown.

St Helena was also the setting for an infamous medical intrigue, still not conclusively resolved at the time of my visits. This mystery related to the most famous of St Helena's prisoners, French statesman and military leader Napoleon Bonaparte, who rose to prominence during the French Revolution in the late 1700s and led several successful campaigns during the French Revolutionary Wars. He dominated European and global affairs for more than a decade during what came to be known as the Napoleonic Wars, most of which he won. He was defeated at the Battle of Waterloo in 1815, after which the British exiled him to St Helena, where he remained imprisoned until his death six years later.

In April 1821, a month before his death, he dictated his last will and testament. Proving that he was one of history's most accomplished manipulators, he added these words: 'My death is premature. I have been assassinated by the English oligopoly and their hired murderer.'

The day after his death on 5 May, an autopsy was performed in the presence of sixteen observers, seven doctors among them. They came to the unanimous conclusion that the cause of death was stomach cancer, but this did little to quell the doubts fed by Napoleon himself as to what had really happened. Had he been poisoned, and if so, by whom? The British government? French rivals? Was it even Napoleon who'd died in the dark and dingy Longwood House?

For almost 200 years such questions have been discussed, disputed and recycled, and have been the subject of numerous books, films and research studies. Then, in January 2007, an article appeared in the journal *Nature Clinical Practice Gastroenterology and Hepatology*, written by a professor of pathology and internal medicine from the University of Texas Southwestern Medical Center. With other researchers, he applied modern pathological and tumour-staging methods to historical accounts, and concluded that Napoleon died of a very advanced case of gastric cancer arising from chronic ulceration caused by the bacterium *Helicobacter pylori*. The immediate cause of death was probably massive gastric bleeding.

Another snippet of medical history was that the famous Dr James Barry had worked here, in the General Hospital in Jamestown, around 1837. Dr Barry was later to make gender history when it was discovered on his death that he was, in fact, female.

A plaque on the wall of my consulting room in the General Hospital of St Helena stated that the original construction was in 1742. Nowhere in South Africa had I worked in a hospital with such deep roots.

I as a community doctor had the privilege of meeting 'Saints', the name given to the folk of St Helena, from across the spectrum of island life. Most of their diseases were familiar but their names were unusual, and I soon learned a source of information as to their origins.

Many of my patients had first names as surnames: Benjamin, Henry, William, Joshua, George. These names, I realised, had come from the brutal slave trade. Slaves had never had the dignity of their own given names, and were given a first name only, chosen and pinned on them by their owners.

The importation of slaves, mainly from Madagascar and Asia, was made illegal in 1792. Phased emancipation of the 800 resident slaves on St Helena began years later, in 1827 – still a full six years before the British parliament finally banned slavery in the colonies.

In 1840 the British government established a naval station on St Helena to suppress the African slave trade. Hundreds of slave ships carrying their tragic cargo from west Africa to the New World were intercepted by Royal Navy vessels, their load of slaves and goods landed on the island, and the ships destroyed. Queen Victoria selected Jamestown, the main settlement on St Helena, to establish a Vice-Admiralty Court to try the crews of the apprehended slave ships.

Over the following nine years more than 15 000 freed slaves were landed on the island, and by 1870 the number stood at 25 000. Many arrived in a sorrowful, sickly state, and their time in refugee camps did little to restore them to health. Their return to their homes in Africa proved almost impossible, as slavers kept no detailed records as to where they had collected the slaves, and the slaves' knowledge of their local geography was insufficient to relocate them. Thousands died.

As the numbers of landed slaves increased to a level that St Helena couldn't accommodate, some 16 000 were sent on to the Cape Colony and the British West Indies, and used as labourers. A thousand opted to stay on St Helena, initially as unpaid labourers, but in time they integrated fully and here their names live on.

I turned my attention to my next patient, a smiling, smooth-skinned, round-faced, oriental-eyed man. His name was Yon. His medical issues resolved, I enquired about his name. He mentioned his Chinese ancestry but seemed vague and shy.

Later, a visit to the museum informed me that in 1806 the Governor of St Helena, Robert Patton, requested the importation of Chinese labour, and by 1818 their numbers stood at 650. A callous decision in 1836 decreed them to be no longer required and requested their return. Some were allowed to stay, and Chinese Lane in upper Jamestown bears testimony to this random exploitation of people regarded purely as units of labour.

My next patient had a mischievous twinkle in his blue eyes and greeted me in tortured Afrikaans. I smiled and stole a glance at his surname: Piek. He volunteered that he was descended from one of the 6 000 Boer prisoners-of-war who'd spent the years 1900 to 1902 living in the world's first overseas concentration camp. Even his medical problem was evidence of his heritage: he had atherosclerosis and coronary artery disease, illnesses with a high prevalence among those of Afrikaans descent.

The General Hospital in Jamestown, with a Christmas Bugs Bunny ready to entertain the patients.

Later that day I took Mary and Anna on a walk of discovery to the site of the Boer camp on Deadwood Plain, where the prisoners had lived in tents or small huts they fashioned themselves out of biscuit tins. They proved to be a typically resourceful lot and interacted easily with the locals. They contributed greatly in the form of labour on the island, and were given many liberties to establish small industries like a brewery, a coffee house, a woodwork shop and some leisure groups including a string quartet, a male choir, craft societies and the inevitable sports teams. Two were allowed to marry local girls.

Living conditions must have been grim at times, though, and a large cemetery at Knollcombes is evidence of the deaths of 180 young men of typhoid. Their names are inscribed on two obelisks that stand at the foot of the hillside. I saw my own surname inscribed there, and thought again of the invisible tracks we wanderers carve across the world and over those of our forebears.

After the peace treaty of the Second Boer War, also known as the South African War, was signed in May 1902, the relocation of the St Helena prisoners commenced. 'The imprisonment of Boer prisoners-of-war in St Helena has indeed benefited the island materially,' notes an article in the *St Helena Guardian* on 23 October 1902, marking the final shipment of prisoners back to South Africa. But some chose to stay on the piece of earth to which they'd been banished and yet had grown to love. They left behind their genes and their names, like Piek and Vanguard and Smit.

I was hoping to see a patient with a name containing some permutation of Dinuzulu kaCetshawyo, the last Zulu king, who led his army against the British in 1890, after they had annexed Zululand in 1887. He was defeated, captured and sent to St Helena, along with an entourage of twelve, including two wives. While on the island for seven years, he fathered eight children, but there's no trace of them now.

The sixth Sultan of Zanzibar, whose seizing of power there led to the shortest war in British history – 38 minutes, on 27 August 1896 – was finally captured in German East Africa when the British invaded in February 1917. He was exiled to St Helena with his support crew of seventeen, but, sadly, no stragglers or offspring of these occupants were my patients either.

The last royal prisoners on the island were three Bahraini princes. Sentenced to fourteen years for offences against the state of Bahrain in 1957, they were incarcerated on St Helena with the permission of Britain, and stayed at the searchlight station at Munden's Point for four years. I visited their jail. It was perched on a rocky promontory with a magnificent view over James Bay. There was no sign of any additional security measures: obviously, escape was highly unlikely.

St Helena was seen as so ideally suited to being a place of incarceration that while working there I heard the strangest of rumours: Nazi Germany had had a plan to use it after they'd invaded Britain – King George VI and Winston Churchill were to be exiled there!

※

My major discovery as a doctor was that St Helena had an efficient and well-run health department, with a 54-bed hospital, six rural clinics, a maternity department, a well-equipped surgical theatre and, best of all, a full-time dentist.

My work there yielded thankfully little in the way of scary, mouth-drying adventures in medicine for me, due largely to my very competent colleagues on whose help I could always rely. Dr John Sharpe, an experienced surgeon, and Dr Carol Coates, a South African-trained anaesthetist and generalist, astounded me with their skill and courage. They also made me question some of my views honed in palliative care. I was accustomed to placing quality of life and symptom control first, and death was an inevitable end for my terminally ill patients.

When I assisted John and Carol in an interminably long surgical intervention in a healthy but elderly patient with a ruptured aortic aneurysm, I observed them try every manoeuvre they knew to save his life in a setting where many might never have attempted it. I was moved and humbled by their efforts. The patient succumbed but they had given him every possible chance. They added to my vista of what could be deemed possible, and morally justifiable, in medicine.

I was the family physician on the island, with my main area of responsibility being the outlying clinics and care facilities such as the retirement home and the centre for disabled patients. It felt like a working holiday despite regular night and weekend calls. Having competent and enthusiastic colleagues was such a bonus, and a source of valuable knowledge. My learning curve for acute medicine was steep but exciting.

My need to perform active cardiopulmonary resuscitation in the preceding years had been minimal, but on St Helena I was often on my own when patients were rushed in, blue around the mouth, with no pulse or a thready heartbeat. I rapidly improved my resuscitation skills, but sadly the success rate of this procedure, even in more experienced hands, is rarely above thirty per cent. I had three resuscitations; only one patient survived.

My short experience on Tristan da Cunha had prepared me for 'island medicine', but the much larger population of St Helena had a kaleidoscope of problems that were amplified by its isolation. I dealt with mass outbreaks of a salmonella-induced dysentery, trauma from occasional drunken brawls, complications of diabetes, acute depression, and the rare leptospirosis contracted from infected rat urine.

The cause of much of the mental anxiety, deep-seated frustration and depression sprang from the restricted life choices of the Saints. Many young, bright teenagers had to face the reality that tertiary education was unlikely. Mundane, boring employment was more the rule, and their behaviour would spin off into excessive alcohol consumption, promiscuity, unplanned pregnancies and domestic violence.

The unusual pattern of inherited disease or deformity was something outsiders always enquired about, but it proved a topic that carried a social stigma. Islanders were reticent about their family connections and the faulty genes that were chance arrivals on their shores. Consanguineous marriage – that is, unions between individuals who are closely related – happened, but the genetic relationship between the partners was played down. It was sometimes tragically revealed when the union produced afflicted offspring.

My first brush with a rare inherited disorder happened during a routine visit to a clinic, when my nursing assistant, looking wild and breathless, informed me, 'Doctor Joan, Libby has come in with an attack of her HANO! You must take her at once to the hospital.' Behind her stood a distressed pudgy young woman, hair raked back into a greasy pony-tail, with a soiled pink dressing gown thrown over her shoulders. Her face and neck were swollen, her eyes sunken beneath thick, shiny lids, and her breathing was rapid and noisy.

At first glance she looked like she was suffering from an acute allergic reaction. I had no idea what HANO was, although I was to discover it was short for hereditary angioneurotic oedema. (It's now known as HAE, or hereditary angioedema – the 'neurotic' had a negative implication that implied it had some mental-disorder link.)

'She needs some injectable antihistamine and steroids,' I said to my assistant.

'No, Doctor, that won't help,' she said, and the patient nodded wildly in agreement.

I was obviously missing something – something important. 'Get Libby into my car,' I said to my assistant. 'I'll meet you there in a moment.'

As Libby was ushered out of the consulting room, I got on the phone to Carol at the hospital, who told me what hano was and that there was an unusually high incidence of this otherwise rare condition on St Helena. 'Get her down here – she may need intubation if her larynx swells up too much,' Carol told me.

I'd never driven those twisty, narrow roads of the high hills of St Helena at greater speed. The trolley and Dr Carol were ready and waiting as I screeched to a halt at the hospital entrance. Libby was still breathing, but her eyes were tight shut. She was whisked off to the operating theatre, where the instruments for intubation were laid out. I became the anaesthetist's assistant as Carol administered the drugs necessary for the procedure. A laryngeal tube was inserted and I pumped oxygen into the patient's lungs using a self-inflating ambu-bag.

'She'll be fine in 24 to 48 hours,' said Carol. 'I've done this a few times. Libby knows the problem and is good at seeking help early.'

I marvelled at Carol's calm demeanour as she told me that it wasn't really known what precipitates the attacks, and that at least fifteen patients, all related, had the condition.

'There's another patient, Toby, who has HANO that presents as swelling of his gastrointestinal tract. He comes in with severe abdominal pain and vomiting. If we knew no better, we'd rush him to hospital for an appendectomy ...'

By virtue of its limited gene pool and marriage between relatives, St Helena had a few sufferers of rare and tragically disabling genetic diseases. At my weekly visit to the care facility for handicapped children the kids always raced out to whichever doctor was willing to smile, touch them, hug them and chat to them. The staff were pleasant and kind but individual attention was difficult.

It took great resolve not to avoid going inside to check on the two sets of siblings, both with mental retardation and spastic quadriplegia. They could neither walk nor use their arms effectively, and there was no treatment to remedy the defective genes with which they'd been born.

And genes persist and are transportable, even over centuries. I met two patients on St Helena who suffered from retinitis pigmentosa, a degenerative eye disease that damages the retina, or back wall of the eye. It presents with decreasing vision at a young age and eventually leads to total blindness. My patients had had genetic studies performed by UCT's professor of genetics, Peter Beighton, and he'd been able to confirm that they had the inherited form of retinitis pigmentosa. A sudden memory of Tristan reminded me of a few patients there with this same very rare condition.

I did have one unusual medical adventure on St Helena. It involved waging war on hundreds, perhaps thousands, of insects that were burrowing and crawling within the skin of a dear, ancient, slightly simple woman who was a resident in the home for the aged. She had a condition known as Norwegian scabies, a severe form of scabies characterised by thick crusts of skin that contain large numbers of scabies mites and eggs.

The female of these insects lays countless eggs in the deeper layers of the skin, which hatch to yield larvae that mature rapidly and lay more eggs. The larvae and the tunnelling adults cause a massively itchy rash.

Agnes, my patient, had been treated many times, but she persisted in climbing into the beds of other inmates, with or without their regular incumbents, and thus she infected others and re-infected herself continuously.

I took on a very rigid, disciplined, long-term offensive. The staff predicted my defeat, but they knew little of my dogged nature. I visited the home daily. I covered Agnes in the anti-scabies lotion. I returned the following day to bath her and re-apply the lotion. I hauled her mattress and those of other affected patients into the hot sun. I stuffed bed linen into washing machines – an unpopular move with the staff, as it added to their bed-making load.

Weeks passed and slowly Agnes itched less. She had so many dead mites in her skin that until the layers of skin were replaced naturally by her body, she would have lingering itching.

I like to think that I did eventually win this battle, but I have no doubt that a few hardy insects took cover and reappeared when the coast was clear and I was off the island.

Medical adventures, even if mundane, were rewarding but life adventures on St Helena were innumerable and captivating. There always seemed to be yet another vista to be enthralled by, yet another new fact to absorb. When it was time to leave, I knew I needed to return, and this I did for a five-month period, from May to September 1995.

Mary declined the invitation this time. She was well embedded in her senior-school life at Herschel in Cape Town and academically didn't want to lose any ground. Long-suffering Anna accompanied me and provided the most glaring medical misadventure of my career.

I admit to being a reluctant doctor for my children. I didn't want them to be sick, ever; then I felt too inadequate to treat them when they were. I wanted whatever they had to be minor and easily remediable. They reminded me that my stock phrase to them was, 'Take an aspirin and go to sleep.' They countered this with, 'Take us to a proper doctor!'

Anna returned home from school one Friday afternoon with an earache. Other than this she seemed fine. I was busy and distracted by packing the camping gear for a weekend on the rugged dry southwestern part of the Island called Sandy Bay. A hand to the forehead revealed no raised temperature, and her pulse rate was normal. I had a very quick, very incomplete look in her ear and saw nothing to alarm me. 'I'm sure it'll get better soon.' I smiled and said brightly, 'Here, have half an aspirin.'

What I failed to acknowledge, however, was that Anna is known for her extremely high pain threshold. Years before, she'd taken a tumble off a horse and fractured both forearms simultaneously; she stumbled back to the stables, pale and taut, but had shed not a tear.

We drove across the island, met my friend Gail Thorpe and her children with whom we'd be sharing a tent, and all felt right with the world as Gail and I sipped wine and watched the red solar disc slip from view.

As I crept into my sleeping bag, I shot a glance at Anna. She was curled up on her right side. Her left hand was clamped tightly over her left ear. Was she whimpering?

'Are you alright, Anna?' I whispered.

'No, Mom. My ear hurts,' came the obvious reply.

Any adequate inspection of the affected ear canal was at this point impossible. I had one pathetically dim torch and no other medical tools. My first-aid kit consisted, as usual, of a few aspirin.

It was a long, uncomfortable night for us both. Anna's pain was physical and she endured it with remarkable stoicism. My pain was sheer mental anguish: I had failed the most basic of medical tests, that of listening and caring. My own child was suffering as a result of my failure. The demons raced through my brain, accusing, criticising, tormenting, belittling. There was no escape.

I was up as dawn paled the sky. I apologised to Gail, bundled Anna into the car and headed for the clinic. I sat my patient down, and tried to slow my fluttering heart by methodically laying out my tools. 'When did this start, Anna?' I asked.

'I think something got into my ear two days ago, when we were rolling on the school fields. It wasn't sore then, though, only a day later.'

My guilt heightened. If only I'd stopped to ask this before. I already was part way to the diagnosis. 'And can you hear okay in that ear?'

'No.'

I embarked on a full examination of my patient. Apart from her obvious discomfort and some tenderness to pressure in front of the affected left ear, I could find no abnormality. Her right ear was normal. Gently I pulled on her left outer ear to straighten the inner canal. She grimaced. I eased my otoscope into position. She whined. What met my eyes confounded me. The magnified viewfinder was filled with a glistening grey-black object that was totally blocking the inner-ear canal. The drum was completely obscured, but signs of inflammation and swelling were present in the skin lining the canal.

I pondered. I squinted. I pushed the otoscope a little further into the object to test its consistency. It indented fractionally – then, suddenly, the viewfinder was obscured with dark fluid muck. I felt a rush of nausea. What had I done?

Anna inhaled sharply. 'It feels a bit less sore now.'

Fighting to maintain calm, I looked again … and the penny dropped.

I carefully worked a specialised ear tool, a Crocodile forceps, into her ear and with the tiny pincers at the end I grabbed at the shiny grey membrane and pulled. What I eased out was a bloody, fragmented tick, complete with tiny black feet, whose feast of blood in Anna's ear had rendered it so turgid that my small pressure with the otoscope had caused rupture.

We both examined the remnants in horror and disbelief – but the funny side took over. We roared with laughter.

I completed the consultation with a very adequate lavage of Anna's ear canal, followed by some antiseptic drops, and within the hour we were back with Gail for breakfast, complete with an excellent story, and with Exhibit A (aka tick) as proof.

On a clear summer's day, with only a zephyr of a wind, St Helena lies in a flat turquoise sea. On this particular day the weather was, however, at the other end of the spectrum. The wind hurtled in from the southeast and the rain thundered down. I donned foul-weather gear to stand in awe near the quayside and marvel at the waves crashing over the concrete barriers, throwing up torpedoes of spray that pummelled cars as they fell earthwards.

It came as no surprise when I was called, a little later, as the storm had moved northwards to inflict more damage on Ascension Island, to attend to an injured crew member of a yacht that had just limped into harbour, dragging a broken mast.

I bumped down to the harbour in my bakkie, and there, seated in the customs hall, was Gerhard, a Dutchman, who, unknown to him, would cause an unalterable shift in my perception of the world. He was flanked by a young blonde couple who I learned were his daughter and son-in-law. They looked exhausted and ashen.

Gerhard rose precariously. He stood unsteadily, towering over me, supporting his right elbow with his left hand. He wore a pair of torn khaki shorts, cinched at the waist with some tattered nylon rope. He was slim and sinewy, with thinning, unruly, salt-encrusted hair. His chest was bare and tanned, like the rest of his body, to a deep nut-brown. His sky blue eyes showed his pain – and something else: a new resignation to an unalterable situation. Much later, I identified this unalterable situation as advancing age.

We drove in uneasy silence to the hospital, where I assisted Gerhard into the radiology department. As I prepared him for an X-ray of his damaged right shoulder, he shook his head and muttered, 'This should not have happened. My strength failed. I could not stop myself from falling. They had to save me from going overboard. I am more hindrance than help.'

Later, in the ward, with Gerhard looking more like a standard patient in his hospital-issue pyjamas, and with the magic of opiate analgesia on board, we discussed his diagnosis.

'You've dislocated your acromioclavicular joint,' I told him. 'Nothing is fractured and we'll manipulate it back into place under anaesthesia, and strap it firmly. However, it will take some time to heal and get back to full mobility and strength.' Then I needed to know. 'How old are you?'

'I'm 69.' He didn't meet my eyes.

'You look younger,' I said, truthfully.

He lifted his head and a smile flickered across his face. 'I have always been a strong athlete ... well, until I was 63, and then I felt my muscles fade, my strength go, my back stiffen. But my daughter Coni wanted me to join them sailing around the world. How could I say no?'

Coni made the decision that they would all take a break and enjoy life on St Helena for about six weeks: their yacht, their bodies and their spirits needed to heal.

Gerhard's gaunt frame, his right arm in a sling, became a familiar sight around Jamestown. He maintained a rigorous walking routine – 'to keep in shape,' he said. 'In Holland I would be ice-skating.'

He often sought me out to share a cup of tea, and I coaxed him to tell me of his travels and his work across the globe. He became

Anna running down Jacob's Ladder into Jamestown.

something of a father-figure to me, then 40-something years old. His insatiable curiosity, his self-reliance and his serious attitude towards keeping his body in good working order, despite the ravages of age, had a profound effect on me. For the first time in my life I started to think of growing old. I wanted it badly. I wanted to be afforded the privilege of age, unlike my Pete. I wanted to feel what it was like, to be faced with this uncharted territory and pick my way through it. But, especially, I wanted to retain the mental and physical strength to step out of my comfort zone, make some contribution to the world, and travel.

On the day that the little Dutch yacht set sail for Ascension Island, 1 126 kilometres to the northwest, Anna and I climbed to a high vantage point to watch it slide over the horizon. We'd soon be returning to our old familiar lives in Cape Town, but this island experience had become another piece in the global jigsaw.

The Falkland, Gough, South Georgia and Marion islands were all washed by the same ocean, which stretched up to Arctic latitudes and way south to the Antarctic. Someone someday would hire me to travel there – or so I optimistically hoped.

CHAPTER 4

Australian Outback: 2001–2002

'Tell me, what is it you plan to do with your one wild and precious life?'
— From the poem 'The Summer Day' by Mary Oliver, 1992

FOR MY FIRST GENERAL-PRACTICE (GP) LOCUM for the Queensland Rural Medical Support Agency I was stationed at Tieri, a town with a population of just over a thousand, in Central Queensland. The practice was manned by a single doctor, whose place I was taking. I was delivered by a single-engine plane to the local dirt airfield, puffs of red dust being raised under the feet and tails of kangaroos as they hopped for cover into the surrounding eucalyptus thicket.

As I planted my feet firmly on Australian soil, my spirit soared. This baking, wide-open space, the bleached blue sky above, and the cheerful banter from the pilot boded well. Here, my patients would be predominantly young, fit workers at the nearby coal mine, and their families.

To my huge delight, the added benefits were a well-trained and conscientious ambulance crew who shared after-hours duties with me, daily laboratory sample collections and access to a big drug formulary. This meant I would have the backup of laboratory tests to assist diagnosis and a wide range of medicines to choose from. I was looking forward to practising good, solid, well researched and investigated medicine.

I had only one serious, life-threatening emergency. A young coal miner with a history of multiple abdominal operations presented to me after days of severe pain and vomiting. As I examined him, my heart accelerated and my mouth went dry. He was dehydrated, was running a fever, and had a rock-hard abdomen. Diagnosis: 'acute abdomen' as a result of an intestinal obstruction. He needed hospitalisation, fast, and probable surgery to relieve the obstruction and remove necrotic (rotting) tissue and other sources of infection.

'Looks like one for the Flying Doctor,' said my young, pretty and efficient nursing assistant. Seeing my look of incomprehension, she explained, 'I'll call them up on the radio, and you can have a chat with the doc.'

She left with a rustle of her starched white uniform while my memory circled back to my harrowing experiences of medical radio contact on Tristan da Cunha. But the situations were poles apart: the Royal Flying Doctor Service ran a 24/7 Telehealth Service and the reception was crystal clear.

'What have you got for me, Doc?' came the relaxed voice across the air.

I explained slowly, carefully, in unemotional detail.

'Oh, yeah. Sounds like an obstruction. And sounds like you ain't no Ozzie. A young Saffer, I suspect.' And he chuckled, putting me at ease. 'Tell you what, get that IV line up, get a nasogastric tube in if you can, and I'll be there in half an hour. Give him something for the trip. Scribble down the details too, please.'

In all my years of medical service, I'd never been offered such ready, gracious assistance. My eyes moistened.

'Let's get going. He'll be here before you know it.' My nursing assistant was at my elbow.

How right she was. The small plane was dropping from the sky as we wheeled the patient into the ambulance. Transfer was fast and efficient. I wished my patient good luck, and as the pilot clambered up into the cockpit, he turned, smiled, and quoted the now famous motto of this incredible aeromedical service: 'The furthest corner, the finest care.' He winked, waved, took to the air and disappeared into gathering storm clouds.

The Flying Doctor pilot clears kangaroos off the strip before landing.

❊

The thought process that ultimately led me to doctoring in the Outback had begun, for me, back on St Helena, where the competence and extreme medical versatility of my two colleagues had taken me down my own, often visited, track to a feeling of medical inadequacy. I was attracted to the medicine required in far-flung, under-resourced locations, but was I up to speed for it? Medicine is often a daunting, scary profession. If one starts out acknowledging a lack of training and competence in certain areas, it can be destructive.

Anaesthetics was a special knowledge area I'd wilfully ignored, believing in my early days of medicine that it was a domain best left to the specialists. During my housemanship year back in 1976, a two-week period had been allocated for anaesthetics. I'd chosen to get married and then hitch-hike around Malawi with my new husband in that time!

I'd met Peter Haw, the man I'd wished to spend the rest of my life with, and as he was an engineer employed by Water Affairs and lived in the wilds of Africa working on a dam on the Cunene River, I'd chosen the closest hospital, a mere 500 kilometres to the south, which offered internships – Windhoek State Hospital in what was then still South West Africa (today's Namibia).

On my first day there, in January 1976, I fingered my name badge – 'Dr Joan Louwrens' – gingerly but with a feeling of pride, as I walked briskly through the double doors of the hospital. I was questioning the wisdom of my decision to cycle to the hospital: I'd wanted to look cool and confident and instead I was sweating profusely. This was a poor start.

I'd been informed the night before that I would be manning my allocated wards on my own, as the senior registrar – my immediate superior who had at least two years of experience under his belt – had been laid low by New Year celebrations. The shrill tone of my bleeper alerted me, with a message to phone a certain ward. My heart sank: it was the paediatric ward, and those tiny inarticulate creatures terrified me to a degree way out of proportion to their size.

'It is urgent, Doctor,' the nursing sister told me over the phone. 'The patient is gasping.'

In the months that followed, 'the patient is gasping' became a familiar phrase; it usually meant that the patient was no longer drawing breath of any kind. On my first day I was ignorant of this, however, and headed for the ward. In the corner cot, as still as stone, lay the tiny patient. My hand instinctively reached out to touch the baby. The child's skin was dry and cool.

I turned to the sister who'd met me at the door. 'What happened?' Stupid question.

'Gastro,' came the reply, as she avoided eye contact and scurried off to the nurses' station.

The ward closed in on me. My pulse was racing, and breathing felt restricted in that faecally tainted air. The crying and wailing of the other babies seemed amplified and threatening. I was in a fight-or-flight reaction and it took all my self-control to stay rooted to the floor.

I gently rolled the eyelids over the child's huge, non-responsive pupils and stroked her head. Things got blurry. With the grimy sheet, I covered the evidence of our failure. 'Sister, please bring me the death-certificate book,' I said.

My first meaningful task on my first day of my first year of medical practice was to complete my first death certificate – that of an eighteen-month-old child whom I'd never seen alive.

As I prepared to leave the ward, the sister tugged at the sleeve of my white coat. 'The other doctor is not here. His patient needs drip,' she said.

Aha, I thought; this I can do. Thanks to all those nights volunteering in the emergency department of Groote Schuur Hospital in Cape Town, acclimatising to the blood, gore and chaos, I had become, I thought, a slick operator with inserting intravenous lines.

The sister led me to another tiny patient whose eyes had receded into his sockets, and whose skin looked old and shrivelled. He stank of faeces. He needed fluids fast, or soon I'd be writing another death certificate.

It's almost impossible to insert an intravenous line into the limbs of such tiny, dehydrated patients, and my heart began its downward slither as I realised I would have to insert the needle into a scalp vein. My hands felt like clumsy paws whenever I attempted this delicate procedure, which involves first shaving the child's head to gain better visibility of any veins. Then a portion of a rubber glove acting as a tourniquet is twisted around the small head of the patient, and a frantic tapping of all possible veins coursing across the scalp ensues, invariably accompanied by screams of protest from the patient.

At this point the assistant becomes key, as the little patient's head must be held immobile as the operator attempts to insert a fine needle into a distended vein without piercing its walls. The relief when a red pushback of blood in the attached tube is seen is indescribable. Then the needle and tube need to be securely stuck to the patient's head to prevent any dislodgement of the needle resulting in fluid tracking into the skin of the scalp and distending it in a grotesque fashion.

I took a deep, slow breath, laid out my tools, poured skin disinfectant into a bowl, and methodically cut plaster strapping, all in an attempt to regain composure. The sister looked on, disdain clearly etched on her face.

The child had obviously had numerous previous attempts at inserting a line, as the skin of his scalp was stubbled and nicked. It was a bad sign. But finally, after three attempts and amid a rising panic, I secured an intravenous line and began the slow process of rehydration. This child had a fighting chance.

During that interminable first day I'd felt utterly unsupervised or supported, and wondered if this was just the usual trial by fire at the start of a medical career: my fellow interns looked equally dazed and frantic, and there was no time to compare notes. I tried at one point to raise my senior registrar on the phone, without any success. I wrote out unfamiliar prescriptions, sutured gaping wounds, attended to geriatric patients suddenly stricken by strokes, and was asked to intervene in a dispute between staff members. The demon of incompetency trailed on my heels and whispered taunts in my ear. Was I cut out for this? Was I strong enough, brave enough, bold enough, clever enough, calm enough to be a good doctor? Or would my fear allow reticence and mediocrity to creep in?

Over the following months I progressed over the numerous obstacles of internship, seldom taking the time to reflect or evaluate. I was in survival mode, the details of which remain hazy. What is now becoming clear to me, as I gaze back on that year, is that internship itself is an ill-structured and unsupervised course in adventure medicine.

Perhaps being in an understaffed, consultant-depleted, outlying hospital far from any academic institution played a role. Two events in that year illustrate my point.

In the first, I was on Emergency Department night duty. It was close to midnight, and the waiting room was remarkably empty, as was the nurses' station: it was the very lengthy 'lunchtime'. I was writing up the notes of the previous patient when I became aware of a giant of a man standing in the doorway. In his hand he held a hospital folder. He seemed disoriented and vague.

Just one more of the many mentally unstable clients, I thought, and indicated that he take a seat on the far side of the consulting room. I continued writing. Minutes later something made me look over my left shoulder. The patient was standing right there, wooden chair held aloft in both hands, and it was descending at great speed in the direction of my head. Fight or flight took over, and I dived to the right as the chair crashed down onto mine, sending out a fusillade of pieces.

I was young, strong, fit and nimble in those days. I screamed while grabbing a nearby drip stand, which I brought down hard on the back of his neck. It only served to bewilder him, however, and he lunged with his bare hands for my neck. I got an elbow in his throat, at which point the security guards finally sauntered in, thinking all they'd have to deal with was the usual troublesome, noisy patient.

The scuffle that followed saw both guards attempting to keep the huge patient pinned to the floor as they yelled for the sister. Sensing trouble, she grabbed the emergency trolley and almost skateboarded across the shabby linoleum into the consulting room where, in a flash, she drew up a large syringe of antipsychotic sedative medication. Wasting no time, she thrust the needle straight through his trousers and into his muscular buttocks – she had clearly done this before.

The effect was close to miraculous. In minutes, every aggressive muscle in the patient fell into a flaccid state, leaving him snoring gently on the floor. The sister, sensing a job well done, played to her grateful audience. She pulled herself up to her full height, straightened her uniform and severely reprimanded me for allowing a potentially violent patient into my consulting room without an escort. 'This is not some wild shebeen, you know,' she snapped, and marched out.

The second incident falls into the adventure category of 'hazardous action of uncertain outcome', and it also exposed many of my own insecurities and weaknesses, at the expense of another's suffering. It was a difficult one to move on from.

Our team were on the usual early-morning ward round. The patient alongside whose bed we paused was an elderly rural Herero man who looked anxious and uncomfortable. He could speak no English, Afrikaans or German, the only languages on offer in the team.

Haltingly, through a translator, we gathered that he was passing blood per rectum and that he'd been losing weight.

'He needs a colonoscopy,' announced the senior registrar. 'Doctor Louwrens, it's your turn.'

A colonoscopy is a procedure where a tubular instrument with an attached lighting mechanism is inserted into the anus, and then eased up into the colon so that a direct inspection of the bowel wall is possible. I mumbled that my experience of the procedure was limited and I'd need some supervision.

'It's easy and it's a good time to learn,' came the unwelcome reply. 'You'll manage.'

The colonoscopes in use then were rigid and unwieldy, not like the little flexible camera-bearing ones of today. I'd prepared adequately, and had explained the procedure to the patient as well as possible. He'd placed his inked thumbmark on the consent form. I suspected that he had no clue what he'd let himself in for, or why. Nor had I.

Being the operator of a colonoscope feels a little like being the navigator of a small craft heading down a psychedelic tunnel. Your total attention is focused down the eyepiece. The rest of the world doesn't exist. You try to ignore the sporadic writhing and groans from the patient. Flashing past are slimy images of mucosa, blood and blood vessels, all shrouded by waves of brownish liquid. From this view, a decision needs to be made as to abnormalities present. Does an area show little inflamed pockets called diverticulae? Is there a lump that could be a tumour? Ulcers?

My journey down this man's colon was halted by a narrowing in the bowel wall. It looked like an old stricture. I needed to see beyond it if I was to adequately exclude any other pathology. I applied gentle pressure to the colonoscope. All that was visible was the thickened bowel wall. I attempted to ease the instrument into the small opening and proceed.

Then it happened. I was suddenly seeing not a tunnel but a spacious cavern lined with a clean, glistening membrane. What were those globules of gleaming yellow? Fat?

I began to sweat, as did my patient. I was looking into forbidden territory – the peritoneal cavity. I had perforated his bowel.

In sheer panic, I withdrew the colonoscope. I reassured the patient, who now looked seriously uncomfortable, and instructed the nurse to place him on hourly observations. I went in search of the surgical consultant.

An hour later I was back at the patient's bedside obtaining his consent again – this time for a laparotomy, a surgical procedure where the abdomen is opened by a long incision, in this case in order to enable inspection and repair of the internal damage I'd caused. He looked at me with trust in his dark eyes. Perhaps he thought I'd diagnosed his problem and was now going to set about remedying it. My guilt was overwhelming.

His colon was repaired but he needed to endure a colostomy bag for six weeks, to give the newly joined pieces of colon time to heal and unite. The relatively minor problem that had brought him to the hospital was also diagnosed and successfully treated.

When he returned to have his colostomy closed and so restore his normal bowel function, he greeted me with a huge smile and grabbed my hand to his heart. Swallowing hard was all I could manage.

Twenty years after I'd dipped out of the anaesthetics rotation during my housemanship, the South African Defence Force's 2 Military Hospital in Wynberg, Cape Town, accepted me as a trainee anaesthetist and I enrolled to study for my diploma in anaesthetics.

I still recall the welcoming words on my first day, in February 1996, from Dr Jacobs, one of my senior colleagues. 'Welcome, Joan. You'll find that anaesthetics is terribly easy.' He paused, grinned sheepishly and added, 'And it can easily get terrible.'

How right he was. I was continually on high alert and became compulsive about labelling and checking syringes filled with potent and potentially dangerous drugs. I learned heightened watchfulness of every aspect of a patient's physiology. I was never able to reach the level of confidence of the old hands who could read the newspaper, do sudoku and write shopping lists, and then within a second be calmly resuscitating the patient from an unexpected cardiac arrest. Keeping a cool head was compulsory – a valuable life skill I slowly and painfully acquired.

The night call during my stint in the anaesthetics department was harrowing. I explained to Mary and Anna that there could be occasions when they may find my bed empty and my stethoscope gone in the middle of the night but that our loyal dog Juno was under strict instructions to take good care of them. I was, thankfully, spared any major consequences of this irresponsible maternal behaviour, and in May 1997 I succeeded in passing the diploma exam.

With a sigh of relief, I immediately transferred out of anaesthetics, and was appointed head of department of the Family Practice Unit of 2 Military Hospital. I thought I'd be back in placid, familiar waters, dealing with the day-to-day maladies of all ages, and I looked forward to a quieter, more mundane medical experience. Instead I became immersed in an adventure of a totally different kind.

I had volunteered to coordinate the Infectious Diseases Clinic and so found myself navigating between the pain and stigma of newly diagnosed patients with the dreaded human immunodeficiency virus, HIV, and the misguided and callous political decisions on which their lives depended. Aids denialist Thabo

Mbeki had assumed the presidency of South Africa in 1999, and from then until he was relieved of his duties in 2008, life expectancy declined for every year of his presidency. Despite solid and accepted research that showed that antiretroviral treatment was the one and only intervention that consistently and predictably prevented people with HIV from progressing to Aids, Mbeki blocked funds from the Global Fund to Fight Aids, TB and Malaria, and he restricted use of donated nevirapine, which stopped mothers passing the virus onto their babies. His health minister, Manto Tshabalala-Msimang, famously advocated using lemon, beetroot, olive oil and garlic for the treatment of Aids.

These actions were catastrophic: Thabo Mbeki can be held responsible for the deaths of 333 000 of the people he was trusted to serve, and for the births of 35 000 HIV-positive babies.

My anger at being made so medically impotent simmered and bubbled. I found it heartbreaking to counsel couples where one was HIV positive, but using condoms wasn't an option as their greatest wish was for a child. Every consultation brought pain: the old granny bringing in her parentless grandchildren to be tested; the middle-aged traditional wife who believed she was in a monogamous relationship, but horrifyingly tested positive; the young soldier who wanted to go on active duty out of the country to earn a better wage for his young family, but was prohibited from doing so when he tested positive. I tried with compassion and gentleness to explain this inexplicable disease, to plot the way ahead, yet could offer no hope of any containment or treatment. It felt deceitful and immoral. But my patients kept coming, kept hoping. And too many kept dying.

I had the privilege of a consultation that was a massive 'point of wonder' amid those dark days of my HIV clinics. The patient came and sat in the same chair as those souls wrestling with the diagnosis of an incurable disease. That patient was ex-president Nelson Mandela. As I was head of Family Medicine, I was given the honour of doing his initial consultation, although I had already been primed that he probably needed referral to a specialist.

When he arrived, the waiting room became a flurry of activity. Spontaneous applause erupted. Chairs were pushed back as the waiting patients stood to honour the man who'd given them their first opportunity to vote. And then, with his characteristic stamp of humility, he said, 'It is a mistake to think that a single individual can unite a country.'

He greeted adults and children alike, and took time to smile and stroke babes in arms. He chuckled a lot. I stood in the doorway of my consulting room, overwhelmed by the now famous 'Madiba Magic'. His entourage was so small I had trouble identifying who was protecting this world statesman.

A man stepped forward and formally introduced me to His Excellency, Nelson Mandela. I was so flustered I can't recall if I bowed, curtseyed, kissed his hand or merely blurted out my name. I escorted him in and, as with thousands of patients before him, assumed my place behind my desk and he sat alongside – I like to keep my patients close, within arm's reach. I was staggered that etiquette allowed us to be alone as I questioned him about his medical history and problems.

He was totally disarming and charming. During his examination, as I peered into the depths of his hairy ear canals, I heard myself asking him how he retained his youthful vigour. He was proud of his self-discipline, which saw him rise early and exercise his body and his brain. On learning that I lived in Rondebosch, he mentioned that he loved walking to the legendary Rustenburg Shoe Store during their sales weeks, and stocking up on bargains for the year! For all his fame, he had the warmest of common touches. I also sensed in him his delight in female company.

As the consultation ended, I embarked on something South Africans, perhaps by virtue of their isolated history, feel compelled to do – create a connection. I summoned up my courage and mentioned that my elder daughter, Mary, now a student at Stanford University in the USA, had become friends with another Stanford student, Zinks Dlamini.

His eyes shone with amusement and he laughed. 'Ah! My clever, charming, handsome grandson! Tell Mary to watch out!' And with that he leant across my desk, reached for a piece of scrap paper and a pen, and asked me to write down Mary's name and contact details. 'I want him to tell her of our meeting today. Our children have connected us!'

I did as he requested and mumbled some thanks, and he smiled and grasped both my hands. I watched him leave, my watery eyes betraying me.

※

Dealing with HIV was burning me out – then a gift dropped onto my desk. A letter from the head of the army medical services arrived, requesting me to consider going down, as the doctor, on the annual Antarctic supply voyage on the *SA Agulhas*.

The consideration lasted as long as it took me to gallop down to the personnel office and sign the papers. I rented out our home, farmed out the pets, and obtained permission from my girls, both of whom had away agendas: Mary studying at Stanford in California and Anna preparing for a term exchange at a school in India.

It didn't happen. For reasons I didn't bother to listen to, the voyage was rescheduled for later in the year, at a time when it was impossible for me to make the trip.

I now had to find alternative accommodation for three months. I laid my job on the line (I was past the point of caring) and requested three months' unpaid leave, and that's when I headed for the Outback of Australia, where the chances of seeing a patient infected with the dreaded HIV were virtually zero.

Cardwell, a tropical coastal town in Far North Queensland, in the Cassowary Coast Region, was the location of my third solo practice locum in Australia.

My first day of work saw me loaded with a rucksack of swimming and snorkelling gear, and the plan to head to the ocean during my lunch break. Outside ambient temperatures hovered around 41 degrees Celsius and the humidity gave the air the feeling of walking into a brick wall.

'Have a good lunch. See you later,' I chimed as I stepped out into the empty reception area in my slipslops, floppy hat, swimming costume and baggy shorts.

'Wait!'

This peremptory command came from the normally meek and pleasant receptionist, Linda. It stopped me in my tracks. Perhaps I was breaking some cardinal rule concerning practice etiquette.

She'd risen with such speed that her chair went clattering to the floor. 'You can't just go out there and swim in the ocean!' A look of unspeakable horror had frozen her face. 'You'll die!'

So this was serious. But why?

Linda then regaled me with a litany of all the creatures that would be out to kill me, from the box jellyfish with its potent venom to the stinging stone fish, the poisonous cone snail and the beautiful but deadly blue-ringed octopus.

'Okay, I get it, no swimming in the ocean,' I said to Linda. 'So I'll head a bit up the river that I noticed opening out on the beach.'

'No!' she yelled. 'Are you crazy? The bull sharks will have you for lunch if the 500-kilogram salties don't get you first. And that's if you even make it through the bush getting there, between the snakes and the spiders.' (The 'salties' are the saltwater crocodiles.)

And I thought as a bush-hardened African I knew about dange-

Venomous creatures of tropical Cardwell kept the doctor busy.

rous creatures! 'Right. Thanks,' I said to Linda. 'I'll change and just go for a stroll down the main street.'

'Watch out for those vicious mangy dogs!' she called after me.

I smiled. One thing I did know was that simple dog bites in Australia can't kill – they don't transmit rabies. Still, if I was to survive, or be able to assist any equally ignorant patients out there, I realised I'd better delve into the Australian dangerous creatures and toxicology handbook.

'No venomous animal on the planet kills quicker than this thing.' This was from an article on box jellyfish, which went on to tell me that 64 people had died from their stings since 1884, and that work on an antivenom was still underway. But there was a surprising first-aid action that could immediately be instituted if a sting occurred: the area stung had to be rinsed copiously with vinegar in order to inactivate the stinging cells. And there on the page was a full-size photo of a pristine beach with a yellow box on a pole, and a large bottle of vinegar nestling inside.

My curiosity overwhelmed me. Braving the turgid furnace of air outside, I ran to the beach. Positioned every hundred metres or so were yellow boxes on poles, and each one contained a full bottle of vinegar.

'What an amazing country!' I murmured, impressed not only by the far-thinking health and safety beach officer, but more by the fact that each box still had its intact bottle of vinegar. In my country every last bottle of vinegar would have been lifted to use on the next meal of fish and chips.

Next I learned about the blue-ringed octopus, 'the world's most venomous marine animal' which, the article told me, 'lives peacefully in rock pools and is not aggressive'. 'Despite its small size, 12–20cm, it carries enough venom to kill 26 adult humans within minutes. The toxin is 1 200 times more toxic than cyanide. The bite is tiny and often painless, with many victims not realising they have been envenomated until respiratory depression and paralysis start to set in. There is no antivenom.'

Victims could be saved, according to the article, if artificial respiration was instituted immediately paralysis set in … and continued until the toxin had metabolised over a period of hours. The good news was that victims who survived the first 24 hours usually recovered completely. This was nonetheless a very daunting prospect, especially as the patient remained fully conscious and alert. I made a hurried check of the ambu-bag and face mask in my emergency box.

Now I was totally captivated by what else this 'home of the deadly' harboured. And I wasn't disappointed. Australia has more venomous snakes than any other country. The most venomous snake in the world is the inland taipan, found in arid areas of Queensland. It's estimated to have enough venom in each bite to kill more than a hundred men, but fortunately it's reclusive and placid and unlikely to attack. Still, it managed to kill 53 people between 1979 and 1998, when an antivenom became available.

And spiders? First prize again. The male Sydney funnel-web spider is the most venomous on the globe, responsible for fifteen deaths between 1927 and 1981, when an antivenom became available.

Even plants and trees are out to get you Down Under. There are a thousand species of toxic plants, from the Morton Bay chestnut to the strychnine tree, the milky mangrove and the famous gympie-gympie or giant stinging tree, arguably the world's most toxic plant. This grows in tropical rainforests in Queensland, in areas close to the practice in Cardwell, and as I planned to spend some time exploring those forests, I committed to memory the details of the appearance of its innocent, soft, hairy leaves.

My long-awaited first weekend of freedom arrived, and having packed the car with camping gear, rucksack, hiking boots, food and beer, I drove north towards Cairns in a mood of high expectation. Arriving at my destination, I padded along a damp path strewn with forest debris, muted sunlight filtering through the canopy, The variety in the vegetation was astounding; even more so was the number of plants and bushes armed with vicious spikes, thorns and prickles.

I smiled: the most evil of all, the gympie-gympie, also known as the suicide tree, wouldn't fool me. I knew it could be a bush, shrub or tree, often growing in disturbed soil, and that it had earned its sinister name from the extreme pain its silica-tipped hairs could inflict – so excruciating that the sufferer may choose self-inflicted death rather than endure the agony. Those hairs acted as fine hypodermic needles, and through them, into skin or eyes or mucous membranes, was injected a potent neurotoxin. But of the gympie-gympie I saw no sign.

A colourful fungus on a fallen tree trunk just off the path caught my eye. Camera in hand, I pushed through the undergrowth – and in a flash, my left calf was seared by boiling acid, set alight and electrocuted simultaneously. There were the quivering heart-shaped leaves of the gympie-gympie, shaking, it seemed to me, with mirth.

Standing stock still and willing the pain away served only to evoke a wave of nausea. There was some hope of relief in my rucksack back on the path. With a super human leap I sailed over the undergrowth, fell onto my bag and tore open a side pocket. In a ziplock bag were the tools for my salvation.

The treatment for a brush with this stinger tree is to first remove, intact, all the needle hairs. I placed a wide strip of very sticky plaster over my throbbing calf, pressed it down gently, then yanked. The relief was almost immediate, and on close inspection of the plaster, I saw a forest of the offensive hairs. To neutralise the residual neurotoxin still in my skin, I doused it with a dilute mixture of hydrochloric acid that I'd mixed up for this very scenario.

I cut short my walk, returned home and took to my bed for a few hours. But my treatment had dramatically shortened my ordeal, and made me a committed follower of instructions for Australian wilderness first aid kits.

When it came to the humans in Cardwell, life was relatively easy. I enjoyed the variety of ages and patients across a vast socioeconomic spectrum, from super-wealthy owners of huge sailing boats to the unemployed on the dole needing help with various addictions.

I was just getting comfortable, a little smug perhaps, in my ability to handle what was thrown at me every day, when my greatest medical challenge appeared. It came, stepping into my house, in the form of my younger daughter, Anna, and it plunged me into dark, helpless despair. Despite my best efforts, clouds of these feelings, sometimes huge and stormlike, sometimes disturbing wisps, lingered for years.

Anna arrived in Cardwell as planned, after her three-month exchange at a school in India high in the Himalayan foothills. In the months preceding her departure from Cape Town I'd become aware of her weight loss and a subtle change in her normal healthy appetite. She seemed to avoid certain foods, particularly those with a high calorific value. To my shame, I paid scant attention. I was extended on all fronts, and as Anna continued to excel academically and was participating in provincial-level sports, I disregarded her issues with food as a passing phase.

Just before she left for India, I'd hesitantly tried to engage her on the issue but she was evasive and showed irritation. I was reluctant to dampen her excitement but I did manage to elicit a promise from her that while not under my beady eye she'd be careful to eat adequately and lose no more weight. I wanted to believe her and thought my duty was done.

When she stepped off the bus in Cardwell, my excitement at seeing her was replaced by a horror so severe that I fought for air. Even at a distance, she looked skeletal. Her blonde hair was pulled tightly back into a ponytail, revealing sunken eyes and bony hollows in her face. Her T-shirt hung on her. Her normally muscular legs were wasted.

Horror was quickly replaced by anger: she hadn't kept her promise. I was unable to contain my emotions and on greeting her, instead of being her happy, grateful mother, I blurted out, 'Anna! You've got so thin! What's been going on?'

I harassed her endlessly on the journey home. She sat quietly, seemingly immune to my tirade, and eventually I ran out of steam and we completed the journey in silence. On entering the house, I apologised and hugged my precious bag of bones.

She murmured softly, 'I didn't think I'd lost that much weight.' Without unpacking, she put on her running shoes and disappeared for an hour.

Sleep was impossible that night. I kept getting up to spy on her sleeping form – to check if she was still breathing. This child, in my assessment, was suffering from a terminal illness.

I know that I was overreacting and lacking in objectivity, but I was terrified. There was no one to keep me rational. 'Oh, Pete! Why did you go and die and leave me to handle this?' I wailed, thumping the pillow. 'It's no accident that it takes two to make and bring up kids: one isn't enough. I've failed,' I whimpered irrationally.

But the sun was still going to rise the next day, and I needed to be the responsible doctor, even if all lay in tatters around me. I needed to calm down. I stood in my flimsy pyjamas under the overhead ceiling fan and concentrated purely on the air moving over my head, my skin, my body. I sucked it into my lungs. I counted as I exhaled. I had to deal with this … this …. dare I call it by its full medical name, anorexia nervosa? No! That was in the murky zone of mental illness, that zone where I always felt inadequate, a failure.

In my fifth year of medical school at UCT we'd been plunged into our psychiatry block. We were introduced to those shadowy and often eccentric-looking members of the profession called psychiatrists. I recall how alternative they seemed. Instead of didactic lectures, they seemed to converse with us and include us in their thinking. They seldom informed us of the solutions to problems: that was for us to discover. I was so beguiled by this approach that I realised, only much later, that the reason for their not supplying us with any definitive solutions was that there seldom were any. The outcomes were always risky.

I took the challenge head on. I spent hours in the mental institutions and acute psychiatric wards of Groote Schuur Hospital. I formed what I thought were meaningful relationships with patients, my favourites being with those who seemed young, bright and creative, and who were only temporarily patients.

They drew me into their worlds. They shared confidences and intimate thoughts with me. I felt that I was making a meaningful contribution to their cure and felt flattered. The worlds they inhabited were ones I had thoughts about in my own head; the only difference I perceived was that I knew that they were worlds not rooted in reality, and ones that I didn't have the courage to talk about, but they did. Were they not, then, more sensitive, more expressive, more perceptive, more open to feelings and emotions than I was?

I was back to being overwhelmed by curiosity of the same kind that had paved my way into studying medicine. I wanted to learn more about this world of the mind. I wanted to be part of it. Decision made: I would become a psychiatrist.

It was in defeat that I relinquished this high-flown ambition. At the end of my psychiatry block I felt psychologically battered and inept. For reasons that my logical brain couldn't grasp, I felt a failure. I'd learned that medication was usually the cornerstone of initiating a solid recovery in mentally ill patients, but I still lacked understanding that compassion and logical, realistic reasoning had no guarantee of being part of the treatment.

My moment of reality, illustrating that I could never become a psychiatrist, was a painful one; after all these years an upwelling of guilt still accompanies the memory. Janine was a beautiful, clever, artistic young girl with whom I had a special bond. She was also a patient with chronic depression. Somewhat manipulative, she was very familiar with psychiatric wards and the students who roamed wide-eyed through them.

I was convinced that after our hours of confidences and meaningful exchanges I had, in some small way, made a difference. She'd agreed to compliancy with her medication and was soon to return home. We'd become close friends, and we would maintain contact long after she was discharged, I felt sure.

She and I left the psychiatric ward within the same week. I returned, as a doctor, over the course of my medical career.

She never did. She took her own life days after discharge.

With Anna, I needed to get back into problem-solving mode. A sense of forward progressions, real or imagined, was a tool I'd come to rely on.

The doctor in me took control and began barking orders to the failing mother in me. 'Get moving! Make a list for action tomorrow. You're going to have to talk to Anna, but mostly you must try to listen to her. She's going to say stuff you don't believe or don't understand at all, or that makes you flaming mad. Just nod. Please try to keep your cool. She's an intelligent, kind soul – and probably one you don't understand. Life may have been more difficult for her than you realise. She's never had a father, and she tries so hard to please you, her only parent . . .' and here I howled in anguish.

The night dragged on. I was only capable of making a list of the practical interventions I felt compelled to do. I needed to study this poorly understood illness, this eating disorder called anorexia nervosa. I needed, with tough love, to curb some of Anna's obsessive behaviour, for instance by restricting her excessive hours of daily exercise. She'd have to tolerate my strict observance of what she ate daily, and she'd have to tolerate being weighed. I'd tempt her with all sorts of goodies on a daily basis. I'd set as a goal the gaining of five kilograms in two weeks. (In hindsight this was totally unrealistic for a patient with an eating disorder – but what did I know?)

It wasn't a happy time. Anna remained calm and even-tempered and she seemingly complied. She did, however, volunteer for a local environmental research group and so spent as little time at home as possible. I didn't have the resolve to stop that. I felt lonely and unsupported, and had great difficulty in keeping buoyant.

I tried too hard to tempt her with food treats. I couldn't accept that her preference was for uncooked salads and vegetables – anything with a low calorific value. I came home with items I enjoy – pizza, cinnamon buns, pork chops, sausage and always something for pudding, of which she forced down a minuscule amount.

Time dragged on. Anna did gain some weight but I gained much more. We had a few meaningful discussions, but I realised that Anna was going to solve this her way. And in that I had to trust.

Weeks later, as she boarded the bus to start her long journey home, she turned, fixed her gaze on me and allowed the hint of a smile to cross her lips. She took a piece of my heart with her. This small, tenacious, gifted child would have to heal with no help from her doctor mother.

Sixteen years had passed since Pete's death. Mary, Anna and I were a tightly bound unit, all contributing, all busy, all pulling a load and, I'd thought, all coping adequately. I now questioned this assessment. If I felt that I was operating at almost maximum output, surely they were also? That would leave no space for error. Had this resulted in Anna feeling that she wasn't meeting my expectations? Were my expectations unreasonably high? I didn't know the answers. I ruefully admitted that I, in fact, didn't even know the correct questions.

I'd floundered badly in this medical intervention. It wasn't an adventure. It was a nightmare.

❋

Mount Isa, with its population of about 20 000, in the Gulf Country region of Queensland, was the location of my final locum. It was huge compared with the previous towns in which I'd worked. I was employed in a practice with four other doctors. This was a welcome change and my medical stress level plummeted. Help was always at hand.

Thoughts of my dear Anna and her way forward still swirled through my head. I would need to make some changes when I returned home, but for the time being I was grateful to have my days and nights full of new patients' problems.

Mount Isa is called the Oasis of the Outback and it boasts an enviable quality of life. But not for all. My Aboriginal patients, although catered for financially fairly well by the government, were mostly unemployed. They became my special area of concern. Their problems were many and complex, mental and physical. Obesity and its related illnesses, alcoholism and depression, plagued them, but to my overwhelming relief, HIV had yet to make inroads.

They were part of the Kalkadoon Aboriginal tribe, who'd lived a nomadic pastoral life in this harsh area before its vast mineral resources were discovered and their lands taken from them. They'd retaliated but suffered a huge defeat in 1884.

They loved to talk of their land and their pastoral activities of old. There seemed little chance for them to resume these, and their ability and desire to embrace modern life appeared limited. Issues

Practising ordered, efficient, well-supported medicine in Mount Isa in the outback of Australia.

of land being forcibly taken from an indigenous population were uncomfortably familiar to me, as a South African, and, as at home, highly emotive and controversial. I did my best to listen, empathise and engage any practical help I could in the form of social workers, nutritionists and psychologists.

The big difference between the indigenous population in Australia and that of South Africa is that the former is so tiny and lacks any political power.

✳

Shortly after my return to South Africa, the South African National Defence Force fired me. I was being considered for a promotion but to be eligible I was required go to Pretoria for a three-month basic army training course. I appealed on the grounds that I was a single parent and that I had obligations and responsibilities at home. They were unsympathetic and I was dismissed on the grounds of 'reluctance'.

It actually suited me fine. I'd had a good innings: I'd learned a lot and made some lasting friendships, and I'd left on good terms with my colleagues, if not with the high-ranking officers.

My new medical adventure was a part-time job with the Student Health Service of UCT. All my patients were young bright adults, at a time of their lives when they were on all sorts of journeys of discovery, not least sexual. The HIV scenario with all its myths, fallacies, discriminations, fear, denials and hopelessness took centre stage in my life again. But this time around, I had some access to trial antiretroviral drugs and I hoped logical explanations and intelligent discussions would prevail.

What I failed to appreciate was that the brains of most young students were still undergoing growth and maturation. So I was also back in the realm of mental instability, stress reactions, personality disorders, frank hysteria and psychosis.

This reality hit me full force when a young science Master's student walked in and requested an HIV test. I read in his notes that he'd had numerous tests spanning years. I enquired about the reason for this, and he nonchalantly replied, 'I get tested at the end of a failed relationship and at the start of a new one.'

I must have looked mightily puzzled as he continued, 'I know all about protecting myself from contracting the virus but the two options on offer – using a condom and abstinence – are just not acceptable to me.'

I had to accept that his choice was to gamble with his life.

During this time I embarked on a study course to qualify for a diploma in acupuncture. My motivation was a little hazy, but I wanted to know more about this ancient Chinese form of traditional medicine that was being recognised in the USA by the National Center for Complementary and Alternative Medicine. The term 'acupuncture' was coined by the surgeon-general of the Dutch East India Company in the 1600s but the practice dated back to about 400 BCE. I was impressed that it had survived, and caught on in the West to become the most popular form of alternative medicine used in the USA.

I learned about chi, the life-force energy that circulates within the body in lines called meridians, and the acupuncture points at which these energy lines could be affected. I listened also to the echoes of opposition from the mainstream scientific world, which claimed that acupuncture was no better than a theatrical placebo – a measure designed merely to humour or placate someone, but with no real therapeutic value.

My own moment of evaluation of this ancient medical art arrived in the form of a young student suffering from an acute episode of diarrhoea, nausea and vomiting. Despite his misery and discomfort he was vociferous in his refusal of any form of drug treatment. He distrusted them all and had come merely for rehydration fluids.

'I can offer you an acupuncture treatment.' This popped out before the thought had really traversed my brain.

'That I can accept. Yes, please,' he groaned.

I lay the student on a bed and with professional ease inserted two needles into each of the P6 acupuncture points on his wrists.

Stimulation of these points by chi manipulation, I'd learned, cured nausea and vomiting. I darkened the room and left, returning at regular intervals to agitate the needles.

Fifteen minutes later he exited via the toilet. 'Please come in tomorrow to report how you are,' I called out to him.

That evening I hauled out my acupuncture textbook. I gasped in embarrassment. I'd placed the needles on the incorrect aspect of my patient's wrists. All I could comfort myself with was that no harm had been done.

As I arrived at work the following morning, I noticed my patient, sitting quietly, engrossed in a magazine. I slunk through to my consulting room.

My receptionist popped her head in. 'Doctor Joan, your patient just wants a quick word,' she said, and I looked up reluctantly, to see behind her my patient – smiling!

'Doc! Those needles were fantastic. I'm totally cured. No more vomiting. I even had a morsel of breakfast.' And he grabbed my hand and shook it firmly.

'Such excellent news,' I said, smiling enthusiastically. 'Come back any time.'

And I quietly sent up thanks for the passage of time, the power of positive thinking and the miraculous force of the placebo effect.

CHAPTER 5

Marion Island and the Roaring Forties: 2007

'We all have a "Land of Beyond" to seek in our life — what more can we ask? Our part is to find the trail that leads to it. A long trail, a hard trail, maybe; but the call comes to us and we have to go.'

— Arctic explorer Fridtjof Nansen, in his inaugural address as rector of the University of St Andrews, Scotland, 1926

LIVING IN CAPE TOWN, I SEEMED unable to focus on a way forward. I had no children at home to give me a reason for staying: Mary was doing her Master's in sustainable energy engineering at the Royal Institute of Technology in Sweden and Anna was studying veterinary medicine in Scotland. My small farm in Knysna, my haven, which had nurtured and restored me after Pete's death, beckoned.

I'd be living close to nature again, with endless kilometres of mountain-biking tracks in the adjacent forests. I needed nothing more. With the decision made, I felt a new lightness and energy.

I made no attempt to find a job there but only days after my arrival in Knysna I was asked to do a GP locum. This work felt like a more organised, friendlier version of my previous provincial-hospital outpatients work, and some time off and freedom of movement were a bonus, but I had to privately admit that, while enjoyable, the medical work gave me little sense of purpose. I missed the feeling of commitment and follow-up. Although I loved living in Knysna, and was enjoying my cycling and the wonderful friendships I'd made, I was getting uncomfortable in my comfort zone.

I made enquiries with the Department of the Environment, specifically with the office that staffed the *SA Agulhas*, our ice-strengthened research vessel. It seemed a long shot, but I requested that I be considered among the possible doctors for voyages south. The Antarctic was still on my list.

'Can you leave in seven days' time?'

This was a telephonic request from Gwen van der Westhuizen, the recruitment officer for the *SA Agulhas*. It was not for a trip to the Antarctic, but for the annual relief voyage to Marion Island.

'I'll be there!' – instantly said, with my characteristic lack of appreciation for consequences.

I opened the atlas to check out where I'd agreed to go. Marion Island, along with Prince Edward Island, forms the Prince Edward Islands archipelago. These islands are 1 770 kilometres southeast of Port Elizabeth and 2 300 kilometres due north of the Antarctic ice shelf.

South Africa had established a meteorological station on Marion Island in 1948 and had maintained a continuous presence of meteorologists there ever since, with teams of scientists and technicians coming and going annually.

Our voyage was to facilitate the turnaround of these teams: to collect those who'd been there for a year, deliver the new team for the next year, and drop off other scientists to work there for a six-week summer stint. A team of oceanographers would remain on board, as would I, for a month of surveying and sampling the Southern Ocean.

I had a pressing problem, though. I'd agreed to work a locum for Dr Dee in Knysna for the very time I'd be away, and letting her down was just not on. Fortunately, the medical fraternity of Knysna and nearby Plettenberg Bay had a number of semi-retired doctors and I found a willing candidate who'd worked for Dr Dee on a previous occasion. My relief was immense.

The ensuing days saw me gathering together foul-weather gear and medical information. I had a heart-sinking moment when I realised, with absolute clarity, that I wasn't adequately trained to take on this responsibility. A reality check then reassured me that no doctor could ever be prepared for all the possible catastrophes. My practical side took charge and soothed my uncertainties by making a comprehensive list of contact details of every possible specialist I would ever need to ask for help while meeting the medical needs of the ninety passengers and forty crew members on board the *SA Agulhas* for a period of six weeks.

It had taken twelve eventful years for me to progress from the adventure of medicine on St Helena island to the looming adventures of medicine on the *SA Agulhas* and Marion Island. I was up for the challenge.

A mundane skill a travelling doctor and GP locum learns is the rapid familiarisation process of getting comfortable in a strange consulting area, and quickly memorising the layout and contents

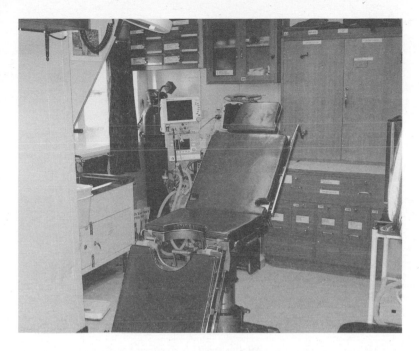

The consulting cabin on the *SA Agulhas*.

of the drug-storage facilities. A patient's life may depend on this.

This area aboard the aging *SA Agulhas* bore the stamp of having survived a host of different doctors carving their way through it over the years. We're an obsessive-compulsive lot; some may say fussy, pedantic and self-opinionated. Whatever the motivation, we often need to change a few things in our working space ... naturally, always for the better!

The consulting room on this ship was on the level of the ocean, so a porthole gave a magnificent view across the turbulent seas outside. The doctor's chair was chained to the desk leg in the event of very rough seas. The bookshelf above the desk had two retaining planks to keep the books from connecting with the doctor's head in inclement weather. All the drawers had wooden retaining strips bolted firmly at one end.

The labelling of the drawers showed the history of a few past doctors: contents of drugs altered and re-altered, surgical instruments listed and then scratched through, some labels in legible handwriting, some illegible, some typed. Only a close inspection would yield the truth.

In the centre of the small room was an ancient somewhat complicated-looking dental/surgical chair with all sorts of wings and folding rests attached. At the head of this was a modern anaesthetics machine which sent cold shivers down my spine. The very last thing I wanted to do here was to have to administer an anaesthetic, unassisted, on an unstable platform.

There was an efficient-looking patient monitor, obviously a recent acquisition. It could record a host of vital functions like pulse, blood pressure, oxygenation, carbon-dioxide levels and cardiac rhythm, and would be called into action only for a seriously ill patient. I sent up a little prayer, to whatever gods may have been listening, begging that I should never have to switch it on.

Across the passageway from the consulting room was an area designated the ward. This was fitted out with three narrow beds, each with its own patient monitor at the head. One of the beds was on an elaborate contraption of gimbals, a pivoted support used on a ship to keep an object upright with respect to the horizon, despite the vessel's pitching and rolling. A bed on gimbals ensures that the patient has a smooth, level ride.

The ward appeared to be very infrequently used and seemed to have taken on the role of additional storage area. Cartons of medical supplies and random kitchen equipment were piled haphazardly on the floor.

Positioned in a gap between the beds was a mobile ultra-modern X ray machine, its thick and complex-looking handbook lying open close to its computer panel. I soon became well acquainted with the technician, Patrick, who was trying to come to grips with all its myriad of functions – and who had painted the long neck of the machine with the skin markings of a giraffe. This was another machine I didn't wish to try out.

I quickly got into the routine of shipboard medicine. The regular crew were my most frequent patients, often with chronic illnesses such as diabetes, obesity and hypertension, which they neglected atrociously.

The first few days at sea saw me inundated by patients with seasickness. What I had to keep a dark secret was that I was similarly afflicted, and my occasional request to be excused temporarily from a consultation was so that I could hotfoot it down the passage to the toilet and lighten my load. I then returned feeling hugely better and proceeded to commiserate with my patient and offer some drug therapy. Fortunately for doctor and patients alike, sea legs and a healthy appetite generally return after three days.

Finger trauma was another common injury, sustained during fishing, rope hauling or food chopping. I got proficient at finger-nail removal, a painless procedure if done with an adequate ring block of local anaesthetic, but always a gruesome sight for the patient.

The medication I came close to running out of was the 'morning-after' pill. I came to recognise those gorgeous, fertile girls, sitting on the edge of the bench outside my clinic, waiting impatiently for

With the young scientists who spent six weeks on Marion Island.

the 8.30am clinic slot. They were savvy enough to know that the sooner the pill was taken after intercourse, the better it would work to either delay ovulation, or interfere with the fertilisation or implantation of a fertilised egg. Pregnancy was the last thing on their agendas.

It was naïve of me to be surprised – the researchers were predominantly postgraduate students, temporary relieved of the constraints of normal life, and nights aboard ship became one long party, with inexpensive alcohol, no driving required and bunks mere steps away.

As the voyage progressed, and papers and reports had to be written, along with some cautionary advice from the doctor, more responsible behaviour emerged and I didn't have to contend with any unwanted pregnancies.

So I was feeling pretty relaxed and confident in my medical role as we neared the end of our three weeks of oceanographic research. We were headed back to Marion to collect the scientists who'd been temporary residents for those few summer weeks. Then the ship would turn north again and be bound for Cape Town.

I was looking forward to setting foot on my continent again – to celebrate with family and friends, to ride my bike through the forest, to see the green of plants, to take my devoted fan club of two eager hounds for a romp, to bury my face in the fur of my cats.

We headed slowly back to Marion. It was a moody, grey day. The fog was down and visibility a mere ten metres. Birds were strangely lacking. The only thing alive seemed to be the sea.

I stood on the deck with the moist air settling in my hair and my breath billowing out in white puffs. This was the ultimate 'middle of nowhere'. The zone of ocean we'd been busy in had no point of reference; it was just a huge chunk of water lying north of the Antarctic and south-southeast of the tip of Africa. No shipping lines passed through it. No planes flew over it. No intrepid yachtsmen ventured into it, as there was no destination here. Perhaps fishing vessels passed through occasionally but in three weeks we'd seen no evidence of these. Even vessels heading for the Antarctic avoided it: they would set out in a more south-southwesterly direction heading from South Africa, or more south-southeasterly from New Zealand, heading for the Ross Sea.

I had a feeling that in all my travelling to weird and desolate places, I'd never been so far from signs of other human activity. This held a unique exhilaration for me but that day it also held something more tangible – the warning of a storm.

There had been a precipitous drop on the barograph: the atmospheric pressure had plummeted from a normal 1 014 millibars to a very low 979 millibars in the space of three hours. A low-pressure zone was approaching, bringing wet and stormy weather.

An inky darkness fell. The captain informed us over the intercom that gale-force winds and ten-metre swells were predicted, that all decks were now out of bounds, and that our ship would be steaming full speed ahead to gain the lee of Marion Island. It could mean 18 to 24 hours of very uncomfortable sailing. There was nothing to do but secure every moveable item in our cabins, fix the guard rails onto the bunks, and hunker down to sleep.

In the small hours of the morning I was awakened by a thumping and groaning, whistling and rocking. Then came the shrill, urgent call of my cabin phone. My heart joined in the thumping.

'I'm on my way. Tell her to go to the surgery and take a seat. I need to throw on some clothes.'

I steadied myself, legs placed wide apart, knees bent, one hand keeping a firm hold on the desk edge. This old grande dame of the seas was pitching wildly. The view from my cabin porthole was alternately grey-and-white angry sea and grey-and-white angry sky.

I staggered down two flights of shifting stairs. The surgery door was ajar. Sprawled across the examining chair was one of the young trainee officers. She was whimpering. Bright-red blood was oozing down the right side of her face from a sizeable wound above her right eyebrow. The white of her right eye looked strangely luminous in its pool of blood.

I reminded myself that head wounds bled copiously and always looked worse than they were, and I began my reassurance monologue. 'Let's take a good look. Yes, we can fix this easily. I know it's very rough, so you're going to help by lying as still as you possibly can.'

I began wiping away the blood and covering the wound as I readied my shifting, clanging instruments. I threw a heavy towel over them. There was no chance of using a gleaming silver kidney dish for the soiled swabs; I tossed them, somewhat haphazardly, directly into the garbage bin, which was screwed to the floor.

My young patient sucked in huge gulps of air and shifted her head in response to each roll of the ship. I needed a stationary target.

I took an unconventional step. 'Jessie, I don't like to do this but I'm going to have to strap your head down. The ship is just rocking too much and this cut is so close to your eye.'

She screwed her eyes shut and nodded.

I reached for the roll of wide white orthopaedic strapping Elastoplast and fashioned a tight swathe across her forehead and around the headrest of the examining chair. A sudden unpleasant memory from my medical-student days snapped into my head: chronically depressed patients were similarly strapped down, in preparation for the violent, visually traumatic, somewhat controversial electroconvulsive therapy, or 'shock therapy'.

'Okay. Small needle prick. The local anaesthetic stings a bit.'

With measured concentration and slow, premeditated movements between the ship's rolling and tossing, I achieved the dance of suturing, and Jessie departed with a large plaster over her right eyebrow but a smile on her lips. An uncertain watery-grey dawn was breaking as I washed the last traces of blood off the examining chair.

I made my way up to the bridge, where all the power and wonder of this raging of the elements was revealed. The incessant, shrill howling of the wind was deafening. As far as the eye could see there were massive white-crested swells, breaking haphazardly. As the ship's bow descended into a trough, thumping through the water, there was a creaking and shuddering. The water then surged skywards in a giant white plume, reaching thirty metres up to the top of the crane mounted on the deck which was used for loading and unloading cargo, while the bow disappeared under tons of water. Slowly, painfully, the bow then eased upwards and the foaming water cascaded over the decks and sides.

This torture continued as the ship made progress at a rate of five knots, a feeble nine kilometres per hour, despite the massive engines cranking over at virtual full bore. My flimsy sea legs were buckling under the onslaught and I made my way back to my cabin. Through a porthole in an outside door that had a view over the poop deck – that small, high deck above the main stern deck – I was horrified to watch as this level, normally so high above the water, was also intermittently immersed under crashing waves. I noticed a thin trail of water seeping under the outside door.

My bunk, positioned along the long axis of the ship, yielded another novel experience. Lying horizontally, I see-sawed between a head-down and a head-up position, with a sideways gyration in between. At first I felt weightless, then my body pressed heavily down onto the mattress, only to slide up to weightlessness again. I felt as though I was tied to a rollercoaster, grimly anticipating the changing force of gravity on my body.

Approaching the research base on Marion Island.

Beyond my porthole, the birds, oblivious of my suffering, utilised the strong winds and eddies for their pleasure. Six southern giant petrels were gliding in formation as they swooped into the troughs, aimed skywards, reached stalling velocity, then swooped down again. I watched their wings; they didn't beat. The larger albatrosses were in cruise mode, enjoying the wind in their faces. Delicate tiny prions were busy close to the surface of the swirling water, darting and diving and flapping.

I reached over for my book, *Endurance*, the heroic tale of Ernest Shackleton and his stricken ship. As I read, I couldn't imagine battling through conditions like this, and far worse, day after day, just to stay alive for an unknown future. It filled me with hope for the resilience of the human spirit.

Many hours later, as the barometric pressure rose and the force of the wind abated, the familiar silhouette of Marion Island floated into view. I felt a deep, humble gratitude.

In the early hours of 1 May, as the *SA Agulhas* was sitting out the winds – which were still gale force, and the swells reaching up to eight metres, despite being in the lee of Marion Island – a Mayday was received. The distress call had been relayed via the Australian sea rescue services to our South African Maritime Rescue Co-ordination Centre based near Cape Town, and then radioed through to us. We were the closest and best-equipped vessel to assist in this emergency.

The *SA Agulhas* was instructed to turn north and head back into the foul weather at full throttle. The bulk of her passengers remained blissfully asleep.

The first I was aware of something amiss was around midnight, when the sound of a helicopter aroused me from a deep sleep. Was I dreaming? Our helicopter pilots would never fly at night – or was there some freak weather condition or other emergency that meant urgent action was required?

Too exhausted from riding out the previous 36 hours of the storm to think clearly, I dismissed it and went back to sleep – only to be awakened a short while later by the violent rolling motion of the ship. Loose objects were flying around my cabin. We were on the move. Still, I remained unconcerned, thinking that the scientists were up to some specialised night sampling.

I rose early, noting the faint glow of the sun in a pewter sky, and realised to my disbelief that we were headed north – and there was no island in sight. Puzzled, I headed for the bridge. Radio static and urgent conversation spilled out.

'Good thing you're here, Doc,' said the first mate cheerily, looking up from the radar screen. 'You're needed.'

I was filled in on the scant details. Following the distress call, the helicopter had flown across from the island in treacherous nighttime conditions, and on board now were all the chopper staff and Tom the paramedic from the island. We hadn't been in direct contact with the stricken yacht, but had had information relayed to us that of the crew of four, one was lost overboard, one had a broken leg and a third had a serious head wound. The yacht was large — 57 feet — and had lost its aft mast when it pitchpoled — twice. Each time, as the yacht careened down a monster wave, it had capsized end over end, the stern pitching over the bow. It was absolutely the worst kind of capsize.

The *Agulhas* would attempt to rendezvous with the yacht and remove injured personnel. My mind went into overdrive. This was going to be some medical adventure! I was unsure whether I was relieved or disappointed that it had already been decided that the medic, and not I, was to be dropped onto the yacht by helicopter when we were within flight range, to assess the situation — he was younger and stronger, and the practical side of the decision was that the doctor was being protected from injury, as she was about to become seriously useful.

The day stuttered on between garbled radio contacts, frequent weather checks and much anxious speculation — and a very bumpy sea.

Finally, 'This is Dale Petersen, captain of *Cowrie Dancer*. Can we speak with your doctor, please?'

I got a clearer picture of the medical status of the crew. The captain had the injured leg, but it wasn't an open fracture: no skin was broken and there was no gross deformity, which indicated that

143

it was probably reasonably stable. Given the information he provided me with – he was unable to bear weight but was relatively pain-free when lying still – I tentatively diagnosed a possible fracture of the pelvis or the neck of the femur.

I then spoke to Carol, a young South African engineer, who was struggling to stem the flow of blood from a head wound on the third crew member, Nick, an Aussie. She sounded exhausted but calm.

Part of the problem was that these two remaining partially able bodies, Carol and Nick, had to continue working to prevent the broken mast from bashing the hull, and were also attempting to keep the yacht on a course towards us, which was proving impossible. The bleeding head wound was almost of secondary importance.

'Sit him up,' I told her over the radio. 'Inject some local anaesthetic and stitch up the wound. You can do it. Use a simple continuous overstitch, just like ordinary sewing.'

'Sewing isn't my strong point – but will do. Over and out.'

The following day, as if a switch had been flipped, the sea lost its fury. The skies cleared and the sun shone with a sympathetic gentleness. The helicopter lifted with power and grace, and disappeared over the horizon to fly the 55 nautical miles to the yacht, a half-hour trip.

To get there would take us four and a half hours of steaming. Although it felt like a fruitless exercise, almost every passenger spent those hours perched on a good vantage point, scanning the sea surface for the bobbing head of the missing crewman of the stricken yacht.

The golden orb of the sun was dipping below the western horizon as I picked up the speck of a yacht through my binoculars. The water was flat, the sky alive with colour, the full moon glowing orange in the east as the sea licked its edges.

For the past few hours the helicopter had been doing a grid search for the missing crewman, returning frequently to the ship to refuel. It had been fruitless. There was no chatter on the ship. The mood was uneasy. The interminable waiting was getting to me too.

'Doctor Joan! Doctor Joan! Report to the bridge immediately.'

Responding to the urgent summons, I made my way up the outside stairs, each step forcing a new scary medical scenario through my head. I knew I'd soon have three, maybe four traumatised survivors to care for.

'Hello, Doc.' The captain flicked his gaze briefly to me and then looked back at the bow. He wore a puckered frown. 'We can't bring the yacht alongside the ship — it's too tricky and dangerous. And we'll be unable to lower anyone onto the deck of the yacht due to the configuration of the masts. I propose that we lower the second mate, Gavin, and the medic close to a rope trailing in the sea behind the yacht. They'll have to swim and grab it, then haul themselves through the sea and clamber aboard. We'll fetch the injured, once stabilised, in the small inflatable, the rubber-duck. What are your thoughts?'

My thoughts were jumbled, jagged and nausea-inducing, but I smiled, nodded and replied, 'All is ready for all four of them in the sickbay.' I didn't mention that although I longed to see that bobbing head hauled out of the sea, I doubted my own ability to save someone who'd been in the cruel, cold sea for more than 48 hours, in only a life jacket and regular foul-weather gear.

Gavin made the transition from helicopter to yacht easily; my binocular viewing of Tom, the medic, had me momentarily worried that I may have a fifth patient, but eventually he was hauled, fairly water-logged, onto the deck by Nick and Carol.

We waited for the order to lower the rubber-duck. It seemed to be taking too long. How long did Tom need to put up a drip, give intravenous morphine and secure the injured captain on the stretcher?

What I failed to appreciate was that the *Cowrie Dancer* was to be abandoned and await possible salvage - if she lasted that long. She needed to have all hatches battened down, cargo secured and sails stashed, and a functioning EPIRB, an emergency position-indicating radio beacon, put in place. This battery-powered radio would transmit a continuous signal, detectable by satellites operated by a consortium of rescue services, that could be used by a potential rescue team to locate the yacht.

At last the rubber-duck was lowered into the water. Four crew in full foul-weather gear were aboard.

I headed to the sickbay and opened the double doors through which a stretcher could pass.

An hour passed.

It was dark when I saw the small craft returning. The transfer of the patient-bearing stretcher from duck to deck looked precarious but the crew were very calm and very skilled. Dale Petersen, captain of the now-abandoned *Cowrie Dancer*, finally made it to the sickbay, to a relatively stable bed, where his long road to healing would begin.

Nick and Carol arrived on the next dinghy delivery. My real work was about to start.

'Doc, whatcha see down there?'

Nick lay semi-recumbent on the examining chair. It had been a few hours since their arrival on our ship, and the priority had been celebratory eating and drinking since then. He had a beer in his hand. That was okay by me – it served as a diversion.

Carol hadn't been able to stitch the wound closed, and I was struggling to shave away Nick's blood-soaked and tangled hair to expose it. I finally got reasonable exposure – it was a massive twelve centimetres long and ragged, filled with congealed blood, long slimy clots and dirty hair. I quickly injected a local anaesthetic and began cleaning and digging down, looking for viable tissue. I needed to trim the edges of dead skin and scalp tissue.

My scalpel hit skull. I knew I needed to do a careful examination to look for a possible fracture. I started to sweat as I swabbed away the new bleeding I'd started. I slid my gloved finger into the wound, down to the smooth surface of the skull, and ran it with increasing pressure along the length of the wound. Nick felt nothing; I felt just smooth bone – no obvious fracture.

Good medical practice at this point would have been to leave the wound unstitched, as too much time had passed since the injury and the chance of infection was high. I chose to go against what I'd been taught as the wound was just too big and messy, and it was too difficult to apply a satisfactory dressing. I inserted 25 stitches and smothered the wound with antibiotic ointment, then covered it all with a light dressing before replacing Nick's grubby red beanie, which seemed to be his comfort blanket.

'Let's take a look tomorrow, Nick. Well done. You were a star patient. Here are the antibiotic capsules. You need to take two twice a day, and some painkillers if required.'

He gave me a lopsided grin and rose unsteadily. He had to be helped by the diminutive Carol, who had purple bruising around both eyes, a small cut on her lower lip, a painful and swollen right hand, and an obviously sprained left ankle. She also had shadows in her eyes that told of a horror she couldn't verbalise.

'I'm fine, Doc,' she whispered, without making eye contact. She didn't want to talk about her ordeal yet. I put my arms around her and hugged her gently.

For a moment she rested her head against my shoulder, then pulled back. 'I must check on Nick.'

'Sleep well, Carol.' What else could I say?

Captain Dale Petersen was my next pressing concern. His morphine dose was wearing off, and I needed to X-ray his suspected fracture with our brand-new machine. My frustration reached mammoth proportions when the technician, Patrick, and I just couldn't get a decent image. The machine was too new, too untried and untested, and Patrick, although a wizard with all things technical, admitted that this was a new challenge. He grumbled that 'management' should have called in an expert to teach him how to use it before departure.

I realised that I'd have to rely on my clinical diagnosis for a few days, until we could get an acceptable picture to send to my orthopaedic surgeon friend, Garth, in Cape Town.

Getting Dale comfortable and pain-free was a priority. Good nursing was now important, and I was the nurse. He also needed frequent changes of position, and massaging of his legs to stave off deep-vein thromboses: I would also be the physiotherapist. My roles would be many.

What neither of us could address at that moment was the profound grief that Dale was experiencing. John, his best friend and sailing companion of many years and many adventures, had died in a manner too appalling to contemplate. He'd taken reasonable precautions during the storm in that he'd been tied to a stanchion – a sturdy vertical pole on the perimeter of the deck, used specifically for attaching lifelines. But the stanchion had snapped when the yacht went over, and when the yacht righted, he was gone. He'd made a grave omission: he had no electronic tracking beacon on his person – something that, back in 2007, would have been a large and cumbersome instrument requiring special attachment. (Today it comes in the form of a wristwatch.)

The little yacht had been a second home to Dale and John. They had circumnavigated the globe in her over a period of seven years. She was more like a living creature than an inanimate object of wood, steel and fabric. Now she was abandoned, probably to finally give up the battle and sink to the ocean floor.

'And she'll take with her my huge cargo of fantastic South African wine,' Dale lamented in an attempt to add a touch of humour. His guffaw morphed into a fit of coughing.

I massaged his calves in silence. Then I rolled him over gently and massaged his buttocks where he had early signs of pressure damage. He was a brave and stoic 66-year-old but so much could go wrong. We were heading back to Marion Island to collect the scientists and the departing team. Then there was the journey back to Cape Town, which could be as short as six days but double that in bad weather.

Although the teamwork involved in the rescue had been amazing and the entire ship had felt united in their efforts, I could already sense a retreat away from occurrences in the sickbay. Folk were fearful of what could happen. Dale's medical, nursing and psychological care now fell solely on my shoulders – for however long it took, he'd be connected to me via a bell directly to my cabin.

I masked my fear with lots of action. I drew up charts of medications and entered into long discussions about these with Dale. I massaged; I did physiotherapy exercises, breathing exercises, arm-strengthening exercises. I frequently changed the dressings on his minor skin wounds. I did bed baths, then smoothed his skin with moisturising cream. I delivered the weather forecast twice a day. We talked, I played music, we played Scrabble, we sat in companionable silence, we cried a little. We become friends. But we both wanted this to end.

We finally achieved a good X-ray, which I sent to the orthopaedic surgeon. He confirmed a fracture of the neck of the

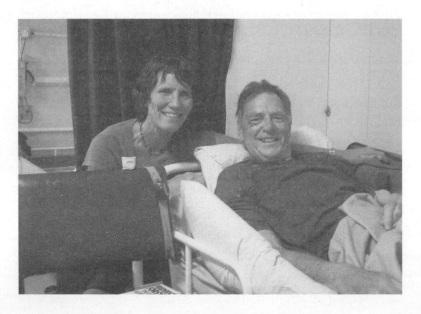

With Captain Dale Petersen in the ward of the *SA Agulhas*.

right femur and the treatment advised was an immediate hip replacement at Vincent Pallotti Hospital in Cape Town.

The weather had the final say in when this happened - a hurricane in the Southern Ocean dictated our return route to Cape Town. Our tracks were circuitous and zigzagged in an attempt to keep our game little ship out of the eye of the storm.

There were times I feared for our safety. I regularly wrote emails home to my loyal vicarious armchair travellers, and on 8 May 2007 I told them, 'If you had scrutinised the weather map at 00:00 this morning, and selected the very worst weather location to be in in the southern hemisphere, the spot would coincidently have been the exact location of our dear *SA Agulhas*.'

I was once again filled with a sense of awe and wonder at the raging of the elements around me as we experienced Beaufort Scale Force 12 conditions, defined as 'devastating hurricane winds', The wind speed was at an average of 70 knots, with gusts of up to 110 knots, and the swell had reached eighteen metres, with a ship horizontal roll of 52 degrees. I staggered around the sickbay, balancing pills and bedpans, and feeling like a cross between a cripple and an astronaut.

A quick trip to the bridge revealed the full extent of the spectacle. Standing in front of a small open hatch in the window, my ears were assailed: the screech of the wind, the thump of the waves against the bow, the loud creaking and groaning emanating from every side of the ship, the distant crash and tinkle of glass as untethered objects flew off to destruction.

The sea was complex in its contours of white-crested mountains and deep, dark valleys. Covering every surface of the water were intricate string-like patterns of wind-blown foam and spray. As a wall of water thundered down onto the deck, sending graceful plumes of spray upwards, the scene became a white-out as the ship bucked and rocked.

'My patient, Dale, has had to develop an amazing degree of acceptance,' I related in my email. 'Cape Town, a comfortable hospital bed and freedom from his pain are ever receding. Our speed over the course of the morning has dropped from an already slow 5 knots to 1,2 knots – and this is now in a southwesterly direction in an attempt to hit the swells front-on. The thought of these massive swells hitting side-on is untenable.

'And so we wait. The wind will drop. We will resume our course in a northerly direction. We long for a respite for our tired bodies constantly in brace mode. However, in a way that I find difficult to explain or justify, I find it thrilling and an affirmation of life itself.'

On the morning of 15 May, after thirteen days at sea since leaving Marion, we finally docked in Cape Town, where the hospital ambulance was ready and waiting. Dale was strapped onto a stretcher and loaded into the back, and the ambulance headed out of the harbour with sirens blaring and lights flashing. I felt strangely empty.

Dale underwent a successful total hip replacement but had the post-operative complication of a deep-vein thrombosis which resulted in a pulmonary embolus that almost cost him his life. I knew that the blood clot would have started its sinister formation while still at sea; I had certainly dodged a bullet in handing him over before the complications set in.

He had superb care in the ICU and was soon discharged on crutches.

I visited him years later at his home in Perth, Australia. He was fit and buoyant, and he took me on a speed walk to show me how full his recovery had been. The lure of the ocean hadn't diminished and he was back on yachts and was working on a whale-research vessel.

In a quiet moment, savouring a glass of excellent Australian wine, he held my gaze and said that I'd saved his life. I put him right. He was lucky to have had the *SA Agulhas* and its well-trained, top-notch crew as the ship closest to his yacht disaster. Our South African ship had responded and pulled off the rescue with professionalism and compassion.

I smiled and acknowledged the pride I felt for my country and its maritime activities. I had, for a brief but eventful voyage, been a small part of it.

CHAPTER 6

The Silk Route: 2008

'Life is like riding a bicycle. To keep your balance you must keep moving.'

– Albert Einstein (translated), in Walter Isaacson's 2007 biography, *Einstein: His Life and Universe*

As a child in Rhodesia, I had regarded a bicycle as a utilitarian object: it got me to school and back. But now that I was a fit 50-something, it became the tool that gained me employment. I'd landed the job of expedition doctor along the Silk Route, a 10 500-kilometre journey by bike across eight counties, starting in Istanbul and finishing in Beijing.

I was feeling upbeat as I posed for the group departure photograph in front of the shimmering Bosporus, with fifteen riders and four staff. I'd learned a thing or two about endurance cycling, and the medical maladies peculiar to this. During the Cape Epic, an eight-day back-road mountain-bike route from Knysna to Cape Town which I'd cycled with my daughter Mary earlier in the year, I'd seen countless varieties of gory saddle sores and had learned the best treatment. I was on top of things – or so I thought.

The warning signs were there, but I was blind to them as I revelled in new discoveries in Azerbaijan. This part of the former USSR was fascinatingly different, and I imagined everyone to be entranced by it. We'd emerged from a trying two weeks as Russia had invaded Georgia, our destination after Turkey, resulting in the closure of all Georgia's borders with Turkey. An undesirable backtrack by bus to Ankara was followed by a flight to Baku, Azerbaijan, and then it was back on to our bikes for an untried circular route, to return to Baku and await our scheduled ferry crossing of the Caspian Sea to Turkmenistan.

But the war in Georgia had disrupted all transport and it became a waiting game. Our confirmed ferry booking had come and gone, and we were informally camped in filthy, steamy conditions, with the temperatures reaching 40 degrees and 90 per cent humidity, on the docks at Baku, between railway lines and dilapidated trucks.

'This is totally, utterly, fucking ridiculous!'

The use of an expletive from Simon, usually polite and softly spoken, the archetypal middle-aged English gentleman, shocked me more than anything. Uncharacteristically, I was at a loss for words. I stole a glance at a grubby seagull tearing at a plastic packet of rotting bait. A rat scurried past. Things were bad.

Most of the cyclists who'd been forced to endure this un-scheduled turn of events had gamely taken it on as an adventure, showing resilience and a quirky sense of humour: to pass the time they held fly-swatting competitions, then set out to find the cheapest beer, of which they consumed copious quantities, followed by the re-telling of grossly exaggerated foul toilet experiences.

But in Simon, and a few others, I'd noticed an increasing moroseness, a withdrawal and a reluctance to engage with anyone.

'But all will come right when we get back on our bikes,' I reassured myself. Today was proving me wrong.

'I demand some action!' Simon shouted, breathing heavily. 'I refuse to eat until there's a contingency plan. Where is James?'

James, the tour leader, was lying in the shade of a truck, drinking beer, but I knew he had no more information than I had. Meeting Simon's wild gaze, I lowered my voice and said slowly, 'I am sorry, Simon. This is unpleasant and unexpected. We are all doing the best we can. We expect to set sail in a day or two,' – my fingers were crossed behind my back – 'but we cannot leave the dock or we will miss—'

'This is bullshit!' This shout came from a towering figure behind me. George, a 50-something Canadian physical-training teacher, was almost spitting with rage. He kicked a plastic water container into touch.

I began to sweat even more. I, their carer, their doctor, had failed them. I'd missed the warning signs. They were angry, dehydrated, depressed and bordering on irrational, and all I seemed capable of doing, in their eyes, was offering false reassurance and another beer.

Thinking that some action was better than nothing at all, I said, 'Okay, guys, I hear you. Come with me.' I walked with them to a spot where a dishevelled tree overhung a stretch of slightly cleaner-than-usual water. 'Let's talk.'

As they poured out their grievances and all their symptoms of stress, especially troublesome insomnia, I came up with a tiny plan. I had one small thing to offer. Evening was approaching. The air was cooling slightly. The light was more sympathetic. 'Wait here,' I said.

I ran to buy two ice-cold lemon drinks from a vendor I'd discovered just that morning. I then scrabbled around my open-air

Camping on the Baku dockside in far-from-ideal conditions.

bedroom and found my own personal emergency medical kit. I heaved a sigh of relief when I found what I was looking for, still amazed that I'd thought to include sleeping tablets, as I'd never personally used them. Drugs can be good.

I ran back with my loot. I thrust the cold bottles into their hands and handed each of them a tablet. 'Drink this. Settle down this evening and then take this tablet. It won't change much, but I promise that you'll have a good night's sleep.'

The god Hypnos was on my side that night. They both slept soundly, and awoke more refreshed and positive.

But the real miracle that morning was that we boarded a ferry, albeit in disorganised haste, and set sail for Turkmenistan. As a perennial optimist, I thought that getting moving again would cure all ills. Wrong again.

Things did move on – from bad to considerably worse. We reached China and cycled from the western border near Kashgar to Beijing on the east coast, through the Taklamakan Desert. The harsh, flat, desolate vistas seemed to infiltrate the minds of George and Simon, who both plummeted into dark, lonely recesses of depression and paranoia. Gone were my blissful days when crawling out of my tent each morning and riding my bike were the only requirements. Now, I had to restore the mental health of my two patients or the entire tour could disintegrate.

Simon was overtly depressed, and suffering all the accompanying physical symptoms of abdominal pain, headaches and insomnia, while George had declared a personal and vindictive race against Ben, a young, cocky, fast-cycling, bright American who'd made it into Harvard Business School despite his origins as a Vietnamese refugee.

It had been a seriously bad day of cycling, with an icy headwind mocking our efforts. My head hurt. The lunch stop, usually a time of revival and friendly banter, was solemn and silent – and the bread was stale. I noticed Simon crouching behind a boulder, far from the rest of us. I followed him back to the road and cycled the rest of the day with him, coaxing monosyllabic responses to what were probably inane questions from me but mainly in silence. His black mood was intransigent.

That night he disappeared into the distance to pitch his tent. I took a deep breath and marched towards it.

'Simon!' I called.

No response. I sat in the dust outside his tent door and waited.

Finally he pulled back the nylon fabric between us. 'What?' He looked tormented.

'Simon, you're making yourself, and us, sick.'

He flicked his head and dropped his gaze.

I pushed on. 'Simon, you have three options. One, you and I can go in search of a Chinese doctor and, with luck, buy some Chinese medication for depression. Two, you can lighten up. Let things roll a little. Stop looking for fault. Try developing a thicker skin. Look up at the stars not down at your feet. I'll help you.' I paused.

'And the third option?' he asked.

I breathed in deeply: 'You must go home.'

'Never!' he said immediately.

I had one sleeping pill left, which I handed to him. There seemed nothing else to say.

The next morning he set out, wordlessly, beside me. To his credit and my huge relief, it appeared he'd chosen option two. I pushed reassurances and coping mechanisms from my limited repertoire, and pointed out anything beautiful I saw along the way. The days that followed were hard for him but he was courageous. He had several relapses but the slope of the graph of recovery was upwards.

We were three months into the trip, in a remote, bleak, windswept part of China. It hadn't been a good day. After eighty kilometres of battling against the wind, the challenge of erecting tents in the gale remained. In the fading light, dispirited and hungry, we crept into our tents in an effort to keep them pinned to the ground.

I was woken by movement and light in the tent next to mine – that of the oldest cyclist on the trip, 72-year-old Henk. I'd grown to like and respect him, and we'd had many searching conversations and as many good chuckles. Dutch, stubborn and stoic, he'd blazed his own trail through life and had tackled this trip with the same attitude, and with a saddlebag loaded with reference books, food, cameras and binoculars.

I waited. He knew where to find me.

The flashing light, rustling of packets, and zips opening and closing persisted for a while, then all went quiet again. Not urgent, I thought to myself, highly relieved.

Henk was at my tent door at first light. He looked troubled. He was holding up the index finger of his right hand, and when I examined it I saw two puncture wounds, inflamed and swollen. They could only have been inflicted by an animal.

'What happened here, Henk?'

'There was a mouse in my tent, eating my speculaas biscuits. I wanted to get him out. I picked him up. He bit my finger.'

'Come, let me clean and dress that for you,' I said. Buying thinking time, I walked slowly to my medical box and sat my patient down alongside a flimsy folding table. We took up our places on either side.

As I worked, Henk asked a question that made the blood begin rushing in my ears. 'What about hondsdolheid?' He used the Dutch word for rabies, which is identical to the Afrikaans one and means 'dog madness'.

'Henk – have you had the hondsdolheid vaccination?' I asked.

He looked almost offended. 'Of course!'

Relief. But various questions and scenarios still circled through my brain. Did he stand a chance of still contracting rabies from this bite? What was the incidence of rabies in China? Were small rodents carriers? Did Henk need a booster vaccine? If so, how was I going to access this in rural China? Would local clinics even stock it? My ignorance felt overwhelming and I hoped it didn't show.

'Okay, Henk, this is going to be alright – your vaccine protects you,' I told him. 'And the chance of that mouse being rabid is very, very small.'

What I learned in later years was that only half of this statement was correct. While small rodents like rats and mice have never been found to carry rabies, and there has never been a report of a human contracting rabies from a mouse bite, people already vaccinated against rabies require a booster vaccination if a bite from a suspected rabid animal has occurred.

Today, China, with its population of eighty million dogs, has the second-highest number of reported rabies cases in the world, and over 2 000 deaths a year. There has been a steady improvement in the rate of vaccination, from a dismally low level in 2008 of 20%, and the aim is to achieve 70% vaccination. China is now the world's largest consumer of rabies vaccinations.

We'd pulled into a service road running parallel to a large irrigation channel. Orchards stretched out on either side. The setting sun poured gold across the water. The mood was buoyant as we went about our evening rituals. Tantalising aromas wafted from the outdoor kitchen.

Shrieks of delight rang out as hot, dusty bodies plunged into the channel and were submerged for the first time in many weeks. No-one had saddle sores or diarrhoea. I even heard a chuckle from Simon.

During dinner, George stood and said he'd like to address the group. We hardly paused between mouthfuls as he started to list what seemed petty grievances. Then his anger bubbled up and over, and he began shouting, pacing, pointing fingers, accusing. The staff were inept, ill prepared and useless; leadership was lacking; and his arch-rival Ben was a lying cheat.

What I – and Ben – had failed to grasp was the seriousness of the contest and the pathological hatred with which George was conducting it. To my horror, he aimed a punch at Ben, who dived for cover as others physically restrained George. James and the cook led him away, beckoning to me as they did so.

How had I missed the warning signs of this outburst? I'd been aware that George had become withdrawn but he'd remained civil and ridden hard every day in constant competition with Ben. But now I realised that he was intensely angry – and it hit me that he was angry with himself. He was accustomed to being a strong leader, a man with coping skills to teach others, but this journey with its physical hardships and unpredictability had exposed hidden weaknesses that he'd had to confront.

'Joan, he has got to go home,' James told me. 'He's mentally unstable and he's jeopardising the entire expedition. I've had it up to here with him – and a few others.' James drew his flattened hand across his neck. He was in no mood to negotiate.

'Give me 24 hours with him, please,' I said. I knew that George had his own private mission to make it to the end of the cycle tour, to Beijing, and if he also failed in that, I dreaded the consequences.

James glared at me. I knew he thought I was being too soft, that this was all going to slide into a messy disaster.

'Twenty-four hours,' he agreed, and added, 'and I can intervene at any stage. I have a job to complete, and one maniac isn't going to spoil it for us all.'

My consulting room on the Silk Route.

Telling George, with a firmness I didn't feel, that I'd meet him at his tent, I made a detour past my own. My personal emergency medical kit yielded yet another treasure: a crumbly, recently expired 10mg Valium tablet. This sedative/tranquilliser could buy me time.

'You're this close to being sent home,' I told George, holding my thumb and index finger millimetres apart. 'You and I can get through this, but I need your full cooperation. Right now, lie down, take this tablet, read a book, and be prepared for a slow ride with me tomorrow. And stay away from everyone else.'

That night my thoughts twisted and tumbled, mocking me. I'd never excelled at psychiatric interventions. Now I was faced with a paranoid patient with an anger problem. He was also a towering, immensely strong man.

I recalled a medical article I'd read by a Zimbabwean psychiatrist, one of the beleaguered twelve trying to deal with a population of about sixteen million. He was creating an informal system of therapists from the community. His most successful were the grandmothers, because they were good at listening and guided their charges to a solution rather than directing them as to what to do.

In the days that followed, George and I cycled side by side. I modelled myself on a caring, non-judgemental grandmother. He talked, I listened. He bared his soul. His anger problem stretched way back into his childhood. Although married, he'd never trusted himself to have children, but he'd always kept his cool as a teacher. He admitted to being pathologically competitive, always trying to prove that he was good enough.

On our bikes, there was a hidden energy in the rolling motion and a lack of constant eye contact that made painful disclosures easier, and this 'saddle counselling' proved remarkably effective. George, seeking me out as a cycling companion when he needed a listening ear, slowly found his own way to deal with the catalysts of his anger.

On an icy, grey day in November 2008, we all rode onto Tiananmen Square in Beijing. Our mission completed, I searched the expressions of George and Simon. While they weren't bubbling over with exuberance like the others, what I did see was a lingering vulnerability and a glow of pride.

I felt a kinship with them. We'd battled together to rise above the odds of crippling mental disorder and we'd triumphed.

CHAPTER 7

Gough Island: 2012

'I am a citizen of the most beautiful nation on earth. A nation whose laws are harsh yet simple, a nation that never cheats, which is immense and without borders, where life is lived in the present. In this limitless nation, this nation of the wind, light and peace, there is no other ruler besides the sea.'

— *The Long Way* by Bernard Moitessier, 1971

BERNARD MOITESSIER WAS A FRENCH SAILOR best known for his participation in the 1968 Sunday Times Golden Globe Race, the first nonstop singlehanded round-the-world yacht race. In the latter half of the race he had the fastest circumnavigation time; he just needed to return to the start line in England to claim victory.

He chose not to. He continued on to Tahiti and in doing so rejected the concept of the commercialisation of long-distance sailing.

His resignation from the race came in the form of a message to the London *Times* correspondent, delivered by slingshot onto the deck of a passing ship. It stated simply that his reason for sailing on was 'because I am happy at sea and perhaps to save my soul'.

I was now also sailing on – on the maiden voyage of the magnificent *SA Agulhas II*, a brand-new red-and-white ice-breaker, the showpiece of the South African National Antarctic Programme. This was her first official 'relief voyage', destined for Tristan da Cunha and Gough islands, and for oceanographic data collection to a latitude of 50 degrees south.

Gough Island, lying at 40 degrees south and 9 degrees west, 2 600 kilometres from Cape Town, is a dependency of Tristan da Cunha and part of the British Overseas Territory of St Helena, Ascension Island and Tristan. Its remote location has long been of interest to explorers and researchers, and particularly to orni-thologists, as it hosts some of the world's most important breeding seabird colonies.

However, it wasn't the birdlife that first attracted South African researchers. Its location was recognised as being invaluable for the collection of meteorological data which from this part of the world was usually provided by weather reports from ships crossing the Atlantic from South America. Hence in 1955 a UK research expedition called the Gough Island Scientific Survey allowed the South African Weather Bureau to set up a rudimentary weather station on the island. This was manned by meteorologist JJ van der Merwe and, in conjunction with the station on Marion Island, the Gough Island weather data contributed to an ambitious international science effort known as the International Geophysical Year of 1957–1958.

South Africa leased from the British government the land on which the weather station was built, and has maintained a continuous presence there since 1956, managed by the South African National Antarctic Programme. As part of this lease agreement, a South African National Antarctic Programme vessel does an annual resupply trip to Gough, and also calls in at Tristan da Cunha on the inward and outward journeys to deliver passengers and freight.

I'd applied to be the ship's doctor on this, the 58th resupply trip, and was accepted, perhaps on the strength of my participation in the Marion Island rescue. I imagined that they saw me as a safe bet: I knew exactly how bad it could get in the raging South Atlantic, and yet, due to a masochistic temperament, I'd elected to return.

Our departure on 6 September 2012 was on a shimmering spring day, and as this new *Agulhas* had been dedicated to the life and songs of the famed Miriam Makeba, our send-off was exuberant, action-filled and noisy. There were brass bands, vuvuzelas, dancers, singers, sea cadets, and battalions of schoolchildren waving our beloved colourful South African flag. Two aggressive-looking bull-nosed tugs eased us out of the berth and past the breakwater. The pilot boat pulled alongside and its captain skipped down the rope ladder, turned to wave, and gave us his final salute and blessing.

I sought some quiet in my state-of-the-art cabin complete with en-suite bathroom. I had the words of Moitessier in mind: 'perhaps to save my soul'. I wasn't in need of soul saving, but since the Marion Island adventure, the open horizons of the ocean had often washed through my thoughts. I was in need of a new medical adventure.

I knew that this was a good place to be right now. Aside from anything else, it would give me time to study for my upcoming exam for a diploma in tropical medicine.

My porthole view of the sea showed it at its best: deep blue and gently rippling. A seagull cruised by. It was what kept bringing me back: the call of that distant horizon, the sharp edge of the unknown, softened by the call of the seabirds, air that feels like a balm, and the promise of new knowledge and unexpected experiences.

We were sailing west, into the setting sun. We'd left behind all signs of humankind. Twenty years had passed since I'd been on this same bearing, headed for Tristan da Cunha, with my two young daughters, on a small Danish cargo vessel.

Was I now any better equipped to deal with this journey? I was reminded earlier by a passenger, Tina Glass, a returning resident of Tristan, that it was her baby I'd delivered in those first few days after my initial arrival on the island. I hadn't delivered many since. I noticed one pregnant woman among the returning Tristan passengers, and I instantly broke out into a cold sweat.

But one passenger I was delighted to meet, given my insecurities with mental illness, was an experienced psychiatrist. He was to spend time on Tristan, unravelling the unique psychiatric issues of this small, isolated, complex community of 270 souls.

I climbed the steel stairs up to a viewing area on the topmost accessible height of the ship. Called the monkey island, in modern ships it usually lies directly above the navigating bridge. When ships had masts and sails, it was located three quarters of the way up the main mast. On this state-of-the-art vessel it was enclosed in glass and had comfortable seating – the perfect vantage point for ornithologists. The four who were on board were all there, rattling off, with enthusiasm, the names of specks of white, black and brown as they glided past.

I noticed the bird that had first entered my life twenty years before and which had made reappearances on my voyages to the point that I now regarded it as a talisman, an observer, real or imagined, of my life. It was the bird with the largest wingspan of all birds in the world today – the wandering albatross. Little did I realise then that it was still working its magic.

The ornithological team was to spend time on Nightingale Island, a speck of land 39 kilometres from Tristan which is uninhabited except for a few days in the year when Tristanians spend time there harvesting the greater shearwater chicks from which they extract a rich oil. This team was to study the rock-hopper penguins on Nightingale as their breeding had been severely affected by an oil spill from a bulk carrier wrecked earlier in the year.

Another tiny land bird that made Nightingale Island its home was the endemic Wilkins's finch. There were only 200 remaining and the team wanted to know why.

I was inspired by their dedication. I learned that Annabel, one of the ornithologists, although German by birth, had studied, worked and travelled the world in her quest to learn more about birds. I mentioned my frustration at not yet having got to the Antarctic to see its penguins. 'I'm still trying to get there on a South African research vessel,' I told her. 'My attempts to get onto a tourist expedition ship have failed. One of the reasons they give is that I'm a little old.'

Annabel made a scoffing noise. (I loved her for that!) 'You must try this new Canadian company, One Ocean Expeditions, who are running ships to the Antarctic and the Arctic. I was recently the ornithologist on a trip. Their doctor was ancient, and not too mobile. I think they're struggling as they're so new. Here, I'll give you the email of the boss.' She tore a piece of paper off her

The perilous descent of the rope ladder.

clipboard pad and scribbled down the information. 'Most of his staff is Canadian, but he really likes Saffers. Tell him I referred you. He's really bad at replying. Just keep trying.'

The Southern Ocean was kind to us and our luck held. We approached Tristan on a clear, sparkling day when the towering sea cliffs and the volcanic peak with its 2 062-metre summit were clearly visible.

Helicopter crews swung into action. I watched from a high deck as a skilled chopper pilot eased his bird slowly down to the loading deck, where the deck hands hooked the loads enclosed in nylon nets onto the thirty-metre cable hanging below the helicopter.

Back on Tristan da Cunha twenty years later.

Seconds later it was swooping in seemingly joyous abandon towards the island, where the load was carefully lowered and released. Then the chopper soared skywards again, to join the many giant petrels, yellow-nosed albatrosses and predatory skuas on their surveillance flights.

'Doctor Joan. Doctor Joan. Report to the bridge please.'

These announcements always sent me into a tachycardia. Hurrying towards the bridge, I thought to myself that at least now we were close to Tristan and could always call on the assistance of the doctor ashore. But this call was merely to help the captain in the selection of the passengers who would be flown to the island, rather than descend the very precarious rope ladder onto the deck of an erratically bobbing launch.

I chose the important people, the old, the fat and the infirm to be whisked across by helicopter. But I didn't get it right. There was a large young trainee scientist who exhibited an undue amount of anxiety at having to descend the rope ladder. I thought she was overreacting and would rise to the occasion. She didn't. She lost her grip on the rope ladder and plummeted into the icy water, into the gap between the launch and the hull of the ship. Only the quick thinking and strength of the two Tristanian crew saved her from being crushed. She was manhandled back up the ladder into my care, and an immediate hot bath followed by a vigorous massage. She never did get onto Tristan.

My own descent down the ladder was hugely fearful. How I wished I'd placed myself firmly in the important persons category!

Setting foot on Tristan again after twenty years was an incredible privilege. Little had changed. The houses, many built from black volcanic rock, the dogs, the cows, the views all looked familiar. Only the number of cars had increased. The folk who came up and greeted me warmly made me feel young again. My godson, Jason, the second babe I'd delivered, now nearly 21 years old, bent over to enfold me in a tight hug. His mother, calm as always, smiled serenely.

I went for a slow amble with Margaret, my erstwhile house-keeper, and we remembered with nostalgia Sogneus, her husband, with whom I'd climbed the peak and who'd been subjected to my suboptimal dental care. He'd suffered a tragic death, not on Tristan, but in a modern hospital in Cape Town, of post-operative complications following a routine procedure. She'd waved farewell to him as his ship departed and had never seen him again.

The ship's hooter sounded. It was the call for the stragglers on the island to head back to the small harbour, scramble onto the launch, risk life and limb on the rope ladder, and prepare to depart for Gough Island.

Margaret thrust a package into my hands. I knew what it had to be: Tristan women are famed for their knitting. 'Just something to keep you warm, Doctor Joan. We still think of you often.'

I hugged this kind, caring, gracious woman, born and raised on a remote piece of rock in the Atlantic Ocean. How extraordinary it was that I, and my girls, had been a small part of her life and that of her three children.

Back on board, I watched with some sadness the settlement of Edinburgh of the Seven Seas fade. Then the summit of Queen Mary's Peak wavered and disappeared. We were headed for Gough.

A greater level of seriousness and preparation now pervaded. A safety briefing on the heli-deck took us through the motions of a simulated chopper crash and the extrication of the potentially seriously wounded pilot.

I was asked to be part of the presentation and was introduced by Dudley Foot, an extraordinarily experienced helicopter pilot and coordinator of all airborne activities. A man of few words, he stated, 'The more you sweat in peace, the less you bleed in war,' then he nodded for me to proceed. My mind ran riot as I stumbled through the unfamiliar presentation, trying to appear calm and experienced in my demonstration of applying a cervical collar and strapping the patient to a fracture board. The audience nodded confidently – but we all knew that the real thing would be terrifying.

Environmental safety was another concern. Gough and

Inaccessible islands were declared a UNESCO World Heritage Site in 1995 and were of particular concern to the Overseas Territories Environment Programme of Britain. On board were two professional rock climbers funded by the Royal Society for the Protection of Birds. They'd been tasked with tackling an alien-vegetation invasion that had spread over the cliffs, threatening the breeding sites of many birds. The culprit was procumbent pearlwort, an innocuous-looking but rapidly spreading northern-hemisphere plant that had been inadvertently introduced via Marion Island where it had become a major uncontrollable menace. I looked forward to watching these lithe young men with good legs dangling from the ends of ropes, chopping out and poisoning the offending plants.

To prevent any possibility of a repeat of the biological invasion, before setting foot on Gough we underwent a kit-cleaning party. With music blaring and impromptu dancing, we scrubbed our boots and outer gear with a chlorine solution, and scrutinised velcro fastenings for any lurking seeds or soil – the scientific term for these nasties being 'propagules'.

The post-doctoral seal researchers, many of whom I'd met on my Marion Island sojourn, joined the scaremongering by regaling us with stories of seal attacks and bites, and graphically illustrated their point with photographs of lacerated and bleeding limbs. One of them rolled up his trousers and pointed to a nasty scar and deformed calf muscle. 'I got too close to an angry subantarctic fur seal,' he said.

I implored them to be careful.

'We'll make sure we stay away from the four-ton elephant seals,' one joker said, and they all laughed. I didn't.

Also on board was a quiet English couple with whom I seldom had the chance to chat as they were always high up on deck, braving every permutation of weather, with binoculars constantly at the ready. They were ornithologists also employed by the Royal Society for the Protection of Birds, and were working on the feasibility of a project to eradicate another lethal threat to the bird life on Gough – mice.

These small rodents had been introduced 150 years before by passing sailors, and today, after surviving on a high-protein diet of seabird chicks, they were fifty per cent larger than their ancestral relatives. It was estimated that two million seabird chicks were lost annually to these monster mice, which can gnaw away at a ten-kilogram albatross chick over a few nights until it succumbs to its accumulated wounds. The Tristan albatross and Atlantic petrel were on the brink of extinction thanks to the predations of these rodents. The eradication plan would rely on the helicopter distribution of rodenticide, a method that had proved very successful on other remote islands like South Georgia.

In the first grey light of dawn, as my porthole was being lashed with rain, the profile of Gough Island hove into view. I trained my binoculars on a white speck in the distance – Gough House, home to the overwintering team of eight intrepid souls who monitored weather, did bird counts and environmental assessments, and kept the diesel engines running. There was also a paramedic tasked with keeping the team healthy. Their solitude was about to be disrupted by the visiting scientists and weather boffins, and the seasoned southern-sea veterans from the Public Works Department who annually do all the repair work and machine servicing on the island.

Many of the members of the team leaving were perched on the roof of Gough House, binoculars focused on us, their ticket to the real world again. But it would still be three weeks before their departure.

The heli-deck presented an interesting spectacle. The seasoned scientists sat quietly on crates and chatted. The novices, preparing for their first helicopter flight, were fully kitted out in foul-weather gear, life jackets firmly in place. They listened attentively as the pre-flight drill was explained, then lined up on command like well-trained hounds. I marvelled at the good fortune in my life that had allowed me to be spectator to all this.

Meanwhile, the weather gurus on board were agitating for a rapid unloading. We were soon to be battered by a massive storm.

Once all had been offloaded, the much-diminished number of ship-based scientists – oceanographers and climatologists – and the crew and I would set off on a 'buoy run'. This would take us to a latitude of 50 degrees south, a personal record for me and one that held the possibility of iceberg sightings. The prime purpose was to drop weather buoys at specific points. These would relay back weather indices for a year before being replaced by the following year's voyage. Along the way, more expensive instruments would be released at set grid points into the air and into the deep.

This would take three weeks, after which we'd return to Gough Island to collect the visiting scientists, and the overwintering team who would have survived a busy time, working, socialising, packing up, bidding their island home farewell and generously sharing their living space with the not-always-welcome visitors.

I was suddenly awake. My cabin was in total darkness and the ship was in its gentle, rhythmic at-anchor mode. Yet there was a muffled sound – a sense of movement beyond my porthole, out towards the inky blackness of the open ocean.

I sat up. I peered through the porthole – and caught my breath in utter amazement. As far as I could discern in the night glow were birds, swooping, diving, twirling, fluttering – the white feathers under their wings quivering, catching the minute fragments of reflected light and scattering them. There were thousands on thousands of them, clearly visible less than a metre from my nose, and fading in hordes into the darkness. In their frenzy, many struck the side of the vessel, and fell, dazed, into the water or the decks below.

I was mesmerised. I couldn't identify them although I presumed most to be the birds I knew to swirl in flocks at sunset around Gough Island – broad-billed prions. We'd been warned to keep all blinds closed at night if lights were on inside, as the birds would fly inexorably and relentlessly towards the light, heedless of any obstructions en route. There was a faint glimmer from the bridge above, and I watched as the officer on duty, also a privileged spectator of this avian display, turned off all the lights he could. But the birds continued, stripped of normal control and survival instinct. I eased myself back onto my bunk, filled with a sense of wonder at what I'd witnessed.

First light saw me bundled up against the biting wind, out on deck, surveying what looked like the wreckage of an aviary. Feathers, fluff, excrement and a few bewildered owners of such lay scattered. I spotted a young petrel wedged into a corner. It seemed unharmed but moved with difficulty as I coaxed it to the edge of the deck. The wind ruffled its feathers; it raised its head and in seconds was soaring to freedom.

I made my way to the highest viewpoint. Evidence of the night invasion was everywhere.

At the entrance to an electricity station stood a crewman, shaking his head in amazement. 'Morning, Doc. Can you believe this? Last night an alarm from an electricity failure went off and when I came to investigate and opened this door, these birds, thousands of them, flew into me. I could hardly breathe they were fighting so hard to escape. They're used to crawling into burrows… they must have crawled along the drain under the door, then found themselves trapped and unable to find the way out again.'

He knelt down and peered into the gloom of the small room. 'See – there are still some stuck behind them wires, and in the light fitting, a nd u nder t he m etal fl oor pl ates.' He wo uld have to extricate and free them. 'I'll need help with this job.'

Later I watched as three burley crewmen facilitated the rescue. One, on his hands and knees, rummaged with a stick under the instruments. The second reached down as the birds emerged, lifting the creatures with some apprehension and passing them to the third crewman, who placed them carefully on the deck, watching with a protective eye until they flapped their way skywards. What a wonderful, gentle diversion from their noisy, harsh, inanimate engine-room world!

The conversation for the rest of the day was of little else. Our captain, who'd spent countless years in these seemingly desolate southern waters, declared that he'd never seen such an over-whelming, awe-inspiring sighting of birds.

For me, it was my 'point of wonder' for the day, and a once-in-a-lifetime event.

Another first on this maiden voyage of the *SA Agulhas II* was the planned launch of the sea-gliders. These hugely expensive, torpedo-like items were a revolutionary tool in oceanographic research and their launching was a historical first for South Africa and the Southern Ocean.

The launching had been postponed on a few occasions due to tumultuous seas, and finally, in somewhat unfavourable conditions, the go-ahead was given. As a spectator, I was already uneasy as I watched a shocking-pink torpedo being winched into the churning water aft. Without warning, a massive wave reached up to grab it, ripping off one of its fins.

Gavin, the project director, gave the order that the damaged

Glider retrieved, the crew attempts to bring the craft alongside in rough seas.

glider had to be retrieved. The rescue craft was on standby and in seconds it was winched over the side, with two experienced crewmen in survival suits and a somewhat inappropriately clad Gavin.

All seemed fine initially. The craft bobbed and danced over the turbulent, frothy waves, the wind buffeting from all sides. With some difficulty, the glider was hauled aboard.

Then I watched in fear and trepidation as attempt after attempt was made to come alongside the ship. Waves crashed over the seaman clinging to the bow as he tried in vain to secure ropes front and back. The craft, in a horror moment, lurched sideways, attempting to disgorge its crew into the wedge of sea between ship and boat and into certain injury as waves and steel would splinter flesh and bones.

I turned away, feeling nauseous, the vision of three patients or, worse, three mangled corpses hovering before me.

After what seemed like hours, with multiple repositionings of the ship, the steel cable was successfully clamped into position and in seconds the craft was tethered like an obedient old nag to its allocated spot on deck. The three intrepid heroes clambered out. Hyperventilating, I staggered down to assist Gavin, who was grey, frozen and speechless.

The large tattooed seaman was on an adrenaline high and declared with an expansive grin, 'I want to do that again!'

'Not on my watch,' I muttered.

My next episode of hyperventilation occurred during my long-awaited hike through the trenches of mud edged with tussock grass and strangled tree-fern vegetation on Gough, which receives a mammoth 310 centimetres of rain annually. We had returned to Gough and had two days in which we could explore the island. Our destination was Seal Beach, home to a four-ton female elephant seal and a population of young subantarctic fur seal cubs.

We'd donned waterproof gear, gloves and gumboots, and were making reasonable progress over the humps of tussock grass at the base of which often lurked the deep ankle-breaking burrows of breeding shearwaters. The phantom-ship cadence was still in our legs. We paused at the top of a cliff and gazed down at the pebble beach below. A familiar uneasiness set in.

The leader of our party wasn't a newcomer to Gough. She'd done this before. 'The descent is a bit tricky but there's a rope to hang on to.'

I cast surreptitious glances around at our party. Most of us were confident and in good physical shape – with one notable exception: the large young woman who'd fallen off the rope ladder while attempting the descent to the launch at Tristan.

I made a weak attempt to assert some authority. 'Anyone who feels they don't want to do this can return to the base.' And I laid it on a bit thick. 'Once we're down, we have to get back up the rope, and there'll be no-one to assist. Is everyone happy to do this?' I looked squarely at the large lady.

With a defiant gleam in her eye, she held my gaze and nodded. I was too feeble to go with my gut feeling and insist that she not attempt this dangerous exercise.

Getting down was uneventful and I scolded myself for being overanxious.

Much later, I was still entranced by the antics of the seal pups when I heard a wail wafting down from the cliff face.

'I can't hold on any longer! Help me! I'm going to fall!'

There, visibly shaking, hanging on to the rope for dear life, was the large young woman. Halfway up, panic had set in, and her feet, instead of supporting her weight, were flailing around, kicking at knobs of moss.

Her colleague just below her was a calm, strong, young ocean-ographer who just happened to be an endurance athlete. He ascended with ease and grace to the level of her lowest foot, kicked out a foothold, and pinned her boot to the boggy soil. 'Now put some weight on that foot,' he ordered. 'Keep holding the rope but relax a bit.' And then, a little more fiercely, 'Just calm down.'

A second saviour had now reached her and held the other foot in place. I climbed at speed to reach them. 'You'll have to keep climbing up,' I told her. 'We'll help you. There'll be a hand on each foot and on your bum but you must move your hands up and help pull. Hold on to the rope or any firm handhold, like a rock or a good piece of vegetation. We won't let you fall.'

I said this all with more confidence than I felt. A battle of strength from the three of us ensued, with some cajoling, some stern commanding and occasional foul language. The large lady's whimpering was background accompaniment.

When we got her to the top, I was in far worse shape than she was. I lay on my back, eyes closed, with my head centimetres from an aggressive yellow-nosed albatross female sitting on her eggs in her mud-packed nest. In warning, she banged her beak like a castanet. I ignored her, watching the stars and tracers traversing my closed eyelids.

Disaster had been averted – again – but I felt I was to blame for not preventing it right from the start. At some crucial moments I needed to be a bit bossier. My hyperventilation slowed. Hard lesson learned.

That night was the handing-over party at Gough House – and it was the mix of human life that made me marvel. The individuals, men and women from a range of different cultures, who staffed this island for a year, did so with relish. They showed good humour and a massive amount of tolerance, empathy and mutual respect. Problems and misunderstandings inevitably arose, but they had to be resolved. There was no escape. It was a party of great spirit, friendly banter and positive feeling, with lots of food, drink, music, dancing and laughter.

I stepped outside every so often, listening to the cries of the birds, and reminding myself where I was, and just how few people had ever had the pleasure of this unique experience.

A day later we were on our way back to Cape Town. We called in at Tristan, where we deposited some additional cargo and the Tristanian who was part of the Overseas Territories Environment Programme team for Britain, then continued on our way.

The highly skilled and experienced paramedic of the departing Gough team was on board, adding to my feeling of security in all things medical. The return voyage was starting to feel like a holiday. I was sleeping soundly.

However, peaceful, uninterrupted nights for the remainder of the journey home were not to be. That night, almost on the stroke of midnight, a prolonged, ear-piercing, urgent alarm sounded throughout the ship. Is this a practice drill? I wondered as I fumbled for the light switch.

The captain's voice came through the intercom. 'Please remain calm. Dress warmly. Proceed to your muster point and await further instructions.'

He sounded as if his jaw was in spasm, and was squeezing out the words. This was no drill. I hurriedly donned my foul-weather gear, grabbed my asthma meds and a bottle of water, and headed into the corridor.

The fire doors to the stairwell had already slammed shut, but not soon enough to exclude the pungent smell of smoke rising up from the nether regions of the ship. A fire on board – a captain's worst nightmare.

The scene then went into fast-forward. Crew members in their neon-orange overalls, boots and hard hats moved past, opening doors to the deck in response to curt radio instructions. The inebriated stragglers from the evening's 'Hilarious Hat' party, in various stages of inappropriate dress, milled around in small agitated groups on the deck. Thankfully, we weren't forced to board the lifeboats: word came through that the fire in the dining room was under control and the emergency was over.

Later, on the deck, warm mug of tea in hand, the loom of the moon reflecting off a calm sea, I tried to imagine what it would feel like bobbing around on a black ocean in a crowded lifeboat as the doctor of 94 panicked souls. Plain terrifying. Gratitude washed over me.

The night after the fire I met my next patient – one who would keep me working and involved right up until Table Mountain slid into view. I had inadvertently locked myself out of my cosy cabin. The hour was late and I could find no responsible being to assist, so I resorted to slinking off to 'my clinic' and climbing, fully clothed, into one of the three beds on offer. I was tossing and turning on the crackling, plastic-shrouded hospital-bed mattress when I became aware of a frantic tapping on the clinic door.

I was considering my options, when the door swung open to reveal a crewman whose face was only vaguely familiar. He was breathing deeply but rapidly, shaking his hands vigorously and periodically fingering his lips. 'Help me, Doc, please,' he panted. 'I'm going to faint. I'm having one of my panic attacks.'

I leapt out of bed, grabbed his arm, and helped him onto the nearest bed as his knees began to buckle. I clamped the oxygen monitor onto his forefinger. As I suspected, his blood-oxygen levels were normal. 'Are your fingers tingling?' I asked. 'Do your lips have pins and needles?'

He whimpered and nodded. The emergency drug box was close at hand. I grabbed a lorazepam – a benzodiazepine medication with tranquillising effects, used to treat anxiety disorders. 'Put this under your tongue. You're hyperventilating, so I'm going to hold a paper bag over your mouth and nose. Breathe into it. Be conscious of slowing down your breathing. I'll count for you. When your breathing is normal again, your level of carbon dioxide will be corrected and all the tingling and faintness will go.'

Slowly, his breathing settled and his colour improved. He kept his eyes closed, but tears began to slide down his cheeks.

I now recognised him as one of a pair of seamen who'd settled a dispute with an exchange of blows and had been brought to me to patch up the damage. 'It's Jerome, isn't it?' He nodded again. 'We need to talk now.'

What followed that night, and every night afterwards, until we docked, was an unconventional counselling session. He wanted to see me only after hours. He didn't want to make eye contact; he wanted to lie down on a bed in the clinic. And I listened to him on one condition: that he would accept referral to a psychologist on his return to Cape Town.

But we did make huge progress. He had a chronic anxiety/anger problem, complicated by episodic heavy drinking. The thought of returning home to a wife whom he saw as disrespectful and an emotional bully was the recent trigger. He had at times taken his anger out on his children and then been overcome with remorse. He himself had been abused by his father. He'd never sought help for his problem. He was too embarrassed, and his escape was always returning to sea.

After our final evening of counselling, one in which he finally chose to be seated opposite me, he thanked me and accepted the letter of referral. 'I'll do this, I promise,' he said.

I lay on my bunk that night and wondered if I'd achieved any success. It was one of the downsides of this type of intense medicine, practised within a limited time frame: I seldom got follow-up, good or bad.

CHAPTER 8

Antarctica: 2013

'At the bottom of this planet lies an enchanted continent in the sky,
like a pale sleeping princess. Sinister and beautiful she lies in her frozen
slumber ...'

– Rear Admiral Richard Byrd, *National Geographic*, 1947

AN ICEBERG LOOMED, VAGUE AND BLURRY on the distant horizon of a gunmetal sea. It was the first I'd ever seen, but I was viewing it from a familiar platform – the monkey island of the *SA Agulhas I*.

We were headed due south from Cape Town, to Crown Bay on the ice shelf of the Antarctic continent. My role was familiar – I was the ship's doctor – but I felt like a walk-on player in this unfolding historical drama. On board we had actors of towering magnitude: Sir Ranulph Fiennes, known as 'the greatest living explorer', and his friend and fellow polar explorer, Dr Mike Stroud, a consultant gastroenterologist and expert on human endurance.

There were also five more brave souls who would attempt to cross the Antarctic in winter, a feat never achieved before. Sir

Ranulph would lead the expedition, but his friend Dr Stroud would not be joining him this time. He would remain involved at a distance, analysing the medical data from the participants collected by the expedition doctor. Sir Ran planned with this effort to raise thousands of pounds for the global charity Seeing is Believing, which aims to eradicate avoidable blindness in developing countries.

There were sixteen support staff on board, all tough, and somewhat eccentric in their training and experience, but all extraordinarily fascinating.

I wasn't part of the expedition. I'd been recruited as crew of the *SA Agulhas*, which had been leased to this expedition at a very favourable rate in exchange for permission to take along 55 naval cadets from throughout Africa. I was to be their doctor and – a new role for me – their gym instructor. I'd have agreed to anything to get onto the voyage!

We, this wonderful old ship and I, had already had our challenges. Our departure from Cape Town had been on a gift of a day – sparkling, clear, windless and sunny – as we were escorted out by seals, gulls and gannets. Table Mountain as the backdrop was soft and benign.

But shortly the Cape rollers were there to tease and try us. An engine failed, leaving us pitching and wallowing as all power was shut off during repairs. It was touch and go as to whether we'd have to return to Cape Town, but Smit Amandla Marine, the organisation that runs the ship, forbade such an action: 'fix it at sea' was the order.

What they, and the majority of the passengers and crew, didn't know was that the chief electrician, key in the repair, was already a patient of mine, suffering from extreme overindulgence during his shore leave. Through the grubby veil of seasickness, I was busy hauling out all my magic concoctions, fortunately from an already-familiar pharmacy, injecting him, inserting pessaries and running in fluids, in an attempt to get him on his feet and compos mentis enough to be of assistance.

That first night we went to bed not knowing in which direction we'd be heading on awakening. An ignominious return, after our wild, celebratory departure, was too dreadful to contemplate. Thankfully, the engine room stalwarts saved the day and we moved off at midnight, albeit slowly, against heavy seas and winds of 50 knots.

In the succeeding days the ambient temperature began to plummet. Excursions onto deck required beanies, gloves, boots, down jackets and waterproof outers. The cadets, who hailed from much warmer climes, like tropical KwaZulu-Natal, Ghana, Angola and Cameroon, began to fret and look uncomfortable.

We were all called to attend a lecture by Sir Ranulph and the polar veterans at which advice on how to deal with the extreme cold was issued. Frostbite, a condition in which the cells within the skin, muscles and tendons freeze, rupture and die, was dealt with at length, and Sir Ran held up a misshapen hand as a graphic example of the damage it can do. On an Arctic expedition, his uncovered hands endured prolonged exposure to extreme cold, leaving him with severe third-degree frostbite in three of his fingers.

On his return to civilisation he had sought medical advice about his blackened and hardened digits. He'd been urged to wait to allow some possible healing and return to function. The pain he'd suffered was unbearable, however, and, he calmly informed us, 'I went off to the hardware store, bought a hacksaw, and removed the offending phalanges myself.'

The audience was stunned. I was surreptitiously taking notes, as attending to all cold injury was my responsibility. I had to keep it quiet that I'd suffered frostbite in my toes while on a cycling race through the Eastern Cape of South Africa during winter. Shifting my toes in my boots reminded me that they'd never returned to normal function.

But now I had a medical challenge of an entirely different nature on my mind. I stole a glance at my patient, a young cadet from Ghana, sitting in the row ahead of me. The skin over his cheeks and forehead glistened, an ominous sign that his body temperature was still elevated.

Later, I knocked on his cabin door and he bade me enter. 'Joe, how are you doing?' I asked.

'A little better, I think, since the pills.' He spoke softly and with effort. He had fear in his eyes.

I took his wrist. His pulse rate was still too fast but it was significantly improved. I checked his eyes. There was no sign of jaundice. He wasn't anaemic. I palpated his abdomen: his liver and spleen weren't enlarged.

This was all positive and I sighed with relief. The worst scenario was that this young man could've succumbed to his disease. The best – and luckiest – scenario was that the doctor on board had just passed a diploma in tropical diseases and had made a presumptive diagnosis of malaria, confirmed by a testing kit found lurking with the urinary catheters. I sent up thanks that some bright and diligent medical-stores supplier had made sure the standard medication for malaria had been added to the pharmacy.

To be diagnosed with malaria at 45 degrees south would normally be unheard of, laughable and ridiculous, but this young man had boarded the ship about twelve days prior, in Ghana, where it had stopped en route to London to collect the expedition team. Joe had already been incubating the disease then. He would make a full recovery but I mused that he should go down in *Guinness World Records* as the patient diagnosed with malaria at the southernmost point ever!

Shortly after my visit to Joe's cabin, a young Cameroonian patient came to me, complaining of chronic insomnia: she was working on overcoming a fear of wild seas. I asked why, given this phobia, she'd chosen a maritime career. She quietly explained that this opportunity had arisen unexpectedly, and as she had been born to the fifth wife in a stressful polygamous marriage, she'd grabbed it, hoping to find a better way to live.

And south, always south, we continued. John, a New Zealander, was the ship's master and ice pilot. A professional seaman and specialist in navigation, he had the heavy responsibility of guiding the ship through the different types of ice, sometimes as thick as three metres deep, we were expected to encounter. En route to the Antarctic the ship would first pass through pack ice containing large pieces of floating ice before reaching the 'fast ice' which extends out from the shore and is attached to it.

He informed me as we crossed the latitude of 60 degrees south that we were officially 'beyond the confines of the world'. Apparently, hundreds of years ago, the boundaries of the world were proclaimed by none other than the insurance industry. Any ships proceeding beyond 72 degrees north and 60 degrees south were deemed 'out of the world' and therefore uninsurable.

I reflected on the inexplicable desire I'd had for the last thirty years, to travel this far south to visit the great desolation of the Antarctic. My *Seabirds of the World* reference book bears the inscription, dated 5/11/1984, in the neat hand of my late father-in-law, Charles Haw: 'Pete and Joan – May this book give you joy on your Antarctic trip.'

That trip had never happened. It was to have been on the first Antarctic tourist vessel, the *Lindblad Explorer*, and a last treat together for Pete and me, but Pete's rampant disease got the upper hand. Now I thought of him often as I struggled to identify those fleeting glimpses of white and black as petrels, shearwaters, prions, gulls, albatrosses and other annoyingly similar birds darted, glided and flapped between the waves.

Apart from being the doctor and the gym instructor on board, I had another duty: I was part of the expedition crew's birdwatching team. We spent an hour, morning and evening, collecting bird-sighting data which would be compared with that collected on the trans-global expedition 33 years before, when Ranulph Fiennes travelled around the world along the Greenwich Meridian, crossing both poles in the process. It was an exhilarating but freezing exercise. Holding binoculars in hands covered only in thin gloves to allow some dexterity quickly became uncomfortable.

My thoughts wandered to the efforts of those early explorers. It was Edmond Halley, the renowned British astronomer and mathematician, in 1609, who was given the credit of being the first to sail across the Antarctic convergence, also known as the Antarctic polar front, a curve continuously encircling Antarctica where the cold, northward-flowing waters meet the relatively warmer waters of the sub-Antarctic. The convergence varies in latitude seasonally but averages around 55 degrees south. Halley was the first man ever to build and command a vessel not for trade, not for war, but purely for scientific discovery; his aim was to measure magnetic variation.

At latitude 51 degrees south he recorded the first-ever-seen tabular iceberg with its clifflike sides and flat top. Not in his wildest imagination could he believe that the towering ice plateaus were floating objects – he saw them as ice-covered islands.

More than 150 years later, starting in 1772 and extending to 1775, Captain James Cook, in the *Resolution*, made three voyages in the Antarctic summers to circumnavigate the world below 40 degrees south. He discovered South Georgia but returned stating fairly definitively that Terra Australis Incognita – the 'unknown land of the south' – was a myth. There was no land down there, he said, and even if there was, it would be totally inaccessible due to impenetrable ice. This effectively put paid to further exploration.

In 1819 Captain William Smith of the English Merchant Navy, trading between the east and west coasts of South America, was driven south by a terrifying blizzard, in the process sighting the islands we now know as the South Shetlands. These were home to millions of seals – and so began the race to harvest these defenceless creatures. Amid the slaughter of a quarter of a million seals in the summer of 1820–1821, James Weddell, a Royal Navy man by training and a sealer by trade, spotted the coastline of the Antarctic peninsula.

It took a further twenty years before a select few from France, the USA and Britain set foot on the mainland proper, in the name of scientific discovery.

Some of the naval cadets who attended my gym classes.

Now we have the Antarctic Treaty of 1959, a great triumph of science over national pride. It regards the Antarctic as the most pristine of the earth's landmasses. Its only human use now (and hopefully for all time) is the pursuit of knowledge, an ideal that has no borders.

It had taken two weeks to cross the Southern Ocean from Cape Town to the Antarctic ice shelf and into an entirely different and mind-blowing world. In 36 hours the *SA Agulhas* was due to arrive in Crown Bay. Then would begin the serious business of unloading the mountain of equipment that was to support the six-man team for a potential year on the White Continent.

Two Caterpillar bulldozer-type vehicles, each weighing twenty

tons, would be deposited on the ice using the large deck crane –
one of the reasons why this vessel was one of only a few suitable
for such an expedition. These vehicles would haul multiple custom-
designed sleds loaded with thousands of litres of fuel and
provisions, and a living and workshop caboose. A staggering seventy
tons of equipment would be hauled by each vehicle, up mountains
and over yawning crevasses, in almost continuous darkness. This
expedition wouldn't have the luxury of any airdrops of provisions,
as no plane could safely fly here during the winter months – when
temperatures drop below -68 degrees Celsius, there's the danger
of fuel freezing and ice depositing on aircraft wings. The
adventurers would be entirely on their own.

The learning curve was steep, and in this the doctor was
included. I met my cadets every morning (which at this stage was
ill defined, as the sun never set) at 6.15, and worked them until
they sweated and groaned. Some I saw later in the clinic
complaining of exercise-induced abdominal or chest pain – but one
woman had a story that was a lesson to all doctors. Her history of
coughing went back ten years during which, despite some
desultory investigations, nothing abnormal had been found. It took
a caring pharmacist who observed her frequent purchasing of
cough medicine to delve further.

He heard how, ten years earlier, she had inadvertently swallowed
the tip of a ballpoint pen. He referred her to a pulmonologist who,
on conducting a scan of her chest, explained that she'd inhaled, not
swallowed, the pen tip, and it had lodged in a lung. At the time of
this trip she was twelve weeks post operation, and had a huge, raw
thoracotomy scar to show, but she was experiencing no further
coughing.

As an avid fan of polar literature I'd devoured many beautifully illustrated books on the Antarctic; I thought I knew what to expect. But I wasn't prepared for the range of emotions I felt when standing on the deck at minus ten degrees, squinting up at a dazzling ice wall towering overhead.

The sounds and subtle movements left me gasping. Stretching far to the horizon were the ice sculptures, the dark water between them offering stark contrast. Closer to the ship, a gentle heaving tilted and rocked the ice layers, and at the bow, the plates of ice were being ruthlessly, split, fractured and churned. A deep resonating scraping hiss with interspersed staccato cracks provided the background music.

The entry channel to the potential offloading site was blocked with ice too thick for this game little ship to penetrate. She was an ice-strengthened ship but not an ice-breaker. A change in wind direction was needed to clear out the approach channel, or an alternative landing site to the east would be sought.

And that was only half the story: 'Getting in is optional but getting out is mandatory,' was the grim but accurate summary from our captain, David Hall. This point was illustrated by a member of the expedition team, who told a story of a ship similar to the *Agulhas* having been trapped by changing ice conditions, then crushed and eventually sunk in a matter of half an hour.

The drill was to keep the ship's propellers churning and free from ice, by nosing the bow into the ice wall and maintaining a gentle forward pressure without actually moving forward. The deep-blue ice wall was virtually within arm's reach and I watched as Adélie penguins played on and around it, diving and bobbing, at times pursued by crab-eater seals, the most common variety here.

Later we were forced to move off the iceberg as a very real danger of a massive chunk of ice hurtling onto the deck developed. Frustration mounted over the next few days, as the ship was forced to chug painfully slowly up and down and around icebergs. Captain Hall, who'd visited the Antarctic coastline countless times, was unfazed. He'd developed a respect and patience bred from acknowledging that nature always rules.

The period of offloading, so eagerly awaited by virtually the entire crew and expedition team, was for me a private hell. The scope for serious injury was limitless and help was farther away than I'd ever experienced in my entire career: Tristan da Cunha seemed positively suburban by comparison.

We had no helicopters on board and were beyond the range of anybody else's. A specialised plane could have landed on the ice about 200 kilometres from us, but then to get a patient to it on a snowmobile was inconceivable. It was a two-week trip to Cape Town, so a ship on a mercy mission could have come down to us – but there was no other suitably ice-strengthened vessel in South Africa.

Facilities on board were reasonable; I was the weak link. I had to deal with my spiralling negative emotions, reminding myself that I was well trained but that no doctor knew it all. I was conscientious and hardworking; I'd proved myself in difficult situations before, and, after all, I was all they had. I would have to do. I had to have faith in the skill and training of those around me, too; they were all I had, and they would pull this off successfully.

I spent the bulk of the unloading days just watching, as if in some way my keeping vigilant would lessen the chance of disaster. The crane hoisted load after load from the deck, swinging it out

The 'air transport' between ship and shore.

over the ice-studded sea, then lowering it rapidly onto an ice surface that was used and grubby from the passage of machinery and boots. Figures in bright-orange overalls, green gumboots, blue hard hats and yellow gloves worked fast to clear the drop area. Skidoos and towing vehicles were continuously on the move, hauling goods up to a low ridge two kilometres away, where the massive Caterpillar bulldozers crouched in silence.

When I could stand it no more I embarked on exercise circuits, climbing every possible staircase on the ship and trotting repeatedly across every deck.

Many times the ship had to move away from the ice shelf due to rising swells or unfavourable winds. The disruption of the offloading resulted in irritation and frustration in everyone – except me. It was at these times, chugging through the ice floes, that I could relax and delight in the Antarctic magnificence. In the evenings the slanting rays of the never-setting summer sun lit up Crown Bay until it sparkled like a nest of jewels. Tiny ripples became tipped with diamonds and ice rubies lay embedded in turquoise silk. From the highest deck at midnight, I watched as the sun caressed the horizon and then wheeled eastwards in preparation for its full reappearance at dawn.

These long hours of daylight were a bonus. The team preparing to cross this Antarctic continent over winter would be noting the slight shortening of the daylight hours, knowing that when they set off in autumn, the nights would be getting progressively longer until, in mid-winter, the sun would not rise at all.

On one of these butterscotch evenings I was privileged to see three emperor penguins, standing at their full height of over a metre, scrutinising four smaller Adélie penguins scrambling onto a floe. A territorial penguin dance followed and finally an evening truce was reached. Balance and harmony prevailed.

The captain insisted that I remain aboard during offloading but gave me one small reprieve on a particularly icy day when I was given permission to deliver flasks of hot chocolate to the shore workers. I was invited to climb aboard a large wooden box, which would then be hoisted by the crane high above the deck, rotated over the floating ice floes, and lowered quickly once over the solid shore ice.

As I stooped under the box railings to embark, the grinning bosun greeted me. 'Welcome aboard,' he said. 'May luck be with you.'

And luck was indeed with me. Having delivered my flasks, I hitched a ride with Adrian, one of the ice veterans, on a tracked Sno-Cat called Snowflake. He was towing a sled loaded with drums of fuel, headed for the mustering area for the equipment, a journey of about two kilometres marked out with flags warning of crevasses on either side of the well-used track.

'This is a slow trip,' he yelled above the din. 'The old girl can't do more than eight kilometres per hour.'

I smiled as I read a sticker on the windscreen: 'All occupants of this vehicle are required to wear seatbelts.' The dashboard fan aimed at the face of the driver also seemed a trifle redundant; the ambient temperature was -5 degrees.

The terrain flattened out as we reached the rows of fuel-filled cargo sleds. Beyond these stretched a featureless, flat, white expanse to the distant, totally horizontal, horizon. The sky was blue, washed and embroidered with fine knots of clouds. A pair of dark-brown Wilson's storm petrels were swooping and diving like bats, the white bands across their tails glinting in the sunlight. The singing silence so acclaimed in the Antarctic wasn't here – the droning mobile crane lifting drums off the sled made sure of that. But nothing could have spoiled this first glimpse of the White Continent for me. My imagination raced off across the snow and tasted the sanctuary, the purity and the timelessness of this last unspoiled wilderness.

My second shore visit was a snow carnival. I escorted the cadets off the ship and onto the ice for their first shore leave. We clambered down a rope ladder, and as feet hit snow exuberance took over. Colours, particularly those of our well-loved South African flag, flashed across the white as cadets posed, snapped pictures, hurled snow, sprawled, jumped, fell, laughed and sang. Exclamations as to the sheer wonder of it all rang out.

How easy it is for the beauty of the natural world to unite us in joy. And how easy it is for the power of the natural world to cause havoc and destroy. An event of unimaginable tragedy was narrowly averted by our incredible captain. In the midst of all the frivolity, he became aware of a subtle change of movement of the surge under the ship and a gathering of sea-ice around the hull. He blew the horn, signifying the vessel's imminent departure from the ice shelf. The cadets, amid a fair amount of grumbling, had to race for the ladder, and within minutes the ship was groaning with the effort of the bow pushing and jolting through thickening ice.

We'd put a fair distance between us and the ice shelf when the sound of the breaking and cleaving of the ice floes was drowned out by a thunderous roar. We watched in disbelief as building-sized pieces of ice tumbled off the shelf into the water, sending jets of spray skywards. The spectacle took agonising minutes to pass.

Later, through binoculars, I appreciated the full extent of the fall. Mounds of fractured ice now lay against the ice shelf, which had shifted fifty metres inland. The flattened offloading area had disappeared, all 200 square metres of it. All the flags demarcating the safe areas, between which the cadets and I had been frolicking, had vanished. The unthinkable horror of what could have been left me gasping.

Offloading took more than three weeks but finally the expedition team was ready to leave. They took the final flight in the box, and stepped onto the snow. A feeling of unity and optimism prevailed. The cadets sang their good wishes. The last farewell was poignant with hugs, fixed smiles, damp eyes and words that seemed to fall short of feelings.

The six stood, sharply contrasted against the blinding snow, arms held high to wave as the *Agulhas* slowly eased herself off the ice shelf. We remained on deck, waving, until they became mere pinpricks of colour.

The familiar red stern would then have slipped from their view, the only bond remaining being in thought.

We were to learn later that this plucky, enthusiastic, dedicated team didn't make it. Disaster struck soon after our departure. Sir Ranulph went off for a practice ski run, breaking his own rules of never going alone. The weather turned foul, with a mean and sudden edge. A whiteout with swirling snow and almost zero visibility followed. He fell awkwardly, and his 68 year-old body didn't have the flexibility to right itself. He needed to remove his ski, an impossible task while he was wearing gloves. He removed one for just a few minutes in order to extricate his foot from the ski and get back into a vertical position. It was long enough to cause irreversible frostbite on a few fingers of the hand that still had all five.

Miraculously, Sir Ran found his way back to the caboose, where the other five members of the team were huddled, waiting in trepidation. Their doctor, a man who'd spent a year on a British base in the Antarctic, was very familiar with severe cold injury, and with a heavy heart he recommended that Ranulph abort his mission with the expedition and get the last plane off the White Continent before winter froze it and sealed it off completely.

This entailed a race against time, and a 200-kilometre ski-mobile journey to the closest summer base, which belonged to the

My first steps on the White Continent.

Belgians. From there Sir Ran was flown out to South Africa, where he received medical treatment, after which he travelled on to his home in England.

The remaining members elected to proceed, and set off with the Caterpillars and their heavy load of sleds, with a skier ahead scouting a safe passage. The days grew so short that, between darkness and snow storms, negotiating a way over yawning crevasses became either too dangerous or impossible, necessitating lengthy diversions. Fuel usage soared to a point at which there was concern that if they needed to return in an emergency, it wouldn't be possible.

They battened down the hatches after covering a distance of 300 kilometres and sat out the rest of the winter – a full six months. They tried to persist with ongoing medical and climatic observations, and sent upbeat email posts to their massive following. However, it defies description how difficult being confined in the tiny space of a caboose for those long, dark months must have been.

Finally, in September, as the days lengthened, they made their way back to the Belgian summer base, took the first return flight off Antarctica to South Africa, and from there, flew home.

CHAPTER 9

The Arctic: 2013

'From where, therefore, comes that peculiar lure of these polar regions that is so powerful and tenacious ...? From where comes the otherworldly charm of these provinces, however desolate and terrifying? ... Amid this desolation and death, I have experienced a more vivid pleasure of my own life.... Here is the sanctuary of sanctuaries, where Nature reveals herself in all her formidable power .... The man who penetrates his way into these regions feels his soul uplifted.'

– Jean-Baptiste Charcot (1897–1936), *Journal de l'expédition Antarctique française*, French medical doctor and polar scientist

I WAS ON A ROLL – literally. Feet apart, I stood on the highest deck of a Russian ice-breaker, kitted out in the bright-blue down jacket uniform of my employers, One Ocean Expeditions, flexing each knee in turn as the ship rolled gently from side to side. Our position was at 78 degrees north, near the archipelago of Svalbard between Greenland and Scandinavia.

I was the doctor on board the *Akademik Sergey Vavilov* for six weeks, taking care of the well-heeled, predominantly geriatric but still sparky passengers as we traversed the waters of the far-north Arctic zones.

It was a mere four months since I'd returned to Cape Town from the Antarctic across the Southern Ocean, and I marvelled at my luck. Sifting through the mountains of emails awaiting my attention, I'd found a reply to my enquiry from the company that Annabel, the young ornithologist on the *SA Agulhas II*, had recommended to me. As a matter of some urgency, they needed a doctor for the imminent season in the Arctic. Could I fill the post?

I took a flight to Longyearbyen, the northernmost settlement in the world. The town and its population of 2 100 are located on the island of Spitsbergen, named by its Dutch discoverers in 1596 for its lofty, pointed, snow-streaked peaks. This is the largest and only permanently populated island of the Svalbard archipelago in northern Norway, and is the jumping-off point for many tourist ships, including the massive cruise ships to which many of my ancient fellow airline passengers tottered off with their walking frames.

To my huge relief, the *Akademik Sergey Vavilov* wasn't one of these; it carried only 95 passengers, who were my responsibility, and a Russian crew of 44, whose health needs were taken care of by a Russian doctor with whom I shared the very spartan onboard surgery. An 'expedition ship', we were distinct from those vessels with passengers who view the Arctic glory largely from the safe vantage of a deck. Our passengers were encouraged, twice a day, to attempt the precarious descent to a rubber-duck bobbing alongside, and then head off to a landing on Arctic soil for a hike and viewing of its incredible wildlife.

Our passengers were also treated to rubber-duck trips into small coves and inlets, and through ice sculptures of towering beauty, to get close to nesting birds such as puffins and eiders. Calving glaciers could be seen from water level, from a respectable distance, as the huge blocks of ice tumbled off without warning, causing waves of terrifying magnitude. The potential for injury, I reflected, was therefore fairly high.

That said, these Arctic waters felt far less remote than those near the southern pole. Help in the form of a mercy lift by helicopter was usually within reach. It was also comforting to have my Russian colleague, Dr Luba, available in the event of a major catastrophe.

I was delighted when I learned that the ship's doctor was expected to go out on the first rubber-duck of every landing, along

A polar bear off the port side of the ship.

with the guy with the gun who had to do a reconnaissance survey for the presence of polar bears. I took ashore a well-equipped medical kit and an automatic external defibrillator (and hoped fervently I'd never have cause to use it). Then I was free to join any of the walking groups, the birding party or botanising group, returning to the ship on the last rubber-duck.

Two days into the trip at 5.15am the intercom in my cabin crackled into life. I surfaced from the depths of slumber, apprehensive, as these rude awakenings in my profession usually spell disaster. This time, however, it was to announce the presence of a polar bear on the port side.

Within minutes, the entire ship's company, hastily clad in an assortment of foul-weather gear, had scrambled onto every available deck space. Slowly, as the hours passed and the sun rose higher in the sky, the ship edged through ice floes, watched cautiously by four huge creamy-coloured bears. They paraded around us with those languid movements peculiar to their species.

I was deeply moved by the spectacle, which felt like a celebration of life itself, but the feeling was tinged with some sadness as I felt their vulnerability. Watching from the other side of the ice flocs was another tourist ship, and their every movement was followed by a rapid fire of camera clicks. Man and man-made climate change are forever altering the ecosystems of these animals. Would my grandchildren have the privilege of seeing them?

The next morning I was again wakened at 5.15am, this time by a loud banging on my cabin door. I threw on my jacket, fixed my expression into a welcoming one, and opened the door.

'Good morning, Doctor Joan. I do hope I didn't disturb you.'

'No, I was awake,' I lied as I tried to place the well-dressed middle-aged English gentleman who stood fidgeting in the doorway, avoiding eye contact.

'Can I see you for a moment, please?'

I then recalled that this was Harry, the wealthy occupant, with his wife, of the most expensive suite on board.

'Yes, of course. Go into the surgery,' I said, and pointed to the door across the passageway. 'I'll be there in a minute.'

I shut the door and frowned. One of the pet hates of doctors is to be shaken from that deep sleep just prior to awakening. It starts us off on the back foot and without all our armour in place. And it's especially annoying when it does not seem to be an emergency.

'Get over it, Joan,' mocked that unsympathetic voice within me. 'You chose this.'

I plastered a smile on my face, and stepped back out of my cabin and across the corridor, into the brightly lit surgery. 'Now, how can I help you, Harry?' I asked.

He hadn't sat down, so I indicated for him to take the seat next to my desk. He looked at me then and smiled, but it was tight and without warmth.

'Doc.' He glanced down at his hands, which were clasped together. 'I just want to end it all.'

For a split second my head spun in confusion. What did he mean? Then I looked into his eyes, which were brimming with deep pain and hopelessness.

This man was on the brink of suicide. I had lived through the unspeakably painful suicides of three university friends, but I had never in all the years of my medical career been faced with an unexpected declaration of this nature. And here, now, surrounded by water and ice in every direction, I was, and it was my sole responsibility.

As I rifled urgently through the files in my head on how to deal with such an emergency, my training, ingrained over the years to the point of being automatic, took over. I embarked on taking a 'history', medical jargon for the story of the presenting complaint.

I listened and engaged with Harry in every possible way over the next half hour. His story wasn't new, and followed a familiar pattern. His childhood had been harsh and lonely, and lacking in parental love. In his teens addictive behaviour had emerged, but he'd overcome this to become a highly successful businessman, albeit one who consumed vast quantities of alcohol. Depression had been his companion for many years, in spite of his having a loving and caring wife.

He'd been under psychiatric care for so long that his London-based psychiatrist had become his greatest support system. He was vulnerable without her regular input, and saw all the unbridled excitement and joy in his fellow passengers as something he couldn't connect with. He felt like he was spoiling everyone's fun and that the world would be better off without him.

This sentiment was one I'd heard many times from suicide-prone patients. They can't see that their death would cause any pain. They see it only as a favour to their loved ones, and the only positive contribution left for them to make.

'And Harry,' I asked gently, 'what medication are you on now?' I was dreading his response as I felt sure he was on massive doses of anti-depressants and mood stabilisers that I'd never heard of before, let alone prescribed.

My question seemed to break his train of thought and he looked puzzled. I saw a gap. 'Let's go to your cabin and check them out.'

He nodded, rose, and shuffled down the passageway into his suite, as I followed. He found his sack of medication and spilled it out on the table. I made a comprehensive list and then asked for the contact details of his psychiatrist. It was only with her help, I knew, that Harry and I would get through this.

'Harry, you and I need to make a pact right now,' I said. 'You need to lie down and stay in your cabin until I return. I won't be long. I'm going to chat to your wife and I'll phone your psychiatrist later when she wakes up. I'll help you, and together we'll get you home to London in a week.'

'That seems so far away,' he whispered. 'Nothing to look forward to …'

'Nothing at all?' I ventured.

He was sitting, elbows on the table, his face in his cupped hands. After a long silence, and without raising his head, he muttered, 'I watch for the fox. I like to see him trotting along my garden wall. He seems so confident, so free …'

I waited until he looked up, then said, 'There are foxes here in the Arctic. I'm hoping we'll get to see one.'

So started a week of high anxiety. I sought out Harry's wife, hoping to gain greater clarity. She was aware of his intentions but it was obvious that this state wasn't new. It had happened a few times before. Each time she'd coaxed him through it. Now she just seemed emotionally drained, exhausted and resigned to the possibility that she could soon be a widow. Perhaps there was even potentially an element of relief in that status.

I informed the expedition leader and the captain. There's a protocol to be followed in a situation of this kind: all the crew are placed on 'suicide watch' but it has to remain hidden from the passengers. It's an onerous additional burden for a crew already working long hours.

I made daily contact with Harry's psychiatrist via satellite phone. She was sympathetic and made subtle changes to his medication while suggesting that it was mainly up to me to use my powers of persuasion to get Harry to believe that these changes would make all the difference. We both knew this wasn't really true.

I met with Harry at least twice a day and related my interaction with his trusted psychiatrist. I spent many long hours counselling and trying to put a positive spin on his good fortune in being here, surrounded by such natural magnificence. I encouraged him to go out with the kayaking group; he'd paid extra for this special activity. I was sure that just being out there, exercising, surrounded by mind-blowing beauty, would in itself be therapy. What I came to realise, however, was that his level of preoccupation in the murky recesses of his mind allowed hardly any other stimulus in.

During the next week, Harry sought me out a few times when he became desperate; he *was* trying to stay alive.

I had one single notable success. We were anchored off Alkefjellet, a group of castle-like cliffs that rise in stepped ramparts a hundred metres out of the sea. Millions of clamorous strings of Brünnich's guillemots laid eggs on these ledges and stood guard over them, defending them against the aggressive marauding glaucous gulls and skuas. The sky overhead was darkened and noisy with birds.

Guillemots aren't enthusiastic flyers, and the young often choose to leave their nests before they're fully fledged. They spin, flutter and fall into the water below, and their fathers then swim south with them to Greenland, returning only years later to reproduce. There are many casualties in this process, with bird bodies strewn across the boulders at the bases of some cliffs. This adds to the wildlife extravaganza. Wily Arctic foxes have learned that there may be easy meals waiting, and so regularly negotiate the cliffbases, looking for bodies or chicks in nests.

As we were lining up to board the rubber-ducks to view this spectacle from the water, a call came in to my radio from the first boat out. 'Arctic fox spotted doing his tour of inspection.'

I made a hasty decision and raced up to Harry's suite, where I found him in his usual position, languishing on a sofa. 'Harry, you're coming with me,' I told him. 'Get into your outdoor gear and bring your camera and your long lens. I'll meet you on deck at the head of the gangway.'

He started to mount a protest, but I took him firmly by the arm, opened the door and herded him through it and down the stairs, saying, 'We're going to see a fox!'

The mood was enthusiastic and Harry was greeted warmly by the group. The sea conditions were perfect. Nothing could have detracted from the sheer wonder of this outing. The sun warmed our faces as we looked up at the spectacle of thousands of guillemots wheeling and screeching overhead. Gulls soared and banked between them. The cliff faces were a mosaic of black, brown and dark green, and there, clambering over boulders near the water's edge, was the Arctic fox, scurrying and sniffing constantly.

In winter, its highly insulating pure-white fur makes it a target of man's greed: the Arctic fox only starts to shiver when the temperatures drop to -70 degrees. It can smell its favourite food, lemmings, lying frozen under seventy centimetres of snow. In the

Birdwatching off Alkefjellet.

depths of winter when food is scarce, the Arctic fox bravely follows polar bears and waits patiently at their kills to partake of the leftovers.

This incredibly hardy little animal has managed to outwit man's intrusion and destruction of its territory and its population remains abundant, yet is always difficult to observe. And here one was, resplendent in his camouflage summer coat of brown, grey and white.

I sneaked a look at Harry. His eyes were hidden behind the viewfinder of his camera, but there was a hint of a gentle smile on his lips.

Days later, when the ship glided into Longyearbyen and Harry and his wife disembarked and stood in line for the bus to the airport, he formally shook my hand. I had to give him a quick hug. I watched as they boarded the bus. He took a seat, looked through the window and raised his hand in a farewell salute.

Some time later I was on a tundra walk with another tourist expedition in Svalbard at an historical site, Smeerenburg, which translates as 'blubber town', a whaling station established in 1614 by the Dutch. In its heyday this town had a permanent population of about 200 but it was also a popular stopoff for whaling ships of all nationalities, where the sailors shared the comforts of Dutch bread and warm female flesh. There were remnants of blubber ovens and houses, and a mass grave where victims of a particularly grim winter had been interred.

The high pebble beach was dotted with indigo pools surrounded by lichen-covered rocks where terns were nesting. They took to

A sighting of the rare Arctic fox.

divebombing our heads in an attempt to keep us at a distance. We scurried up a scree slope, tripping over clumps of dwarf willows, the only tree found here. It grows in tight clumps to a mere few centimetres in height, at which point it's relentlessly chewed off by the reindeer.

A sudden dark darting movement crossed my peripheral vision. It vanished. I held my breath and watched. A tiny Arctic fox emerged in a state of perpetual motion. It was no bigger than a hefty domestic cat and its coat was brownish-grey with some patches of winter moult – pure-white fur. It had a proud bushy tail which it used as a balancing bar. The fox flowed over and around the rocks, its muzzle moving continuously between the soggy earth and rock ledges.

It froze. Its head jerked up. It had sensed us, but being inquisitive – and a scavenger when need be – it started an extraordinary circuit which ended about five metres from where we stood. There it sat, dog-like, and scratched both of its short rounded ears in turn, showing off its fur-covered foot pads, a feature unique to this canid (mammal of the dog family). It scanned us, its hazel eyes meeting ours briefly in an offhand manner. Cameras clicked like muted machine-gun fire, until it trotted off, pausing to sniff the ground as it went.

My only regret was that Harry was not with me to enjoy this magnificent sighting of a fox at such close range.

Months later, after I'd returned home to Knysna, I received a postcard from London. On it was a photo of a red fox striding across a wall. I turned it over.

'Thank you, Doctor Joan. The fox made all the difference. Harry.'

I was becoming slick at shipboard medicine. I doled out seasickness tablets, although conditions, I thought, were fairly mild. I dressed blisters, lanced abscesses, stitched the odd eyebrow, sympathised with and medicated those with upper-respiratory viral infections, and treated migraines and hangovers.

And I'm happy to report that my dental efforts had much more successful outcomes than those on Tristan da Cunha. A passenger came to me having broken a filled tooth, leaving the rough edge to lacerate his tongue. He was lamenting that eating all the delicious food on board was no longer a pleasure: the pain was too bad. I sought out a well-groomed passenger whose long and immaculately kept nails I'd admired. I borrowed her metal nail file, and with my trusty headlight, and a gauze swab to grip the patient's tongue, I commenced filing. Minutes later, to my immense relief, I had a beaming customer.

I lost sleep over a patient called Phillip, a tall, slim, beautifully spoken English gentleman who'd popped his head into the surgery between breakfast and boarding the rubber-ducks for the morning excursion. I'd noticed he was always first in line to get out and seemed to be revelling in the Arctic bird life. He didn't want to miss a minute of the action.

'Doctor Joan, I've had a swollen calf muscle for the past few days. I think I tore a muscle on a walk. It's a bit tender, but it doesn't really stop me from walking. Can you give me something for it, please?'

I got him onto the examining couch, and questioned him about previous illnesses and other medication. My careful examination added to my anxiety. I had no way to confirm the diagnosis, but with his advanced age, and the fact that he'd been on a long sedentary flight in the past five days, I was very concerned that he'd developed a deep-vein thrombosis. This in itself posed no great danger, but the consequences of a thrombus, or clot, becoming dislodged and moving along veins and into the lungs results in the very dangerous condition of a pulmonary embolus. The worst outcome of this is death.

If I treated him for a deep-vein thrombosis (as opposed to a simple muscle injury), he'd need heparin, an intravenously administered anticoagulant, and careful monitoring, which required a hospital admission.

I shared my fears with him. He was totally unimpressed with the idea of being evacuated off the ship and to a hospital in Longyearbyen.

'Okay, Phillip,' I said, unhappily. 'Just give me the morning to think about this.'

He left for a thrilling shore excursion to view walruses; I got on the satellite phone to discuss his case with his physician in England. I'd heard of a trial treatment using high-dose aspirin, but I'd never been trained to do this. His physician had, however, had some experience and although he agreed it wasn't optimal, he proposed that in the event of our not being sure of the diagnosis, and as the patient had so few symptoms, we could risk it.

Easy for him sitting so far away, I thought.

I became a regular visitor to Phillip's cabin as I followed the progress of his swollen calf over the next week. It did improve, and he remained cheerful and grateful for the aspirin treatment.

I got him off the ship without further drama, clutching a referral to his physician. A letter from his doctor arrived a few weeks later, complimenting me on my care of our joint patient. All was good with Phillip: a scan of his calf showed no evidence of a thrombus. Who knows what had been there originally?

My third voyage around Spitsbergen broke all sorts of records. On a medical front I didn't issue a single tablet for seasickness, and it was all just a blur of mundane, easily handled problems.

And we achieved the fewest landings of any One Ocean Expeditions voyage – because we kept getting interrupted by polar bears. Twenty were sighted: thin, dirty individuals when stranded on the land, and fat, furry, successful seal hunters on the ice pack.

We'd walked to within smelling distance of a wallow of sixty walruses, shuffling and snorting and clashing tusks in a huge brown blubbery mound. In the distance, off the beach and up on the grassy slopes, grazed thirteen short-legged reindeer. Ethereal ivory gulls, rarer here than the polar bear, were spotted a record-breaking seven times, strutting around the carcasses of polar-bear kills or gliding in small groups like Arctic angels. And we saw an astonishing six species of whale, including a beluga, the white 'sea canary', so called for its strange vocalisations.

I began suffering from a malady peculiar to these extreme latitudes: polarhullah, which translates roughly from the Danish as 'pole fever'. My senses were in overdrive. I wanted to remember every shade of blue, white, silver and grey streaking through the icebergs.

I began to fret that my viewing of the literally millions of Brünnich's guillemots that laid their eggs on the rocky ledges of the cliffs would be my last. We sat again in the rubber-ducks in the water below, the sky overhead darkened and noisy from bird bodies as the chicks launched themselves inelegantly from the ledges and fell into the water below. I had seen this all before, but each time was like a first. It was unimaginable that I may not see it again.

As I sat in a state of awe, a pod of glistening-white ghost-like beluga whales swam under our rubber-duck. It was all so miraculous.

I spent any available downtime on the ship reading about the early explorers of the polar zones. Heroes of three nationalities predominated: Norwegians Nansen and Amundsen, Britons Scott, Franklin and Shackleton, and Americans Peary and Cook, who could never decide who got to the North Pole first. These explorers pushed the boundaries of existence at the edge of the known world.

My personal hero, Ernest Shackleton, said that the polar explorer needed optimism, patience and physical strength; courage and luck for him were optional. Along the way, there were heroes who didn't survive to tell their stories, but died experiencing unimaginable horrors and terrors in a lonely, remorseless land.

Now, on a comfortable, heated ship, those of us 'adventurers' of a more feeble disposition could experience the magic of the polar zones and be fairly sure of a safe return, unlike those early explorers who departed knowing that it could be years before they returned, if at all.

CHAPTER 10

Antarctica revisited, South Georgia revealed: 2014–2015

'The love of great adventure is not an acquired taste; it is in the blood.'

– Lincoln Ellsworth, the first man to fly across the Antarctic, in *The Polar Times*, January 1936

I SLEPT AT 34 DEGREES SOUTH last night, almost the same latitude on which lies Knysna, my starting point on this adventure. But I'd first flown due west for eleven hours, racing the sun.

Mary, whose departure point was also at 34 degrees south – Sydney, Australia – was flying due east into the dawn. We were tying a gossamer belt of jet-stream vapour around the world to pull us together at Buenos Aires, the gracious capital of Argentina.

I'd clinched a job as ship's doctor, again with One Ocean Expeditions, and was on my way to board the ship at Ushuaia, in Argentina. The voyages were heading for the Antarctic Peninsula.

Best of all, I'd managed to arrange for companions: Mary would join me on this voyage and Anna on the following one. My departure date from my home in Knysna, 3 December, was the twenty-ninth anniversary of my beloved husband's death. Pete and I had had plans to visit Argentina, to walk its mountains, to sail its oceans; now I was off to do it with his children. The idea of having my daughters as company, and to share in the magnificence of the Antarctic, put me at peace.

The next day Mary and I arrived in Ushuaia, Fin del Mundo, 'the end of the world', the southernmost town on the planet, lying at 54.5 degrees south. I gazed out from an overheated hotel room at towering black peaks with blinding-white snow trickling, like cake icing, off their summits and forming a fringe around a brooding grey bay. There our ship, the *Akademik Ioffe*, the second ice-strengthened vessel used by One Ocean Expeditions, lay tethered to the dock.

In a few hours we'd be steaming down the deceptively calm waters of the Beagle Channel, to take our chances crossing the notorious Drake Passage and on to the Antarctic. I should have felt a degree of confidence, bred from some familiarity, but I shivered involuntarily as I felt my adrenaline surging, preparing me for another plunge into new unknowns.

Trussed up in my new sky-blue One Ocean Expeditions down jacket, I walked with Mary along the scruffy waterfront of Ushuaia to the Argentinian immigration and customs. I smiled and used my rusty Spanish with the friendly officials. Formalities dispensed with, Argentina welcomed us and we wandered along the quayside, two of many foreigners heading for the ships moored on either side of a broad concrete jetty.

Since the explosion of the Antarctic cruise industry in the 1980s, Ushuaia has become a favourite jumping-off point and has acquired the atmosphere of an expedition base where the operators and the well-heeled rub shoulders with backpack-toting budget travellers and those adventurers (like myself) who can only get here by peddling their skills on expedition ships.

My thoughts went to Lars Eric Lindblad, the Swedish-American entrepreneur and explorer who started all this in 1966 in a chartered Argentinian naval ship. He pioneered tourism to many remote and exotic parts of the world, and by 1969 he'd bought his own ice-strengthened ship for Antarctic tourism, the MS *Lindblad Explorer*. Now about 35 000 tourists visit annually.

This figure made me feel uncomfortable. The International Association of Antarctica Tour Operators, established in 1991 by seven private companies, aims to 'advocate and promote the practice of safe and environmentally responsible private-sector travel to Antarctica.' It's proved to be a gallant watchdog – but how much more people pressure can this fragile continent stand?

I thought of the words of Robert Macfarlane, one of our most expressive nature writers, in his book *The Wild Places*. He says, with hope, 'The wild prefaced us, and it will outlive us. Human cultures will pass, given time …'

Meeting and greeting the new passengers as they walked up the gangway and into the ship for the first time was always a happy occasion. There was a festive air, every crew member looked clean and smiley, and we had no problems to deal with yet. It felt like the curtain was about to go up on an exciting, spectacular show.

I was perhaps the only crew member who looked with a more discerning eye at the folks as they filed by and were escorted to their cabins. I watched how they walked, whether they needed sticks, if all limbs and eyes were present, if they were overweight or too thin, and if they seemed overly frightened.

This was also the point at which I might be accosted by a passenger who had a medical problem they wanted me to know about from the very outset, and this time it was an elderly American wearing a faded baseball cap, an ill fitting T-shirt and well-worn blue jeans held up by an aging leather belt. After shaking my hand vigorously, he looked at my name badge and into my eyes with a relieved smile, revealing a mouthful of teeth that had seen a great deal of mileage.

'Hello, Doc! Am I pleased to meet you!' My heart sank. 'I'm Greg. Can I chat to you now?'

'Give me ten minutes and I'll meet you in your cabin,' I told him, confirming with him that I'd got the right cabin number.

Ten minutes later I found Greg lying flat on his back on the lower bunk in his cabin, his arms folded across his chest. He pushed himself into a vertical position and stood up. 'Doc, I'm not sick,' he said.

I inwardly heaved a grateful sigh.

'I have a small difficulty, though. I'm an old man with quite a few medical problems, but I'm feeling pretty darn good right now. My wife said I should never have come, and she refused to join me, but the sea is in my blood and I wanted to see the parts of it that are frozen.' He grabbed a plastic container off the bedside table and opened it to reveal a compartmentalised pill container with tablets nestling in only the last two slots.

'I take quite a few tablets every day,' he continued. 'This box I kept in my hand luggage for the trip here and the rest of my medication is in my big suitcase – and that's gone astray, with no chance of reaching the ship before we leave.'

He smiled. His watery blue eyes had a certain jaunty look. He seemed remarkably unconcerned. I wasn't sure what disaster I was dealing with.

'Do you have a list of your medication?' I asked him. I was sure we'd be able to supply him from our pharmacy on board.

He fumbled in his jeans pocket to extract a dog-eared piece of paper on which was typed his medication.

I took it. 'Leave it with me. I'll get what you need and catch you later,' I said.

'I knew you'd fix it for me,' smiled Greg.

I headed down to the clinic, smoothed out his list, and started sweating. I recognised maybe two of the nine medications. The list gave the trade names of the pills, all from the USA. I was familiar with South African and British trade names. The ship had no internet available to google these unfamiliar names. And the medication that I could replace from our pharmacy was in different strengths and would need precision cutting into exact pieces to suit the patient's needs.

I consulted Greg's medical form, which all patients had to complete before being accepted for the cruise. His medical history included diabetes, hypertension, cardiac arrhythmias, prostatic hypertrophy, macular degeneration, osteoarthritis, hypothyroidism and glaucoma, as well as a string of previous surgeries. How was this man still alive? I checked his age. He was 86 years old!

In a more controlled environment with more testing facilities enabling me to test basic blood components and electrolytes, I could've tried eliminating a few medications, but I wasn't brave enough to embark on that experiment now. I glanced at my watch. In two hours we set sail. For me, this was bordering on an emergency.

I grabbed the passenger list and scanned it for anyone with 'Dr' in front of their name. I raced up to the bar and lounge, roping in any crew member available to locate the possible doctors on board. We came up with doctors of psychology, oceanography, politics and archaeology.

Finally, I found Dr Angela, a lucky gift as she was a specialist physician in practice in San Francisco. Within minutes she'd written recognisable (to me) names of drugs next to all the American trade names.

The bad news was that we had pitifully few of them in the pharmacy. I had a sudden inspiration: I'd try the Quark Expeditions ship docked across the jetty from us. They'd have a doctor and fully stocked pharmacy on board.

On my way out I informed the expedition leader of my dilemma and that he might need to contact our land agent to help with acquiring medicines from a local outlet, after getting a local doctor to issue the scripts. He rolled his eyes at me.

Luck beamed down on me again. The doctor on board the Quark vessel was a very helpful and pleasant South African who had a phone app to 'translate' the names of our familiar generic drugs into the ones in his pharmacy that were in Spanish. He handed over four packets of drugs on the list and I quickly wrote down the Spanish names of the remaining two: I was taking no chances on the extent of the local doctor's familiarity with English drug names.

Somewhat breathless now, and with less than an hour to our departure, I raced back to the *Akademik Ioffe*. The expedition leader was standing on the gangway, walkie-talkie in hand. 'Well? Any success? I have the land agent standing by.'

'Tell him to get here fast. I'll write down the two drugs we require. Ask him to get a script from his local doctor contact for twelve days' worth. Then he must fill the script at a town pharmacy. Can you arrange for payment?'

'No problem – it goes on the ship's account.'

I was almost hyperventilating as I awaited the appearance of the land agent, hopefully with a packet of drugs in hand. I got word that he was on his way, and the departure of the ship had to be delayed by fifteen minutes. The land agent literally tossed the packet of drugs to me as the ropes were cast off.

I expected Greg to be anxiously waiting for me in the lobby. Instead I found him quaffing a beer and regaling the company with nautical stories. 'Hello, Doc,' he said cheerfully. 'All okay now? So we're on our wonderful way!'

I just managed a nod.

I was now curious as to the level of calmness with which Greg had dealt with this. Was he unaware of the seriousness of just stopping all his medication? Was he okay with the possibility of getting very ill, maybe even dying? How had he stayed so apparently relaxed?

Later, after dinner, as we slid through the muted light and silvery water of the Beagle Channel, Greg came to the clinic to collect his new array of medication. He was in the same old T-shirt and jeans, and I recalled that, of course, he had no luggage. That didn't bother him either, he said. 'I can borrow, and wash and make do. Thanks for the pills. Good job!'

My curiosity finally overcame my good manners. 'Greg, please tell me, what was your job when you were a younger man?'

'Oh, I had a wonderful life in the US Navy. I commanded a submarine for 25 years.'

He waved as he left.

I sat back. I was very happy to be able to look out at the gulls swooping over the waves at our stern, and see the golden orb of the sun edging towards the western horizon.

Spending your life as Greg had done, in a confined metal space deep under the ocean, with little personal peace and no means of escape, must render you somewhat altered. His stress meter must be calibrated way below most of ours, I concluded; his acceptance and fatalistic attitude had become just part of who he was.

I had a sense that everyone who visited this wild place, this pristine icy wilderness, would depart slightly changed: an appreciation, a simplification in perspective, an uplifting of the soul, a sense of stewardship, gratitude.

And it was a change that was best shared.

※

Prior to the completion of the Panama Canal in 1914, sailors wishing to make their way from the Atlantic to the Pacific would have had a choice of three routes, each bearing the name of a great maritime explorer or his ship, from one of the three countries that had vied with each other through the centuries for supremacy of the seas.

The earliest sailed passage was the Straits of Magellan, crossed in 1520 by Ferdinand Magellan, the Portuguese explorer, during his global circumnavigation. This separates the mainland of South America in the north from the islands of Tierra del Fuego in the south. Then, and still now, it's narrow, with unpredictable winds and currents.

Sir Francis Drake was instructed in 1577 by his English Queen, Elizabeth, to 'subdue heathen lands not in possession of any Christian prince' along the Pacific coast of South and Central America. He navigated through the Straits of Magellan and then was pummelled by a storm that sank two of his ships and blew him south of Tierra del Fuego and into an expanse of open water, so raising the possibility of another southern passage. This was subsequently to be known as the Drake Passage, but it wasn't until 1616 that it was officially discovered by Captain Willem Schouten, a Dutch sailor.

Schouten had been hired by a wealthy Dutch merchant, Isaac le Maire, who instructed him to find a passage linking the Atlantic to the Pacific farther south than the treacherous Straits of Magellan, because he wished to break the monopoly the Dutch East India Company held on the route around the Cape of Good Hope. The voyage was sponsored by the Gold Seekers, the moneyed fathers of the city of Hoorn in the Netherlands. Hence, when Schouten rounded the southernmost headland on Tierra del Fuego, which marked the northern boundary of the Drake Passage and where the Atlantic and Pacific oceans meet, he named it Cape Horn.

This Drake Passage was used as a major east-west shipping route between Europe and the Americas for 200 years. Venturing farther south wasn't seriously considered, as Captain Cook had already done his circumnavigation of Antarctica, survived ice, fog, snowstorms, intense cold and treacherous sailing around vast icebergs, and proclaimed that a southern continent did not exist. Even if it did, he concluded that it would never be explored.

In 1819, while rounding Cape Horn, William Smith, the owner/captain of an English merchant ship, was driven violently south by a storm, and he discovered what subsequently became known as the South Shetland Islands. He returned, remarking on the proliferation of seals he saw. So began the unrestrained slaughter of these creatures.

Interest was reawakened, and the following year Edward Bransfield, an officer in the Royal Navy, was instructed to explore further. He crossed a thousand kilometres of ocean, reached the South Shetlands, where he landed on and proclaimed King George Island. He then continued in a southwesterly direction and sighted the northernmost point of the Antarctic mainland. History is divided as to whether he was the first, as a Russian explorer, Fabian von Bellingshausen, was in the area at the same time and also documented the sighting of an icy shoreline, now known to have been part of the Antarctic continent.

The third navigable passage around South America linking the Atlantic and Pacific is the narrow Beagle Channel. This was discovered by Captain Robert FitzRoy, and named after his ship HMS *Beagle* during its first hydrographic survey of the southern coasts of South America, which lasted from 1826 until 1830. In 1833 the *Beagle* again sailed through it, on its second survey voyage. This time it had the young naturalist Charles Darwin on board. On reaching the channel he had his first sight of glaciers and wrote in his field notes, 'It is scarcely possible to imagine anything more beautiful than the beryl-like blue of these glaciers, and especially contrasted with the dead white of the upper expanse of snow.'

The Drake Passage, which stretches for 1 200 kilometres, is the shortest sea route from South America to the South Shetland Islands and the Antarctic Peninsula. Today, expedition vessels, research vessels and even yachts head south across this unforgiving body of water. It has a reputation for being cruel and hazardous, with wild, unpredictable sea conditions attributable to vicious winds and the massive volume of water flowing through a bottle-neck: the Antarctic Circumpolar Current, the largest current in the world, funnels through the Drake Passage as it flows from west to east around Antarctica, carrying 600 times the flow of the Amazon River.

For a doctor, the Drake Passage can be a harrowing two days of treating intractable seasickness – her own and that of the passengers. That's when the journey is called the Drake Shake. The other end of the spectrum is the Drake Lake – when travellers are presented with a boring façade of a grey, oily sea, low cloud and muted light. But they are then also enormously relieved and the doctor is idle and happy.

The other bonus in these calm conditions is the easy sighting of scores of humpbacked whales, attracted by the Antarctic krill that feed off the upwelling of nutrients in the Antarctic Convergence zone. It can also be a feeding frenzy for hundreds of Cape petrels, flashing their boldly patterned black-and-white plumage as they swoop and dive, maintaining a forward speed of forty kilometres per hour. Icebergs begin to appear, often fringed with penguins or sporting an immobile seal basking in the soft light.

All that said, a ferocious Drake Shake is worth experiencing – one with fifteen-metre waves and winds at 10 on the Beaufort scale (a hurricane is 12). It's a rite of passage: beautiful, challenging and terrifying, and a reaffirmation that man will always be secondary to the power of nature.

On this trip, as these conditions loomed, I tried to prepare the passengers without scaring them silly. I prescribed medication before we left sheltered waters. I encouraged snacking on ginger, wearing acupressure or electronic wrist bands, getting fresh air (usually impossible as all decks would be out of bounds) and watching the horizon (usually totally obscured by waves crashing against the windows). I filled my small black bag with pills and patches, needles, vials of potent drugs and swabs.

I kept a smile on my face and snuck into my cabin to lie horizontal when I felt my stomach contents hovering too high. I reassured distressed passengers that it would be for a maximum period of 48 hours before we entered quiet waters, and life therefore was still worth living.

My daughter Anna, who was with me during this particular Drake Shake and who had seen me suffer from debilitating seasickness on many occasions, was amazed at my control. 'Either you've learned a thing or two, Mom, or you've ablated your middle-ear semicircular canals with all your sea travel.'

I giggled as I remembered she'd also once posed the question to me as I was lying prostrate on the deck, wishing for death during a family fishing expedition: 'Mom – what's the definition of misery? Answer – seasickness.' Now I tried to remain cheerful as I visited those many passengers lying motionless in darkened cabins, sucking on tepid ginger ale. A dose of injected cyclizine, a well known anti-nauseant often called Valoid, did wonders – for patients and doctor alike.

I even managed to be one of the few intrepid folk reporting for meals. Although my resilience was purely drug induced, I revelled in the sense of camaraderie that was shared among diners. The dining room was storm-proofed, with every table having hinged edges that could be raised, and all redundant crockery and cutlery removed. Soup was off the menu.

The end chairs at each table were bound to the floor with steel cables, so their incumbents ran the risk of having chairs and bodies hurtling towards them without warning. Chaos could erupt very quickly.

'Here it comes!' yelled a woman across the table. She'd been peering through the intermittently drenched porthole and had spied a wave of mammoth proportions.

It slammed broadside into the ship, which jerked through forty degrees. Table contents became airborne, soaring through the air and smashing on the floor. Bits of carrot, beetroot, lettuce and olives showered down. Chairs slid. Passengers grasped the table, each other, their beer glasses. The tinkling of breaking glass and wild yelps of surprise rang out. Within seconds the ship had heaved back in the other direction and every moveable object became unleashed again.

'Stay seated. Hold on to the table,' came the expedition leader's stern command. 'Staff, please …'

The One Ocean staff, me included, were on their feet, mopping, sweeping and disposing of the debris.

Lunch resumed, with all now well schooled in keeping an eye on the window and one hand firmly attached to the table. The waiters calmly continued serving food.

There were two more rites of passage for those lucky travellers in the Antarctic. They were optional but if the full wonder of the wild was to be experienced, there was really no choice. Both involved the doctor lingering hopefully on the periphery, with fingers crossed, trusting that there would be no calamities.

The first was the 'polar plunge'. This involved immersing the body into sub-zero-temperature water, usually for as short a time as possible. I would always lead by example, both because I loved doing it, and to demonstrate to all passengers, especially those over 60 years of age, that they were not exempt on the grounds that they feared sudden cardiac arrest. For those who still harboured anxiety, I placed the automatic external defibrillator in its bright orange case in a prominent position on the shore and instructed a member of staff proficient in its use to stand by.

On the voyage I did with my small, thin daughter Anna, the polar plunge took place on Christmas Day. The ship was headed for Deception Island in the South Shetland archipelago. This was probably the landmass first spotted in 1820 when the Drake Passage was originally crossed successfully. Its name alludes to its appearance of being a solid island, when it is in fact the caldera of an active volcano, now flooded to form a ring around a protected bay.

On this Christmas Day, we needed a sheltered harbour; the sea was lumpy, a forty-knot gale was blowing and snow was being driven in sheets around us. This atrocious weather threatened our passage into the bay, as it passed through a narrow gap of 230 metres called Neptune's Bellows. It was a breath-holding but successful transit.

The volcano on Deception was active in 1967 and 1969 and effectively destroyed the local scientific stations. The ruins of these and the evidence of the island's whaling industry, which ceased only in 1931, loomed as ghostly hulks in the blizzard. Its current inhabitants, a huge colony of chinstrap penguins, looked delighted at the prospect of company.

As a pre-swim warm-up, I escorted the intrepid guests along the black-lava beach and up to the crater rim. We hauled out every bit

The polar plunge.

of warm-gear reinforcement in our day packs as we scrambled, leaning into the wind, heads down, hoods up, to the high point. There was no view that day. Billows of sulphurous steam rose to greet us, but there were sadly no visible pools of bubbling hot water in which to thaw our frozen extremities.

Back on the beach, our moment of reckoning arrived. My example encouraged the older set to participate – the average age was well over 50 years. It was like viewing speeded-up video footage as layer after layer of clothing was torn off, socks and boots sent flying in haste to reveal pale, pasty bodies. The preferred mode of entry to the sea was a sprint down the lava beach and a wild full-frontal launch into the water. The speed of the film was drastically increased as the bodies came flying out again, setting the blobs of sea ice oscillating.

There was trembling, shouting, hooting and laughter back on the beach, as the shivering flesh was re-clothed as well as frozen hands would allow, and numb, blue feet stuffed again into boots. I looked for Anna. She was silent, blue, and curled up in a tight ball, but there was a smile on her face.

The Christmas camaraderie and laughter in the sauna that followed made for a glowing memory, as did wallowing in the hot tub on the deck, warm gluhwein in hand. In the space of a few minutes, through the steamy haze, we spotted all four varieties of seals – leopard, Weddell, crab-eater and elephant – hauled up on the sea ice, very fast asleep.

Spending a night in a sleeping bag on the Antarctic ice was the other rite of passage not to be missed. It wasn't compulsory for the doctor to be in attendance, but I always volunteered as I found it thrilling, and I believed there was more chance for mishaps with the camping passengers than with those who chose the warmer option of their own cabins.

The campout involved a lot of extra work for the staff but there was so much pleasure in heading out on a rubber-duck, with just young and enthusiastic staff, to set up camp, cut ice steps and set up a mobile toilet on some never-before-trodden piece of Antarctica. All participants while still on board were given a full demonstration of what was expected and warned that there was no ship return before the scheduled morning pickup.

On this occasion we'd made a camp on Leith Cove Island at 63 degrees south. We headed out after dinner, so preparation of food wasn't necessary. However, snow trenches had to be dug, long enough, wide enough and deep enough in which to place a sleeping body out of the wind. Additional wind barriers were fashioned and gear endlessly arranged and rearranged. And it remained twilight throughout — another disorienting factor. I didn't bank on a solid night's sleep.

I lay cocooned in my puffy down sleeping bag, in an inner bag and with the outside covering of a state-of-the-art bivvy bag. I felt sweaty and claustrophobic but I was oblivious to the snow beneath me, so effective was my silver insulating sleep mat. Filling my senses and eradicating any feeling of discomfort was the scratchy, tinkling sound of snow falling on the bivvy hood. The light was silvery and outlined the 62 not-so-happy campers who were doing battle with bags, boots and anoraks, and the decision of what to remove before worming into their snow beds.

The air rang with the nervous staccato chatter of our numerous Chinese passengers, most of whom had erected meticulously constructed lofty Great Walls of China around their sleeping places. I sensed some were freaked out by this, a voluntary experience, but I fashioned a small fresh-air inlet for my nose, rendered my ears deaf and slept.

'Doctor Joan! Doctor Joan!'

Scrabbling through layers of semi-consciousness, I glanced at my watch: 4am. I unzipped the bivvy hood and poked my head out into the still-falling snow. There stood Jim, the Chinese translator. There was a woman in our party who was too cold, he said, and needed to return to the ship.

Before I could respond, another head emerged from a nearby bivvy, and in an Australian accent and with some degree of irritation, informed me that the ship needed to come and collect everyone as the continuous snow had resulted in folk becoming wet and uncomfortable.

Keeping my thoughts to myself, I smiled and apologised and referred them to Ben, the assistant expedition leader. He politely explained, yet again, that the rubber-ducks would collect us all at 6am, then he zipped up his bivvy.

I gathered that this was an unsatisfactory response as a mass exodus from sleeping bags resulted, with much Chinese vocalisation. Ignoring it, I went back to sleep.

At 5.30am Ben's voice woke me. 'Doctor Joan! You're needed near the landing.'

Getting out of my sleeping paraphernalia, now encased in twenty centimetres of snow, was slow and clumsy. A good dose of snow slid into my boots as I pulled them on, and I hastened down to find a hysterical Russian crew member who was pale, shaky and agitated.

There was a total language block but she was very much alive, with healthy vital signs. When in doubt, try old fashioned bodily contact, I thought, so I sat her down on a sleeping mat, hugged her tight to my body and rubbed her back. Eventually her breathing slowed and she calmed down.

Diagnosis was impossible, but later in the day, with her usual immaculate makeup in place, she was again serving at tables.

※

There's a little-known island, South Georgia, which spelled journey's end for adventurer Sir Ernest Shackleton, captain of the ship *Endurance*. In August 1914 the veteran polar explorer set out from London to attempt the first full traverse of the frozen continent in the south. By January the following year Shackleton's ship had become trapped in pack ice, and it stayed firmly in place until October, when the tremendous pressures of the ever-shifting ice sheets cracked her hull, sending the *Endurance* to the bottom of the sea.

The crew abandoned ship and made camp on an ice floe. Their provisions dwindling, they were forced to kill and eat their sled dogs. Shackleton finally ordered his crew into the lifeboats that had been salvaged from the *Endurance*, and five days later they reached a spit of land in the frozen ocean called Elephant Island.

Shackleton knew that in order for his men to survive he would need to reach the larger island of South Georgia to the northeast where whaling stations could offer assistance, so he and five of his strongest men set out once again in a lifeboat. The six men braved the Southern Ocean for sixteen days before reaching South Georgia, after which Shackleton and two of his crew marched across wild and mountainous terrain, covering fifty kilometres in 36 hours to reach a whaling station, and help at long last.

Aside from this fascinating history, South Georgia island has huge colonies of birds and seals, and provides some of the greatest and most approachable concentrations of wildlife in the world.

In December 2014 I secured my ticket to a dream: the position of ship's doctor on One Ocean Expeditions' anniversary voyage commemorating the centenary of Sir Ernest Shackleton's expedition. It proved to be so much more, both good and awfully bad, than I could ever have envisioned.

From the start, it just had to be an extraordinary voyage. The passengers were predominantly well-heeled British public schoolers with direct genetic links to past polar explorers; the passenger list included Alexandra Shackleton, granddaughter of Ernest, and the four grandchildren of Sir James Wordie, principal scientist on the *Endurance*.

Then there was Heather Lane, who had a burning interest in another famous British explorer, Robert Scott, who'd diced with death on his return from the South Pole – and lost. She was the librarian of the collection at the Scott Polar Research Institute in Cambridge.

Lieutenant Colonel Henry Worsley, distantly related to Captain Frank Worsley of the *Endurance*, was a member of staff. He was preparing himself for his pending challenge to make the first solo and unassisted crossing of Antarctica using the route his life-long idol, Shackleton, would have taken had the *Endurance* not become trapped in sea-ice. He was the only man to have, unassisted, hauled a sledge carrying all his equipment along both the Shackleton/Scott route and the Amundsen route to the South Pole.

Our ignominious departure from Ushuaia wasn't a good start. Supper was interrupted so we could go on deck to wave farewell – but the boisterous winds thought otherwise and we remained firmly pinned to the quay.

Much later, twilight lent an ethereal light to our progress along the Beagle Channel as we watched kelp gulls and giant southern petrels swooping across the bow while flightless steamer ducks churned their way to safety. The sheer thrill of being at sea again stroked my soul.

A full day of steaming in a northeasterly direction brought us to the western part of the Falklands and we prepared for our first landing on an island called West Point. Splashes of yellow gorse (sadly, an introduced invader plant) shone off the rolling hills as we approached a landing jetty and small homestead. Sheep grazed mindlessly between gatherings of upland geese, while wild turkey vultures circled overhead, ever hopeful for a tasty gosling snack. Strikingly marked black-and-white Peale's dolphins escorted the rubber-ducks to shore.

But the best was yet to come – a walk to a colony where black-browed albatrosses and rockhopper penguins bred alongside each other. We slogged up a steep hill and into the colony perched on the edge of a cliff covered with tussock-grass. There a sight of elegance, grace, wonder and harmony met us: thousands of black-browed albatrosses soared above and below and around us, crying out to their mates, who stretched their necks skywards from their elevated nests, trying to alert their mates to their location. The squawking, quarrelsome rockhopper penguins milled around in random disorder. How those landlubbers must have envied their flying bedfellows!

Three hours later the situation couldn't have been more different. Fully kitted up in foul-weather gear and floatation jacket, automatic defibrillator firmly in hand and about to board the rubber-duck for the afternoon excursion, I was called to an elderly passenger, Gerald, who'd fallen on his face on the earlier walk and sustained a bleeding nose. This had appeared to respond to immediate first-aid treatment but his nose was now pouring blood again.

My first question revealed the horror of the situation: he was on oral warfarin, a common anticoagulant, for a condition not well known by himself or indicated in his medical notes. The extent of the bruising on his knees and arms indicated big trouble.

With the help of the Russian Dr Luba, I rifled through our pharmacy stocks. There was no vitamin K, the antidote to warfarin. I set about a frantic further search while she put up drips and packed Gerald's nose with adrenaline-soaked gauze – adrenaline causes rapid constriction of blood vessels and could stop or slow the bleeding.

Finally, when I'd almost given up all hope, I found three vials of vitamin K in a container ominously labelled 'for disposal'. They were two years beyond their expiry date. I elected to use them anyway and the treatment worked – for a while.

As I sat down to dinner, a second dreaded call came through. Gerald was bleeding again.

Dr Luba decided it was my problem now and retreated. Sweating, I packed his nose both from the front, up his nostrils, and also from inside his mouth and behind his pharynx. Then I remembered seeing something in the emergency shore medical kit. I raced down, tore it open and there it was: a very aptly named 'rhino tampon', designed specifically for epistaxis – a bleeding nose.

I shoved this large, tightly packed wad of cotton wool up Gerald's nose, trying to maintain a semblance of calm. I admitted him to the sickbay, reassuring him that all was under control. Then I climbed into the adjacent bed, fully clothed, and lay rigid in the darkness. I heard his breathing settle as he drifted off to sleep. I had very little that night.

The following day we were scheduled to stop over at Port Stanley, the capital of the Falkland Islands, and a town of 2 500 people. I conferred with the expedition leader and requested that my patient and I be provided with transport from the quay to the town's King Edward VII Memorial Hospital.

I discussed the plan with Gerald. I needed to have a few blood tests done to check his level of warfarin. I needed to know what his red blood-cell count was, in order to assess the extent of his blood loss. I needed to know what his clotting time was. Pending the outcome of these tests, there was a chance that I'd recommend Gerald leave the expedition and return home to the USA.

This prospect made him distinctly unhappy and argumentative. This was, for him, the trip of a lifetime. Shackleton was his personal hero. He had to visit the grave of the great man. He wasn't going home. He was prepared to take the risk.

What he didn't appreciate was that I wasn't prepared to take the risk.

At the hospital I conferred with the doctor. He performed the required tests on my rather pale patient and removed the nasal pack. Gerald's bleeding tests were now normal and his red blood-cell count, although low, was acceptable.

Although the immediate crisis was over, I remained very involved in Gerald's wellbeing. I took the chance of permanently stopping his warfarin; he was very vague as to why he'd been taking it in the first place. It was a risk, but I felt the dangers of warfarin causing re-bleeding were greater than the danger of stopping it. I made three-times-daily visits to check on him.

He now had seasickness to add to his woes, and was miserable, alone in his cabin, spending the entire day curled up on the bottom bunk with the curtains drawn around him. I tried to encourage him to come up to the lounge.

'Too many stairs,' he said. 'My knee is sore. I feel exhausted.'

Alarm bells sounded in my head. 'Let me examine your knee, please.'

His left knee, which had taken a battering in his fall, was swollen, tense and tender. The skin overlying it had been ripped, and when I removed the dressing the wound oozed, and the surrounding skin was a florid red. I was fairly sure that he'd bled into his knee and now had blood trapped inside his knee joint. But what concerned me more was that the skin overlying his knee was an angry red and warm to the touch. I checked his pulse. Too rapid for comfort. His face was sweaty and hot. He was developing septicaemia, a spreading infection throughout his body.

That comforting hospital on the Falklands lay in a dim past: we were headed south along the South Georgia coast and on to Elephant Island and the Antarctic, with another sixteen days at sea.

'I need to start you on antibiotics,' I told him.

He nodded and rolled over to face the wall.

I made a detour past the lounge, where I sought out Angus, an orthopaedic surgeon who worked in the trauma department of a busy hospital in Edinburgh. I badly needed help and reassurance.

'Hello, Doctor Joan!' he called out when he saw me. 'Come and have a drink with this old doc.'

'Thanks, Angus, but I can't right now. I need to chat to you. Can we talk in the library please?'

'Och, lass, this sounds serious,' he said, and winked, but he accompanied me to the library, where we sat in a quiet corner.

'First, I need to ask your permission to talk to you about a patient,' I began. 'It's not strictly correct that I do this, your being a passenger, but I need a specialist opinion.'

'Fire away. I'll help if I can.'

I told him the full story, formally, as if I were a junior doctor presenting a patient to my consultant on a hospital ward round, and he listened without interruption. 'I don't want to drain the blood from his knee – I'm very concerned about introducing infection and giving him a septic arthritis – but it may help his pain and mobility ...' My voice trailed off.

Then Angus did what I'd wanted to ask him to do but didn't dare: he offered to see my patient. I could've hugged him.

Gerald seemed unimpressed that another doctor had come to check on him. But Angus, an ultra-professional, put him at ease and ended the consultation with a conversation about golf. It had been some time since I'd seen Gerald so animated.

Back in the library, Angus shared his concerns with me. 'It doesn't look good but I would definitely not put a needle in there; you have enough problems as it is,' he confirmed. 'Let's see what the anti-biotics do. I can't really offer any other help except moral support.'

That, for me, was priceless.

In 1775, when Captain Cook set foot on South Georgia – the first person ever – I'm sure he suffered the same weather as we did: a forty-knot gale with frozen rain lashing in horizontal sheets. He 'took possession of the country in his Majesty's name', certain he'd discovered the long-sought-after Southern Continent.

He continued to sail southeastwards along the coast until he rounded a cape and turned westwards. His disenchantment was profound: what he'd discovered wasn't the Southern Continent but a small island. He immortalised the moment in the name he gave this geographical feature: Cape Disappointment.

What Cook had actually discovered was a long, narrow, glaciated island, 170 kilometres in length and ranging from just two to forty kilometres wide, its backbone of jagged peaks reaching up 2 934 metres, with no visible vegetation, and home only to thousands of birds and seals. His report home was unenthusiastic, and he attached little value to the landmass, other than noting 'sea-bears [fur seals] were pretty numerous'.

In 1786 the first sealer arrived to slaughter them. By 1825 over a million pelts had been taken, and the fur seal was almost extinct. The killing officially stopped only in 1912.

At the time of our visit, South Georgia was still recovering from this violent, wasteful plunder, but was regaining its breath-taking magic. Man was now firmly put in his place as observer only, and the thousands of birds and seals were now essentially predator-naïve, with only the beady-eyed skuas hovering in search of eggs or chicks.

On our shore trips we were overwhelmed by tens of thousands of stately king penguins and their brown fluffy chicks, strutting between snorting, grunting grey masses of elephant seals, inter-spersed with feistier, whiskered Antarctic fur seals. Nesting gentoo penguins added to the mix.

In a small shore pond we spotted rare pintail ducks. Their reappearance was a miracle wrought by the vision, dedication and hard work of a few individuals who'd refused to see them pushed off our planet by the Norwegian rat – a species introduced by early whalers. A programme of aerial rat-baiting by helicopters two years ago had been remarkably successful, and efforts were continuing.

Now we were headed for a landing in King Haakon Bay on South Georgia, weather permitting, the site where one of the lifeboats off the sunken *Endurance* had made landing with Shackleton and five companions aboard, after they'd crossed the 1 300 kilometres from Elephant Island on the stormiest water in the world. It had taken sixteen days of hellish conditions, with constant bailing or chipping ice off the deck, minutes of sleep grabbed in a sitting position in fermenting reindeer-pelt sleeping bags, which dropped rancid balls of fur into the food they struggled to prepare on a spluttering paraffin stove.

It was thanks to Frank Worsley's navigation, which was nothing short of brilliant, that the men hadn't missed the thin sliver of land that was South Georgia and been blown into the blue yonder. So extreme were the conditions that Worsley had been able to take only four reasonably accurate sextant readings, and then he still had to be held in position to avoid being pitched overboard.

The mounting medical problems I faced seemed insignificant in comparison, though not to the patients who were suffering them. Gerald was no better. I was baffled as to why there was no improvement in his skin sepsis, given that he was on appropriately massive doses of antibiotics, until I went back to basics and checked on his packets of pills. He hadn't been taking them.

I felt exasperated and unsympathetic until I realised he was mildly confused, along with a creeping depression. I added another medication, and planned to spend more time with him.

I had also in the course of a single day seen three patients with acute chest pain. They were all anxious geriatrics with previous heart conditions and/or surgery, and on a range of specialist medications. The ship didn't have any modern monitoring equipment, not even an adequate ECG machine.

Incongruously, however, it was equipped with state-of-the-art medication to be administered if a heart attack was diagnosed. I was aware that many of these medications needed precise measuring and careful monitoring, preferably in an ICU setting, as they could precipitate abnormal cardiac rhythms or dramatic drops in blood pressure, resulting in a worst-case scenario of death. I knew that I didn't have the courage or experience to use any of them, even had I had a cardiologist at the other end of a satellite phone.

Again, I went back to basics – I took detailed histories followed by meticulous examinations. One patient was suffering from angina and I increased the medication she was already on for this. The other two didn't fulfil the diagnostic criteria for a heart attack, although I couldn't prove this – and anyway, what would I have done if they had?

I gave them each an aspirin and planned to see them later. I found them that evening, joking and smiling, in the bar, gin in hand, pain forgotten. Alcohol is an excellent anxiety reducer.

The Shackleton anniversary festivities proceeded unabated. Lectures, slideshows and rubber-duck landings kept the bulk of passengers invigorated and busy.

A respiratory-tract virus had snuck aboard and was ravaging a swathe of passengers, but most were resolute that nothing was going to keep them from the full experience of South Georgia. It meant, however, that I was often in the surgery, doling out fistfuls of medications, bottles of cough mixture, throat lozenges and sympathy, before racing to board a rubber-duck to assist for a landing. I felt – and looked – more ragged than the clients.

But it wasn't possible to be weary or unenthusiastic on South Georgia. A frozen Eden, it felt like an ongoing process of creation. Its towering razor-sharp peaks etched with snow rose above the black cliffs and beaches that were home to thousands of birds and seals.

Elephant-seal weaners looking for food.

As remote and extreme as the island was, it generated an astounding depth of emotional attachment. Perhaps it was the thousands of elegant king penguins, striking with their black heads, white bellies, grey backs and orange scarves as they strutted past, centimetres from our feet, and proceeded to the business at hand – the feeding of their brown fluffy chicks.

Maybe it was the manner in which the three-week-old elephant-seal pups sought out anything or anyone as a surrogate mother, given that their own had fed them with ultra-rich fatty milk and then gone back to the sea, leaving their offspring to mature and, in time, themselves head for the deep. These weaners wriggled up to us, nudging, looking for a milk-bearing teat, content to snuggle up to our legs and the mounds of bags on the beach. I'd never been approached so intimately by such huge wild animals.

Perhaps it was the beach carpeted with gigantic, lumbering male elephant seals that intermittently raised their upper bodies and began jousting with adjacent competition, packing a punch of hundreds of kilograms as they used their heads as battering rams.

The dainty (in comparison) female fur seals were suckling black furry pups while the bullying males made amorous advances for yet another chance at procreation. Being rejected made the males an aggressive lot and they continued spats with any male competition – or weird-looking visitors like us. They approached fast, with a mean glint in their eyes, giving a breathy bark from an open tooth-lined jaw, and a hiking pole held at arm's length in a rather shaky hand was our only form of defence. I hadn't forgotten the horror stories of the seal researchers on Gough Island, and the graphic evidence one had shown of a fur-seal bite.

What lingered with me especially as I looked out at the golden light on the mountains, and the silvery reflections of the ruffled water as penguins porpoised in the surf in their hundreds, was the sound, filling, it seemed, the entire heavens. There was the plaintive mewl of the clumsy king penguin chicks begging for a fish from their attentive parents, honking like a thousand vuvuzelas, and the gentle nasal snoring of the elephant-seal weaners, the barking and the whining of the fur seals, and the sickening thuds of flesh against flesh as jousting elephant seals expressed the territorial imperative. It was a privilege beyond words.

For me, and for most passengers on this trip, there was a deeper emotional level to South Georgia. Shackleton and his five companions had stared death in the face when they'd finally approached South Georgia during a hurricane which had threatened to smash their little boat onto the rocks of the small Annenkov Island; a 600-ton steamer nearby, caught in the same storm, was sunk. The lives of all the remaining crew of the *Endurance*, surviving against all the odds back on Elephant Island, under two upturned lifeboats, were dependent on the survival of these six brave men. They battled and fought and were washed up, totally exhausted, in a tiny cove, now called Cave Cove. There they lay, recuperating, eating seal flesh, for five days before moving to safer ground at the head of King Haakon Bay.

The whaling station that was their ultimate destination lay on the other side of the island, across huge mountains that had never been surveyed. Winter was approaching and there was no time to waste: during a break in the weather (which turned out to be the very last of the season), Shackleton, Worsley and seaman Tom Crean headed off on an unknown route, with many heart-breaking backtracks. The story of their crossing, a feat of superhuman endurance, is one of the great mountaineering epics of all time.

On 20 May 1916, while still high on the summits, they heard a factory whistle – the first sound of civilisation that had reached their ears for eighteen months. They hurtled, slid and slipped down a frozen waterfall, now called Shackleton's Waterfall (to which the bulk of passengers made a pilgrimage, and which they viewed in quiet awe). The three of them limped into the safety and comfort of Stromness Whaling Station; children who saw these wild men approaching from the uninhabited side of the island fled in terror.

The following day the three men were rescued from King Haakon Bay, but three attempts to rescue the men on Elephant

Island were thwarted by weather and ice. The fourth was successful and the 22 marooned men were picked up at last. Through the outstanding courage and leadership of Ernest Shackleton, every man survived.

Before heading south to Elephant Island we had another significant stop: Grytviken, the site of the first and largest whaling station on South Georgia, and the burial site of Sir Ernest Shackleton. This was the landing that my patient Gerald had pinned all his hopes on. For me, it was a personal pilgrimage of religious proportions.

Gerald had responded somewhat to my ministrations and could walk with a stick. He still looked like he'd been through major trauma, with deep-purple bruises, now edged with a jaundiced yellow, on his face, arms and legs. I hadn't re-started his warfarin, and lived with this anxiety, fretting in private and sleeping poorly at night, waiting for some emergency call out related to this omission.

I assisted Gerald down the gangway. He was quiet and resolute but made it clear that that was all the help he required. He wanted to proceed alone.

I watched him picking his way through the rusting oil vats and disintegrating whaling ships that served as stark reminders of a bloody industry that had come close to causing the extinction of the gentle giants of the Southern Ocean.

Whaling started here in 1904, when Grytviken was established by a Norwegian captain, CA Larsen. He arrived with sixty men and a prefabricated factory and accommodation buildings.

Two years before, he'd visited on a Swedish polar expedition and commented that it was almost possible to cross Cumberland Bay, on which Grytviken lies, 'across the backs of whales'. On the two visits I'd paid to Grytviken, I had yet to see one.

This whaling station had been abandoned in the mid-1960s after a death count of 175 250 whales: it was no longer profitable due to dwindling numbers and economic woes. Even a sideline operation of slaughtering thousands of elephant seals for their oil failed. The whaling station was now open to visitors, along with an excellent museum, all maintained by the South Georgia Trust. The hope was that visitors would leave South Georgia moved and enlightened, and would return home as well-informed ambassadors for and champions of the cause of Southern Ocean conservation.

The highlight of the landing at Grytviken for our Shackleton commemorative voyage was the church service we had in the very whalers' church where Shackleton's funeral had been held. He'd died of a heart attack on the *Quest*, anchored off South Georgia, in January 1922 while heading south on another expedition. There were plans to return his earthly remains to England, the land of his birth, but his widow ordered that his body be buried on South Georgia, where his soul and spirit could still wander to his beloved South.

Our service was especially poignant, and the grandchildren of Timothy McCarthy, Alfred Kerr, Thomas Orde-Lees, James Wordie and Shackleton himself spoke with an emotion that could have been derived only from a genetic link to the incredible survivors of the *Endurance*. I was honoured to be the bell ringer.

From the church we filed to the cemetery, a windswept space hugging the mountain edge, and the resting place of early sailors and whalers who'd perished in the surrounding perilous waters. The gravestones bore mainly Norwegian names and lay positioned east-west, unlike the grave of Ernest Shackleton, which lay with his

At Ernest Shackleton's grave.

head to the south. Alexandra, his granddaughter, led the ritual of every member present having a small tot of whisky, but holding back a few drops to sprinkle on the grave of 'the Boss'.

I stole a glance at Gerald. He was standing straight and sure, albeit supported by his stick, his chin held high, his eyes closed. He'd made it to where his hero lay: a dream realised. He too was a survivor.

I slept easier that night. We still had nearly two weeks on board, but my confidence of delivering Gerald back alive was growing. We were on our way to Elephant Island. I could hear laughter and loud chatter floating down the stairs from the bar. The mood was exuberant; the spirit of Shackleton permeated.

As we lost sight of the towering mountains of South Georgia, the barometer dropped precipitously, the winds increased to seventy knots and waves began crashing over the bow, sending up jets of sparkling foam. Gerald and many others took to their beds, while I lurched from cabin to cabin with my small black bag of pills and potions.

Out in the elements, the albatrosses – black-browed, wandering and light-mantled sooty – revelled in the conditions as flocks of Antarctic prions swooped over the wild waters. Storm petrels danced delicately across the surges, undeterred by their anger – the name 'petrel' comes from St Peter, who was reputed to have walked on water.

The outline of Elephant Island, that piece of frozen rock jutting from the Scotia Sea which had been home to the crew of the stricken *Endurance* for an interminable four and a half months, loomed through the sleet and snow.

In April 1916 these men had sailed and rowed in three lifeboats for seven days – for four of them with no sleep at all – often in knee-deep icy water, dodging icebergs, famished, thirsty, frost-bitten, half-dead. They'd made a pitiable site in their final ludicrous bid for survival. Their landing spot, now named Point Wild, was, according to Alfred Lansing's 1959 book *Endurance: Shackleton's Incredible Voyage*, 'the merest handhold, 100 feet wide and 50 feet deep. A meagre grip on a savage coast, exposed to the full fury of the sub-Antarctic Ocean. But no matter – they were on land. …Solid, unsinkable, immovable, blessed land.'

A hundred years later, on the *Akademik Sergey Vavilov*, even Gerald, huddled in foul-weather gear, made it up to the bridge. Every passenger and staff member was hoping for a landing but the gale-force winds and massive swell prohibited it. We stood, imagining dimly what it must have felt like to be on those small, ill-equipped, lurching, bobbing craft for days. I looked around at the passengers, many of whom had already been my patients. This, for them, had to be an emotional encounter.

I looked up to the snow-covered cliffs where colonies of chinstrap penguins huddled. On the pebble beach, I noted the slug-like shapes of elephant seals. Nature, which had almost destroyed those men, had also generously provided the nourishment for them to live another day: seal and penguin meat, supplemented by penguin eggs, ensured a diet high in protein and fat, as well as the crucial vitamin C.

A day later Elephant Island faded into the shrouds of low-lying cloud. Most of us would never see that piece of rock again, but would remain nonetheless forever enriched by the spirit of Shackleton.

The Antarctic Peninsula and its calm bays and inlets lay ahead. I was looking forward to a much-needed a break from the demands of seasickness. Then Gerald deteriorated again, contracting bronchopneumonia. He coughed up thick green sputum with occasional bits of blood in it.

I took on the role of the physiotherapist: twice a day I pummelled his chest and encouraged deep breathing in an attempt to loosen up infected sputum. I wanted him to cough this up and avoid its causing blockages in the narrow breathing tubes in his lungs.

Then I had to don my surgeon's hat and lance a nasty abscess on the nether regions of a member of the British aristocracy. In ideal conditions, the abscess would have been opened and drained in an operating theatre, under general anaesthetic, but the immediate need was to alleviate her excruciating pain. She adopted a stiff upper lip and endured in the spirit of Shackleton.

We did spend one day in paradise – Paradise Harbour, Antarctic Peninsula. It would be hard to find a more spectacular, awe-inspiring location anywhere else on earth; I had an otherworldly feeling that I was wandering on another planet. We had the gift of seeing it in warm, sparkling sunshine, with a deep-blue sky streaked by layers and wisps of cottonwool clouds. Penguins shot across the glassy sea surface, leaving intricate patterns of ever-widening concentric circles. Crab-eater seals lay basking on small ice floes, revealing life by the occasional flick of a flipper.

We landed at the old concrete steps of a disused Argentinian research station, and crunched up through wet snow to stand between the faded-red wooden buildings. Gentoo penguins were nesting in their lee. The females had laid two eggs on a nest of stones, and the males were in adoring attendance, offering the perfect pebble to aid the nest foundation. They barely registered our presence.

We climbed through knee-deep snow to a vantage point, where we looked down in wonder and gratitude for the gift of such beauty, with the cracking and rumbling of ice calving off hanging glaciers and tumbling headlong into the bay.

As I scanned the tiny buildings of the station below I recalled the story of an Argentinian doctor, years before, who'd been press-ganged into spending a year at this station. He despised it, and was despised in turn for his arrogant and complaining behaviour. Relief was in sight as the annual supply vessel hove into view, bringing replacement personnel – but, unfortunately, not for the doctor. He was ordered to spend another year in 'paradise'. In desperation, he devised a cunning plan. He set the station alight as the vessel was departing, presuming that they would see the fire, return and rescue all the residents, who would have been rendered homeless.

His plan backfired horribly: the fire wasn't spotted – or perhaps it was ignored – and the vessel continued on its way north. Once the fire had been extinguished, precious little of the station remained. What ensued was a grim six months of acrimony and hate – a far cry from the camaraderie that had seen the *Endurance* crew through vicious times.

Sea ice and foul weather blocked our passage to our proposed southernmost point, and I felt an inkling of sympathy for my Argentinian colleague: days of howling wind and icy grey certainly could cause mental instability.

Turning north resulted in disappointment doldrums in the passengers, particularly in the five Wordie family members, who'd been banking on visiting the historic Wordie House, an old British Antarctic research station named in honour of James Wordie and now a national monument.

As we continued north back to Ushuaia, the threat of a wild Drake Passage loomed. Only Gerald showed an upsurge in mood: he'd accomplished his mission. The side trip to the peninsula had brought more physical discomfort for him, however. I'd persisted with regular monitoring and contact, but I sensed his distrust of me. So much had gone wrong. I hadn't cured him. I faced his disapproval alone and with all the evenness I could muster, but it hurt.

Worse, it eroded my confidence in my own ability, which over the years of medicine practised in difficult places had come under severe threat but survived. I hung onto Shackleton's words: 'Difficulties are just things to overcome, after all.'

＊

I'd faced more medical challenges than was comfortable on the Shackleton Centenary Voyage, but we made it back to Ushuaia – and no-one died. The passengers, laden with hand luggage, many sporting One Ocean Expeditions jackets and beanies, were saying their farewells to the staff members lined up at the end of the gangway. Most had had a spectacular, memorable journey and were exuberant and effusive with their thanks. I'd made some good friends, shared many animated conversations and hoped that my medical input had been satisfactory.

I was old enough to know, though, that there was no formula for being a good doctor for everyone. My eyes searched for Gerald. I'd written a comprehensive letter to his doctor back in New York, listing all my interventions and added medications. I'd prepared packets of medication for his trip home. I had to personally just close the circle.

I caught up with him as he was about to board the bus and tapped him on the shoulder. He turned to me in silence. I extended my hand, which he took in a limp handshake. 'Good luck on your journey home. Take it easy in Buenos Aires – not too much tangoing,' I said, cringing inwardly at my feeble attempt at humour.

His face remained a mask. 'I will be careful,' he said. 'Goodbye.'

In that moment, it dawned on me that there was now a real possibility of having to face what doctors fear more than anything: litigation. I knew I'd done my utmost in the circumstances, but that may not have been good enough: Gerald could sue me for inadequate or inappropriate treatment that may have left some degree of permanent damage. The next few months would be spent dreading any formal-looking mail from the USA, or the opening of an email from American lawyers.

There were two postscripts to this trip. First, I never did get a lawyer's letter or email from an American lawyer.

And, second, Lieutenant Colonel Henry Worsley, the member of staff who was a distant relative of Captain Frank Worsley, didn't succeed in making his crossing of Antarctica using Shackleton's erstwhile route. His journey in 2016 ended 1 450 kilometres in, when he was a mere 200 kilometres from his intended endpoint. He called for help, stating, 'I just cannot put one foot in front of the other.' He was flown out to Punta Arenas in southern Chile, where, tragically, he died in hospital of multiple organ failure. In 2017 his ashes were interred at Grytviken, on South Georgia, near the grave of his hero, Ernest Shackleton.

The staff of the *Akademik Sergey Vavilov* were in for a hectic morning. We had to 'turn it around' – render it pristine and in inviting condition for the next cohort of guests who would be embarking later in the afternoon, for *their* trip of a lifetime to the Antarctic Peninsula. Among them was my dear cherished friend and neighbour Estelle.

I'd known her since 1989, when I'd returned from Knysna to Cape Town. Estelle, who had three children, had the luxury of being an 'at-home' mother, where I was a serious, independent, at times lonely, working single mother of two. She'd become my confidante on many issues, and had a forthright and intelligent way of dealing with all problems. She didn't suffer fools or idleness gladly, but appropriate tender compassion flowed easily from her.

She laughed a lot, including at herself, and always tried to get the best out of everyone, even if a little unsubtly at times.

Estelle knew me and my tendency towards dwindling self-esteem – and she would have none of it. I knew that having her as my cabin mate for the next ten days would be extraordinarily good fun, but also deeply restorative. Any medical disaster would be easier to deal with, having her as a layman advisor, but more especially, my loyal friend.

That night, sliding through the oily waters of the Beagle Channel, Estelle and I sat down to dinner, and toasted our good fortune in having this trip together. I kept one eye roving, assessing my potential patients.

The largest single group was seventeen teenaged boys from a prestigious private school in Brisbane. Their two masters looked rugged and healthy. One had asked for a few quiet words with me, and had informed me that one boy had a rare inherited cardiac problem, catecholaminergic polymorphic ventricular tachycardia (CPVT). I'd never heard of it before, but learned that it was a condition characterised by an abnormal heart rhythm. As the heart rate increased in response to physical activity or emotional stress, it could trigger an abnormally fast and irregular heartbeat called ventricular tachycardia.

The boy was well controlled on medication, the master assured me, but they were travelling with a portable defibrillator – just in case. I smiled, reassuringly I hoped, but thought I should make it clear from the outset that the polar plunge and ice camping weren't a good idea – not only for the boy, but for me: I don't think I could've stood the strain.

Just past midnight the ship began rolling precipitously; drawers started slamming and chairs sliding. A violent storm tore into us as we entered the Drake Passage. A wave pounded our porthole, smashing it open and dousing our beds with curtains of icy water. Rapid protective action was taken and I noted that Estelle was relishing every minute. As she was a self-confessed sufferer of seasickness, I'd put her on my personal rigid prophylactic regime, so I chalked up my first medical success of the voyage.

I was less sure about all those boys.

Resigned to my fate the next morning, I climbed the stairs to the lounge. There sprawled fifteen gangly, green, glassy-eyed, greasy-haired schoolboys, clutching vomit bags to their mouths. I rapidly dispatched them to the bunks in their cabins on the third level, where the motion of the ship was less pronounced. Like a practical school ma'am I did my rounds, issuing handfuls of seasickness pills or threatening the big needle, with stern instructions as to hydration and rest, and for them to stay out of public areas until they could adequately control their gastric contents.

Thanks to my sharing of hard-earned personal experience, I succeeded in returning the bulk of them to wolfing down vast quantities of food, accompanied by teenage-boy grunting and burping.

One of my personal pleasures on these shipboard sojourns was having minimal contact with the outside world: we had no cellphone reception, so there was no time-wasting attention to the trivia of social media; there was no TV, so we didn't get news unless something earth-shaking was shared with us from the bridge; and there was only very basic limited internet, which I used for medical purposes and also to entertain the cohort of armchair travellers I'd collected over the years. And to let my kids know that I was surviving.

We'd made a side trip through the Antarctic Sound, to Paulet Island in the Weddell Sea, to escape the gale-force winds. There we witnessed the unbelievable sight and sound of 200 000 nesting Adélie penguins.

It was also there that I received an email that added another swerve to my life. It came, as if from another planet, from the hot, drought-stricken wilds of the Kruger National Park in South Africa. Doctor Nicki, a young colleague I'd befriended during my course in tropical medicine and hygiene, and who was now one of the resident doctors at the park, disclosed that she was pregnant and wanted to know if I was interested in taking her place for three months when she went on maternity leave.

There was not a doubt in my mind that I wanted to do it. I knew it would be busy, demanding, unpredictable and remote – adventure medicine at its best – but I wasn't sure I could handle it. Maybe I needed to take a break, be a small-town GP for a while, dealing with colds, stress, obesity, insomnia and backache.

'Estelle – what do you think? Do you think I can take this on?' I asked my friend.

She put her hand on my shoulder, shook her head slowly, gave me a look that can only be described as pitying, and answered, 'Does your dog bark?'

CHAPTER 11

Back to self

'Physician, heal thyself: then wilt thou also heal thy patient.'
— from *Thus Spoke Zarathustra* by Friedrich Nietzsche, 1885

IN THEORY, I KNOW A LOT about the human body, but I still marvel at its fragility, countered by its resilience and magical properties. On long and potentially dangerous trips where I was the only medical help, the question that often followed was, 'But who will assist if *you* fall seriously ill?'

I like to think that I take reasonable precautions. I exercise daily and attempt to remain fitter and stronger than most others of a similar age. I'm a chronic asthmatic on daily maintenance of inhaled steroids and bronchodilators. Although this sometimes cramps my style, I've never been hospitalised for it.

My major source of disappointment is my failing skeleton: it has just not stood up to the hammering to which I've subjected it. The cartilage I inherited was of second-grade standard and so far I've had to undergo three hip replacements and a number of other orthopaedic procedures.

But I remain hugely grateful to modern medical technology. Without it I'd be sedentary and knitting endless blankets for the homeless.

I try to avoid sharing war stories with potential patients – it undermines confidence. I recall on an Antarctic trip, on the occasion of meeting and greeting the new passengers, a good-looking, tall, elderly gentleman, who, on seeing my name badge inscribed with 'Dr', confided that he'd recently undergone a hip replacement. I commended him for undertaking the voyage and asked when he'd had the surgery. He mentioned the date and I said he needed to take extra care and that I'd be around to assist him at any stage. What I didn't disclose was that I'd undergone a hip replacement on exactly the same date.

I confess that there have been times when an abnormality I've detected in my own body has caused me extreme anxiety, but due to my location at the time, and my position as doctor, I've had to keep it totally private and attempt to deal with the issue alone.

While cycling the Silk Route in Asia, from Istanbul to Beijing, which was prior to my first hip replacement – a probably irresponsible action on my part, given the amount of chronic pain I was enduring – I noticed a black tarry substance emerging with my stool. This substance, melena, is derived from active bleeding higher up in the gastrointestinal tract, like in the stomach. We were in rural Turkey, with rudimentary toilet facilities, usually long drops, which rendered stool inspection easy.

If I'd been faced with this problem in a patient, I would have recommended immediate transfer to an adequate medical facility, and further investigation. I don't take my own advice easily. What I did know was that due to my hip pain, I was taking regular anti-inflammatory medication, and a known side effect of this is ulceration and bleeding from the stomach. I'd had the foresight to include the medication to reduce stomach acid, and so assist healing of any stomach defects. I commenced this treatment, and at the same time stopped the anti-inflammatories, instead taking grossly inadequate paracetamol for the hip pain; and within days the melena had ceased. Problem solved, or so I thought.

The hip replacement transformed my life. There was no more pain and no more need for anti-inflammatories, and I was back on my bicycle within six weeks. I began training for the Trans Baviaans, a 24-hour mountain-bike marathon of 230 kilometres from Willowmore in the heart of the Eastern Cape to Jeffreys Bay, 75 kilometres southwest of Port Elizabeth. On the journey to Willowmore, with my fellow riders in a cramped and hot car, I began to feel sweaty and mildly nauseous. I put this down to travel sickness, my old companion.

At the registration I felt no better, and on seeing a colleague from Knysna I quietly mentioned my problem. 'You're probably getting this vicious flu that's going around. Here,' he said, and rummaged in his pocket, 'I took these new antivirals and they worked wonders.' (Medical colleagues break all the rules when dealing with each other!)

I gratefully took the tablets and swallowed them immediately. Minutes later I was being carted inside, carried by the feet and the arms 'like a dead kudu', one of my cycling teammates later told me. I'd passed out.

I regained consciousness and recovered sufficiently to offload my bike and attempt to get organised for the start of the race the next day. I was concerned, though. I felt lacking in energy and a little breathless, and my pulse was much faster than usual. Riding into the back country where access was only possible by 4x4 vehicles and helicopters began to seem a bad idea.

I announced that I was probably going to be better in the morning and would make my final decision about participation then. When I passed out again in the middle of the night, I had to face the inevitable: I was unfit to proceed with the race.

I was offered a lift back to Knysna but I refused on the grounds that I'd soon be fine, so I'd travel the length of the race, to cheer on my team, with our seconding vehicle.

Later that night, in the pitch dark, in the bush, I had to request a sudden halt and I vomited violently. At the campsite the next morning, I had another melena stool: I was again suffering from gastrointestinal bleeding. If I'd been able to see what had come up from my stomach the previous night, it would have been bright-red blood. When I took the trouble to really take a look at myself in the mirror, a ghostly apparition grimaced back. I was deathly pale. A finger on my pulse added evidence of extensive blood loss – it was rapid and thready. I couldn't blame anti-inflammatories this time.

What followed was hospitalisation in Knysna, transfusion of thirteen units of blood, a gastroscopy (a scope down the throat into the stomach) and a small biopsy to confirm the presence of a gastrointestinal stromal tumour, which no doubt had been present at my first episode of melena in Turkey. This tumour, usually in the stomach, can be benign or malignant (cancerous); it has to be surgically removed and a final diagnosis made by examining its cells carefully under a microscope.

Then came more bleeding and another collapse, in the ward, followed by a laparotomy to stop the bleeding and remove the tumour. I was hugely relieved that it proved to be of only very low-grade malignancy, and its removal was probably all the treatment I required. Still, it was a slow, painful recovery – and I had to do some serious introspection as to my useless diagnostic skills.

※

I grew up in a family that had close to zero exposure to the medical profession. We had no friendly family doctor. We had no need of one – we weren't allowed to get sick, and if we did, we were still sent to school. In my entire primary-school education, I had 100% attendance.

My dad had a scathing disregard for the medical profession. He was a brilliant, precise and dedicated engineer. All the problems with which he was confronted in his work could be solved with deep thought and the application of exacting mathematics. His sole medication for all ills was Zam-Buk, that medicinally sweet-smelling, slimy, green ointment. It could be forced into any orifice – mouth, nose, ears, anus – where it usually burned a little, which meant it was 'doing its work'; it could be smeared on a chest, and it could soothe any skin ailment.

The only thing it couldn't cure was my mother's severe asthma, and I always had the feeling that my dad silently blamed her for this shortcoming. My mom's asthma is what led to my only involvement with the medical profession, and always in a terrified, observational role.

The scenario invariably started deep into a cold night. I would lie rigid in bed, hearing my father's voice commanding my mother to pack her things. Above this, like a background sound effect, could be heard the laboured wheezing of my poor mom as she strained to expel air from her lungs in an attempt to make space for more oxygen to be sucked into those distended air sacs.

Dad would then shake us kids out of bed and instruct us to get ready to drive with him to the hospital. Mom would be waiting in the front seat of our large navy-blue Chevrolet, shoulders pulled up, chest moving only slightly in that all-pervading respiratory wheeze, pupils dilated in fear. I thought she would die, sitting there, on that leather bench-seat of the car, and Dad would keep driving.

We always made it to the hospital. All attention was then on Mom. Us kids – my elder brother George and I – found a corner in which to lurk, and watched as a scene that quickly became familiar played out. A metal trolley with a thin mattress appeared. The head of it was raised. What seemed like a host of white-garbed women converged on our mother. A mask gushing oxygen was snapped onto her face, and that was the last we saw of her as she was whisked through two swinging doors, each with a round frosted-glass window. My father disappeared, I never knew where to.

A long wait then ensued. It was at this stage that I started my game to while away the hours and offer a diversion for my small, anxious brain. I had no idea what all these people did. I needed to figure it out.

The emergency room was the initiation of my knowledge of how folks were 'saved' by this hospital. The workers within it seemed so confident, so focused, so expert, so clever. What tricks did they perform to get my mother into another room, on another floor, into a large white bed, sitting up with a smile of welcome on her face, with my father, unsmiling, in a chair next to her?

I watched carefully for clues. The corridors were a frenzy of activity but it seemed well organised. Food arrived in huge stainless-steel cupboards on wheels, sheets and blankets arrived on trolleys. Foul-smelling liquids were spirited away in containers under paper covers. A tall trolley with doors opened out to reveal rows of small bottles, which on close scrutiny were seen to contain myriads of colourful pills of all sizes and shapes. These were then doled out to the folks in the beds, and seemed to be part of the magical recoveries.

Then a person, usually a man, with a shiny disc-shaped object attached to black rubber tubing hanging around his neck, would stride down the corridor. He seemed to ooze authority and certainty. The women in white hurriedly copied down his every word. My dad told me later that these figures of power were called doctors. He also mentioned, in an offhand fashion, that they studied long and hard at university to assume this position, but that theirs was a lowly, unenviable and unstimulating job, and certainly not one to be sought after.

But my curiosity had become all-consuming: I wanted to be part of this world where everyone seemed busy, competent and respected. And they seemed to get folk well again, those unfortunate ones who needed it. Sickness, then, it seemed to me, was just infrequent, unexplained bad luck, but someone had to deal with it, solve the problem.

I started to imagine myself as one of those rarefied beings, with a thirst for seeking out the riddle of sickness, and so creating a worthwhile spot for myself in the world.

It was a fall from a horse when I was 11 years old that resulted in my first hospital admission. I flew in a spectacular arc from the horse's back and landed on my outstretched right arm. I heard a bone snap.

I rolled and groaned in the dust, watching as my riderless steed galloped off into the distance. I stared in horror at my grossly deformed forearm. Tears flowed, more from fear than from pain, as I felt sure that the management of such an injury would involve chopping my arm off at the elbow – such was my medical ignorance.

Some years later I had a friend in my class at school whose father was a GP. From her comments on the nature of his work, I ascertained that he was a doctor, but not the sort I'd observed in a hospital. He was the figure we lacked in our family. So great was my need to see this person in the flesh that I engineered myself an invitation to spend a weekend in their home. Dr Barber turned out to be the most relaxed, kindest, smiliest senior adult male I'd ever met. I was bursting to ask him about the mysteries of medicine but too embarrassed to expose my ignorance. However, the desire to follow his lead was born. I wanted to be a doctor.

I entered my last two years of school and won an academic scholarship to study chemical engineering at UCT. This choice was largely my father's. He dismissed my suggestion of medicine: it did not require a good brain, he said, and then, if I did qualify as a doctor, I would waste good taxpayers' money by simply getting married and never making full use of my training.

I tried to stave off this final career choice by opting to travel for a year before taking up my place at university. My father was appalled by this idea, and it never materialised, as I had another serious brush with the medical profession: I dislocated my right knee while playing a particularly aggressive hockey match. Two surgeries and a plaster cast stretching from my ankle to my groin saw me start university, in February 1970, as a semi-invalid and despondent chemical-engineering student.

I was one of two girls in a class of 25. We were competitive and stretched our brains but we had fun and many laughs. Even socially, we hung around together. However, I felt like a fraud. I was masquerading as an interested chemical-engineering student, taking up teachers' valuable energy, when in my head and in my heart I wanted to be a medical student.

Eventually, I got up the courage to phone my father. Standing in a malodorous telephone booth, sweating and nervous, clutching a fistful of coins, I made the call. Talking fast to stop my father from interrupting, I told him that I'd changed to medicine. 'I've got permission to take biology and I'll keep my maths going in case ... I haven't yet been accepted into the medical faculty, but if I pass this year well I have a good chance of getting accepted.'

Silence.

'I have to contact the scholarship people. I hope they'll allow me to change my course.'

I heard my father clear his throat. 'You do realise that you'll be working with the wreckage of humanity for the rest of your life?' he said.

'Yes, Dad. But it's what I want to do.'

My father wasn't convinced but he didn't forbid the change: I'd overcome the biggest hurdle and emerged relatively unscathed.

It was a strange, sad incident that reaffirmed my steadfast resolve to study medicine. I'd remained in the engineering class for physics, and I had a chemical-engineering laboratory partner. He was a quiet, likeable, gentle young man from Rhodesia and we worked in comfortable harmony.

On my return to university after the July holidays, I found myself alone at the lab bench. 'Is Gerry still on holiday?' I enquired of the other Rhodesian students.

'He's not coming back,' came a reply.

'Why not? Is he laughing off varsity?' I persisted.

'He was sick.'

'Oh dear. When will he be better?'

A long, awkward pause, then: 'He won't be. He killed himself.'

The lecturer walked in then, and the class started, and we never spoke of Gerry again. But I slept little that night. What sickness had he had? He'd seemed healthy enough. Was this a sickness of the mind and soul? Why hadn't I noticed anything? After all, I'd spent hours working shoulder to shoulder with him. Had I not been open to him confiding any of his concerns to me?

I took this as a personal failure, and one that didn't stand me in good stead in my chosen career. My understanding of physical sickness was increasing exponentially; of the intricacies of mental illness, however, I knew little and understood less. I hoped and trusted that over the years of training and subsequent medical practice, this would be remedied.

Ultimately, I completed my medical degree in the prescribed six years.

※

My medical mentors and teachers may raise their eyebrows when I disclose that I think luck, whatever one deems that to be, plays a role in our lives, and for me specifically in my line of medicine, with the situations I've had to deal with.

It was on a boisterous Drake Passage crossing at the start of a voyage to the Antarctic that I called in all my lucky points. It was lunchtime and I was negotiating the central buffet salad table, plate in one hand, salad tongs in the other. My left foot hooked on the table drape just as the ship made a sudden lurch, and I catapulted to the floor, landing heavily on my recently replaced hip. It was a show stopper, as the plate smashed into thousands of small pieces and bits of lettuce flew everywhere.

I regained my cool as I stayed on my knees and cleaned up the mess but the pain was severe. Had I dislocated or fractured something?

Slowly I attempted to take some weight on my right leg, and it held. A tender haematoma swelled rapidly over my right femoral area and by the evening was a huge, boggy, dark-purple bulge. How lucky that I wasn't on any blood-thinning agents, like warfarin, as a number of folks my age have to endure. How lucky that the point of impact was such that the damage was to soft tissue only. How lucky that my replaced hip hadn't dislocated – a common and difficult problem to deal with on an ill-equipped ship, with no specialised medical help.

Limping for the next week was a small price to pay.

I've been forced into a few situations where I've had to suffice as my own doctor. In many instances the sensible solution would've been to cease the activity I was doing, but this never seemed to be an option for me. This has led to my developing a kindred spirit with endurance athletes and showing a sympathy that other more sensible doctors would not demonstrate. And I've come to respect great strength of purpose as a driving force and ultimately a healing tool.

It was on the Freedom Challenge race across South Africa, a non-stop, self-navigated 2 300-kilometre mountain-bike chase across the country, which has to be completed in 26 days, that I developed excruciating pain, numbness and tingling in both my hands. It was so bad at night that sleep was almost impossible.

Intellectually, I knew what the diagnosis was: bilateral severe carpal tunnel syndrome, aggravated by long hours of gripping the handlebars. This occurs when the median nerve is squeezed or compressed as it travels through the wrist.

I also knew what the appropriate treatment was: surgery on both hands to split the carpal tunnel and so relieve pressure on the median nerve. But I wasn't even halfway to the finish line and nothing was going to stop me from getting there. I tried all the tricks I knew, resorting to potent painkillers and even sleeping tablets, but it didn't help.

I knew that high-dose oral steroids called prednisone might reduce the swelling of the nerve tissue. It wasn't a conventional treatment for my problem, but I needed help. If I decided to take this medication, where would I obtain it?

Late one night I phoned a colleague and longstanding friend. 'Please, Chris, what do you think? Can I do this?'

He'd been following my progress via the tracking device I was wearing and he knew my exact location. He cleared his throat, a mannerism I knew well when he was thinking and at a loss for words. 'It may help but I'm not sure,' he said. 'I've never prescribed it before for carpal tunnel, but if you phoned me, you must be desperate. I presume you've tried anti-inflammatories?' I grinned in the darkness: he knew me so well. 'Do you have enough prednisone with you to start an adequate course?' He also knew I always carried some for a relapse of my asthma.

'No.'

'Okay, I'll write a script and send it to a pharmacy in Prince Albert – you should be there in about three days' time.'

And then he did try, and I knew it was ethically what he had to do: 'Maybe you should pack it in?' he suggested.

'You know that's not a possibility.'

'Yes, but I had to suggest it.'

I lay back in my unfamiliar bed, hands raised above my head in an effort to reduce the pain. Help was close. I also had enough medical knowledge to know that these steroids would reduce all my joint aches and pains, and keep any bronchospasm at bay. And, with luck, they would give me a profound sense of wellbeing. Prednisone is one of the all time miracle drugs. Sure, if I'd been leading the pack and in danger of being drug-tested, they would have landed me in a lot of trouble, but there was no chance of that, I knew.

I finished the race. I've never done anything more gruelling and with a higher attrition rate to my body. But it was a dream fulfilled from which I benefited hugely, having travelled in the back country of my own land, become strong and fit, experienced the wonderful hospitality of the farming community and rural locals, witnessed glorious dawns and sunsets, seen a myriad shades of light, suffered and rejoiced, often simultaneously, slept rough when lost … My cycling partner and I clasped hands and raised them in victory as we teetered over the finish line, belief in ourselves reaffirmed.

A few weeks later I underwent the required carpal tunnel surgery on both wrists and have never looked back.

※

In November 2015 I attended the 40th reunion of my UCT graduating medical class, the class of 1975. I was working my locum in the Kruger National Park, and flew back to Cape Town for the occasion.

Reunions are always a time of remembrance, both warm and painful, of friendships rekindled, a time for taking stock and for looking forward. Our class had produced outstanding doctors, many of whom are now world experts. They'd become citizens of other countries – the USA, Canada, Australia, New Zealand, Israel, Zambia, England and many countries in Europe. This gathering of these highly successful medical professionals from all over the world highlighted for me what we'd endured together as a class.

Today, it comes as a surprise to many to learn that our graduating class was made up of one third black students, mainly those those classified Coloured and Indian. This was contrary to the policies of the government of the time and I never asked how UCT managed to achieve it.

I as class representative had my own challenges as a result. It was still in the days of segregated wards. Under apartheid, black students weren't allowed to examine white patients but white students were allowed to examine black patients.

My go-between with the body of black students was Asgar Kalla, a polite, softly spoken and highly intelligent individual. He now holds the professorship of rheumatology at UCT and Groote Schuur Hospital. He attended our reunion and I dearly wanted to revisit those difficult times from my new standpoint of advancing age and with a view that was continually altering as I proceeded through life.

Asgar and I embraced warmly and exchanged small talk, but only for a moment. Our connection forged as students was still there. I thanked him for his grace in our dealings over the years. I acknowledged how we shared a common trait of growing up in a minority in our country, mine as a white Afrikaner, his an infinitely less privileged one, as a black of Indian descent.

But after graduating, we'd both chosen to contribute, to give our country the chance of growing into a democracy, hoping that we would then have equal opportunities. We'd both married and raised our children here. We'd clutched at the spirit of optimism and self-reliance as we watched our country spin into political upheaval, with the hope that a Rainbow Nation would ultimately emerge. We'd shared that privileged moment in 1990, Nelson Mandela's release from prison, and the speech that this, one of the greatest statesmen in history, gave before he became our first democratically elected president.

It's a sad reality that out of those 142 graduates in 1975, fewer than a third remain living and working in South Africa. I see it as a staggering loss of resources for our country. There are so many factors that alter the course of newly graduated doctors, but our class was particularly vulnerable to the time and the country in which we graduated.

South Africa was then, and remains now, a high-risk country. But it is my country, my home. With all its conflicts, astounding diversity, challenges and incomparable natural beauty, it's the country of my birth, in which I've had the good fortune to grow up and to live now, and where I will be staying.

My feet rest on the red earth of Africa. It's on my skin, in my head and in my heart. Adventure medicine has taken me through all seven continents, but my life's adventures started, and will finish, here in Africa.

Acknowledgements

MY CHILDHOOD WAS PUNCTUATED BY A set of old, well-used adages. I thank my mother for this. 'Many a true word is spoken in jest' was a favourite and was eventually responsible for the seed of the idea for this book. After my intentionally light-hearted presentation at my alma mater's 40th medical class reunion, concerning my adventure medicine romp through the seven continents, I was approached by a smiling, highly esteemed professor colleague who announced that 'adventure medicine' was the next new speciality and that I should write the book for it.

A Wilder Life is not that book but it flowed from this suggestion, and caught me up in the adventure of writing and making some sense of my medical work choices.

The bulk of the time I spent writing was due to a compulsory break following a traumatic cycle accident. It was therefore a solitary process, with minimal outside input and only my animals with whom to converse. Big thanks to my amazing, loyal cycling buddies who broke the solitude and came with moral support, food and drink.

Melinda Ferguson encouraged me early on in the process, and for this I'm deeply grateful.

My dear daughters, Mary and Anna, have become accustomed to the flights of fancy of their mother, but their support and love are rock solid. They may not agree with all the thoughts and emotions I've expressed, but they've been gracious in their acceptance. Anna, in her quiet, practical way, was indispensable during the Covid-19 lockdown, as an IT advisor in the editing process – though she hadn't chosen to be holed up with me for so long!

Tracey Hawthorne shepherded me through the editing with wisdom, patience and an open-minded view. To her, so many thanks, and also for modernising my schoolgirl prose.

Jeremy Boraine, Ceri Prenter and Aimee Carelse at Jonathan Ball Publishers offered quiet support and ideas, and invaluable reassurance, while I floundered t hrough t he u nfamiliar a nd challenging publishing landscape.

But my deepest gratitude goes to the many patients and their families who've afforded me the privilege of entering their worlds in an attempt to heal or comfort. I've learned from them and been humbled by them. Their acts of human kindness have illuminated my world. (I've changed many of their names and situations to protect their identities.)

And to my many colleagues over the years who've taught and assisted me, thank you for contributing, unknowingly, to these, my medical stories.